CW01497288

Deus.
in adiutoriu
meum inten
de. Domine ad adiu
uandum me festina
Gloria patri et filio
et spiritui sancto

REMARKABLE RENAISSANCE BOOKS

John Boardley

BODLEIAN
LIBRARY
PUBLISHING

The aspects of things that are most important for us are hidden because of their simplicity and familiarity. (One is unable to notice something — because it is always before one's eyes.)

Ludwig Wittgenstein[1]

vacua: et tenebre erāt sup faciē abissi.
et spūs dñi ferebat̄ sup aquas. Dixitq;
deus. Fiat lux. Et facta ē lux. Et vidit
deus lucem q͡ esset bona: ⁊ diuisit lucē
a tenebris. appellauitq; lucem diem ⁊
tenebras noctem. Factūq; est vespe et
mane dies vnus. Dixit q; deus. Fiat
firmamentū in medio aquar: ⁊ diui=
dat aquas ab aquis. Et fecit deus fir=
mamentū: diuisitq; aquas que erāt
sub firmamento ab hijs q̄ erant sup
firmamentū. et factū ē ita. Vocauitq;
deus firmamentū celū: ⁊ factū ē vespe
et mane dies secūd⁹. Dixit vero deus.
Congregent̄ aque que sub celo sūt in
locū vnū ⁊ appareat arida. Et factū ē
ita. Et vocauit deus aridam terram:
congregacionesq; aquar appellauit
maria. Et vidit deus q͡ esset bonū. et
ait. Germinet terra herbā virentem et
facientē semen: ⁊ lignū pomifer faciēs
fructū iuxta genus suū. cui⁹ semen in
semetipō sit sup terrā. Et factū ē ita. Et
protulit terra herbā virentē ⁊ facientē
semē iuxta genus suū: lignūq; faciēs
fructū ⁊ habēs vnūquodq; sementē scdm

Dixit eciā de
anime viuen
sub firmamē
grandia. et o
motabile qu
suas. ⁊ omn
Et vidit deus
cens dicens. C
replete aqua
cent sup terrā
dies quītus.
ducat terra a
iumenta ⁊ re
species suas.
bestias terre iu
ta ⁊ omne rep
vidit deus q
mus hoīem
nostrā. ⁊ pres
tilibȝ celi ⁊ best
reptili qd mo
deus hoīem
suā. ad ymag
sculū ⁊ femin
q; illis deus.
mini ⁊ replete

CONTENTS

aproche • aproche

INTRODUCTION
MORE THAN BOOKS

For books are more than books, they are the life, the very heart and core of ages past, the reason why men lived, and worked, and died, the essence and quintessence of their lives.

AMY LOWELL, 1925[2]

In Egyptian mythology, writing was invented by Thoth, the god of wisdom and secret knowledge. He was record keeper and scribe to the gods and, according to one tradition, he authored forty-two books containing the entirety of human – and occult – knowledge. However, before bestowing the gift of writing to humanity, Thoth first enumerated its advantages to Amun, the king of Egypt, insisting that it 'will make the Egyptians wiser and will improve their memories'.[3] Amun, both king and god, objected, suggesting that the very opposite would transpire – that writing would be inimical to memory. Why bother remembering anything when everything is written down! This legend was retold in the fifth century BCE by Socrates, who was passionately opposed to writing in favour of dialectic. When the cognitive neuroscientist Maryanne Wolf wrote that 'the inflexible muteness of written words doomed the dialogic process Socrates saw as the heart of education',[4] she was reiterating Socrates' main objection to writing – that 'reading is not a conversation'.[5] The great irony, of course, is that we only know about Socrates' objections to the written word through the prolific writings of his pupil, Plato.

We cannot say with any certainty when humans began to speak. Estimates range from 200,000 to 60,000 years ago. When it comes to the invention of written language, however, we are on much firmer ground. Speech leaves behind no artifactual traces; its ephemeralness is not preserved in layers of rock and silt and sand. But the written word has literally left its mark, surviving its authors by thousands of years.

1 Thoth, inventor of writing, from the *Book of the Dead of Hunefer* papyrus. This version is from c.1285 BCE.

SUMERIAN CUNEIFORM

Around 3200 BCE, the first-known writing system was invented in Mesopotamia, the region between the Euphrates and Tigris rivers that includes present-day Iraq. The pictographs of this early cuneiform writing appear to have descended from much more ancient inscribed clay tokens that were used to record transactions of commodities such as grain, cattle and textiles. Within the space of several centuries, cuneiform had evolved into a complex writing system that was expansive and sophisticated enough to support the conversion and preservation of the region's rich oral tradition into written literature. This included the *Epic of Gilgamesh*, one of the world's first books, recorded in clay towards the end of the second millennium BCE.

EGYPTIAN HIEROGLYPHS AND CHINESE ORACLES

At around the same time that cuneiform was evolving into a fully fledged writing system, and perhaps inspired by their Easterly neighbours, the Egyptians developed hieroglyphs, a writing system combining logographic and syllabic components. But whereas the Sumerians in Mesopotamia continued to incise their words into clay tablets, the Egyptians moved from clay and stone to a new, more portable and flexible writing surface. Used by the Egyptians from at least the sixth century BCE, papyrus was made from laminated strips of the fibrous pith of the papyrus plant, prevalent throughout the Nile Delta. It was even exported to other parts of the Mediterranean. Egyptian scribes also developed an ink whose basic ingredients – soot, gum arabic and water – are used to this very day. Instead of the stylus, they made brushes with which to write. Papyrus was convenient and portable. The roll (*volumen*, from which we get the word 'volume') served as the dominant form of the book until about the fourth century CE. Elsewhere in the world, other writing systems developed independently. The earliest examples of Chinese writing were various oracles written or incised on animal bones and tortoise shells that date to the thirteenth century BCE. Chinese was later written on strips of bamboo or wood and on silk, until the invention of paper.

FROM WAX TABLET TO CODEX

Writing boards, typically made of wood and sometimes with shallow recesses filled with beeswax and pigment, first appeared in Mesopotamia in the third millennium BCE. Later, they were widely used in the Graeco-Roman world. The Romans called them *tabulae*. When multiple *tabulae* were joined or 'bound' together with leather thongs or cord along their

2 Sumerian proto-cuneiform tablet: administrative account with entries concerning malt and barley groats. c.3100–2900 BCE.

longest edge, forming a kind of hinge, then the wooden codex was born (codex means 'block of wood' in Latin). These wax tablets or proto-codices were compact, portable and reusable. 'It is best to write on wax owing to the facility which it offers for erasure', wrote the first-century Roman educator Quintilian.[6]

Towards the end of the same century, the Latin poet Martial (Marcus Valerius Martialis) famously praised the portability of the innovative new parchment codex. He even named the shop where they could be purchased. But this novel new codex failed to take off. Had it been more popular as a medium for literary works, then writers such as Pliny, who had something to say about almost everything, would surely have mentioned it. The transition from roll to codex, then, was protracted. From the second century the codex gradually began to make inroads and was the preferred format for early Christians, its use spreading with their religion as they went from persecuted cult to official religion of the Roman Empire as decreed in 380 CE. By the late fifth and early sixth centuries, the parchment codex had supplanted the roll book.

THE PRINTED BOOK

3 Wood and wax writing tablets. Byzantine Egypt, 500–700 CE.

The next major milestone in the history of the book was related not to its shape or material form but to its means of production. A truly remarkable discovery was made in 1900 in the Mogao Caves on the Silk Road, in China's north-western Gansu province. Discovered among tens of thousands of texts, many preserved for more than a thousand years, was the *Diamond Sutra*, a Chinese translation of an early Sanskrit Buddhist text (fig. 4). Incredibly, the book bore the name of its printer and the date of its printing: Wang Jie, 11 May 868. It remains the world's earliest surviving printed book. The sophistication and quality of its printing suggest that woodblock printing for texts was already well established by the time the *Diamond Sutra* was printed. Yet another printing innovation followed in the mid-eleventh century, during the early Song dynasty in China, when Bi Sheng (*c.*972–1051) invented reusable printing types made from baked clay. Meanwhile, in Europe, where there was limited demand for books, all texts continued to be copied individually and laboriously by hand.

PAPER

Four hundred years after Bi Sheng's invention, moveable type was invented or reinvented by an enterprising German entrepreneur living in Mainz. Gutenberg's tripartite innovation – a printing press, a hand mould to cast metal letters, and a suitable ink – set off a printing

boom that produced, by even conservative estimates, more than 10 million books in the half-century between 1450 and 1500. However, without yet another ancient Chinese invention, this scale of production would have been unthinkable. From late antiquity and throughout almost the entire European Middle Ages, everything had been written on prepared animal skins (parchment). A single book of several hundred pages required dozens of animal skins. It is hard to imagine there being enough sheep, goats and cows in the world to support the billions of pages that were subsequently printed by Gutenberg and his heirs in the fifteenth century alone. The success, or at the very least the grand scale of printing's success, depended on paper.

The invention of paper, a more convenient substitute for bamboo and a considerably cheaper alternative to silk, is traditionally attributed to the Chinese court official Ts'ai Lun (Cai Lun) in 105 CE.[7] The Arabs learned the secret of papermaking from the Chinese, later introducing papermaking to Europe via Muslim Spain. Paper was only slowly adopted in Europe, but 'in a remarkable shift of scribal practices, in the fourteenth century scribes across Europe began to use paper for manuscripts'.[8] And so it was that, by the time Gutenberg was printing in the early 1450s, paper was widely available and considerably less expensive than parchment.

4 金剛般若波羅蜜經 (*Diamond Sutra*). 11 May 868 CE, Mogao, China. The earliest dated printed book.

BEYOND THE PILLARS OF HERCULES

The chapters that follow trace the emergence of modern Europe from the advent of print to the flowering of modern science through a series of remarkable books. This was a turbulent and profoundly transformative period. Unprecedented economic expansion was fuelled by the growth of international trade, new trade routes and steadily improving infrastructure. The Reformation and its backlash, the Counter-Reformation, dramatically transformed the religious and political landscape of Europe, and signalled the beginning of the end of a thousand years of ecclesiastical absolutism and papal hegemony. The circumnavigation of the globe in 1519–22 by the Magellan–Elcano expedition paved the way for European Christianization and colonization. A century later, in 1619, twenty enslaved Africans arrived in the English colony of Virginia, marking the beginning of modern slavery. This period is also characterized by uprisings and internecine wars – the Thirty Years War (1618–48) claimed upwards of five million lives! Regular and sometimes widespread outbreaks of the bubonic plague also took their toll. Striking in 1665, the Great Plague of London killed 100,000 people,

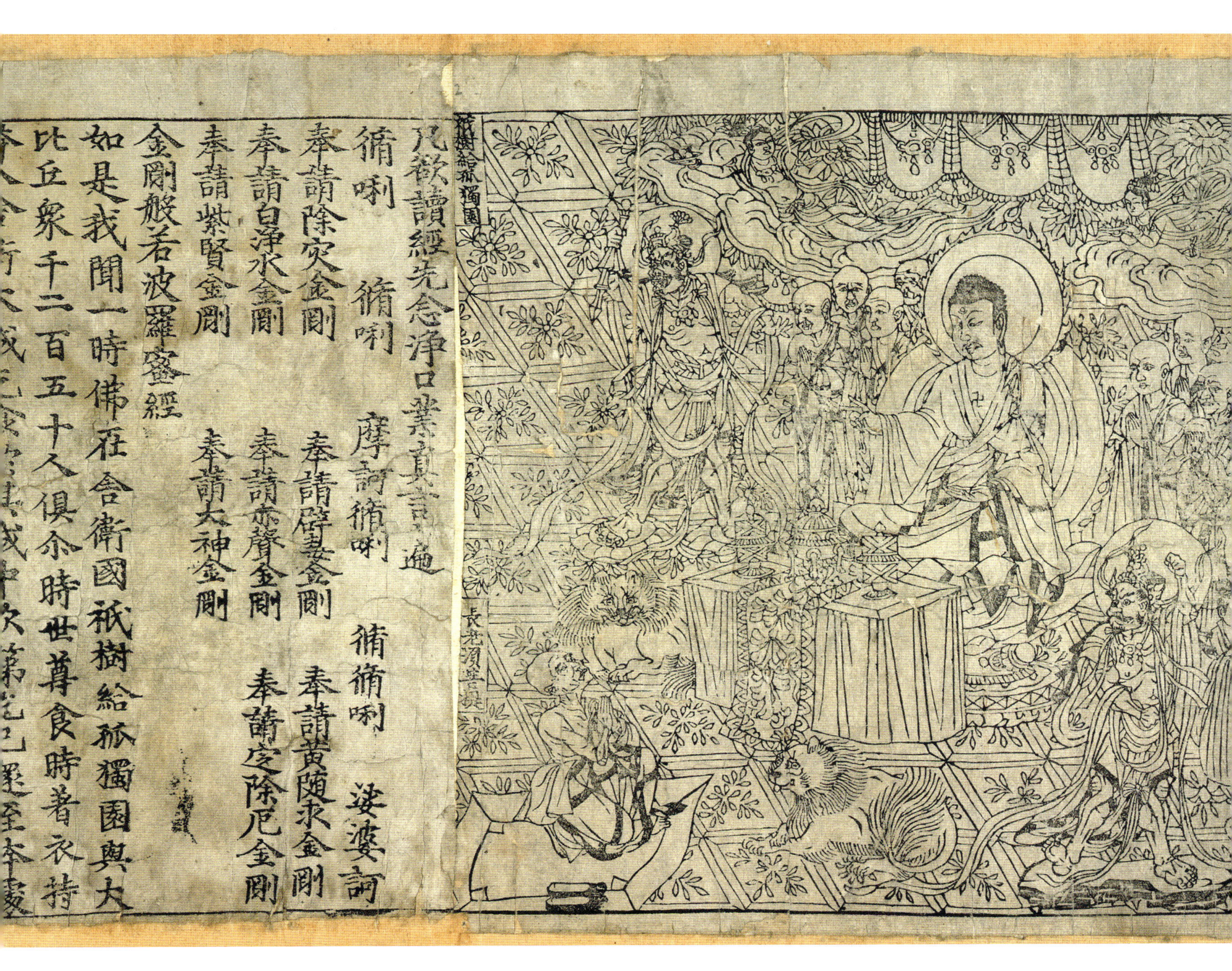

凡欲讀經先念淨口業真言遍

脩唎 脩唎 摩訶脩唎 脩脩唎 娑婆訶

奉請除灾金剛 奉請辟毒金剛 奉請黄随求金剛

奉請白淨水金剛 奉請赤聲金剛 奉請定除厄金剛

奉請紫賢金剛 奉請大神金剛

金剛般若波羅蜜經

如是我聞一時佛在舍衛國祇樹給孤獨園與大

比丘衆千二百五十人俱尒時世尊食時著衣持

鉢入舍衛大城乞食於其城中次第乞已還至本處

about one-fifth of the city's inhabitants, within the space of just two years.

Europe's newfound wealth built new schools, founded new universities and sustained a burgeoning printing industry, which satisfied a continent newly hungry for books. By the end of the sixteenth century, at least 150 million books had been printed. When Gutenberg began printing in the 1450s, only a small minority could read and write. Aided by urbanization and fuelled by economic, religious and intellectual incentives, in subsequent centuries literacy improved markedly, so that by the eighteenth century male literacy had climbed to fifty per cent in some urban centres.[9] This was accompanied by a profound shift in reading tastes. Predominantly religious books for moral edification gave way to largely secular reading for learning and pleasure, including new literary genres like the novel and the periodical.

Just as children exit childhood with the sobering realization that their parents are neither immortal nor infallible, so the great scholars of the Renaissance came to realize that their ancient heroes were flawed. Although by no means the first to say it, the English philosopher Francis Bacon (1561–1626) was explicit in his antipathy towards Aristotle (and his scholastic apologists), cautioning that 'it would disgrace us … if the limits of the intellectual globe should be set by the narrow discoveries of the ancients'.[10] Bacon likened those limits to the Pillars of Hercules – it was indeed time to leave the shallows for the vast oceans beyond.

5 Ships passing through the Pillars of Hercules, depicted in this engraved frontispiece to Francis Bacon's *Instauratio Magna*, 1620.

BUCKLE UP!

The eighteen books that follow, all from Oxford University's world-famous Bodleian Library, are just a small sampling of the many remarkable printed books published and read during the first centuries of printing in Europe. They are eighteen stories that, when taken together, paint a vivid and compelling picture of a world becoming, to use that eternal anachronism, modern. This is the era of Machiavelli and the Medici, of Dürer, Michelangelo, Raphael, Shakespeare, Descartes and, of course, Leonardo da Vinci. In 1490s Milan we watch Leonardo as he takes up a compass to inscribe a circle around a figure with arms outstretched. His image of Vitruvian Man is now one of the world's most iconic and instantly recognizable symbols. We also learn the secrets of the *Divina proportione* (the Golden Ratio), elucidated by his friend, roommate and maths tutor, Luca Pacioli.

Heading to Brussels in 1536, we come across a rather macabre scene. Andreas Vesalius, a

FRANCISCI
DE VERULAMIO,
Summi Angliæ
CANCELLARIJ,
Instauratio
magna.
Multi pertransibunt & augebitur scientia.
Sim: Pass: sculp:
Anno
1620.
LONDINI
Apud Joannem Billium
Typographum
Regium.

young student doctor, aided by the polymath Gemma Frisius, is stealing body parts from decomposing corpses hanging from roadside gallows. What Vesalius learned and published from his anatomical experiments on those various body-snatched parts, some of which he hid under his bed, overturned a thousand years of anatomy, radically transforming our understanding of the human body.

Mapmakers and geographers like Abraham Ortelius and Gerard Mercator raced to keep pace with the Age of Exploration, producing atlases and new kinds of maps for seafarers, like the Mercator projection. As the world underfoot grew larger, so too did the sky overhead. What Galileo discovered when he first pointed his telescope at the night sky in 1609 led some to ridicule him. They scoffed that he had been deceived by his own eyes and that his new-fangled telescopes were producing astronomical chimeras. But once people began to look for themselves, through their own telescopes, they also saw the mountains, valleys and craters on the Moon and the four moons of Jupiter that Galileo had described. These telescopic revelations not only suggested that Copernicus might have been right, but that the cosmos was much larger and filled with a multitude more stars than the thousand or so recorded in star catalogues since the days of Hipparchus and Ptolemy. The Milky Way, long considered an atmospheric or meteorological phenomenon, was resolved through Galileo's first telescopic observations into countless individual stars. The cosmos was undergoing Early Modern cosmic inflation. Consider that between Ptolemy in the second century and Copernicus in the sixteenth, the entire observable universe was estimated to be around 209 million km in diameter. That universe would fit, with room to spare, inside the present-day orbit of Mars! But by the turn of the seventeenth century, Kepler proposed that the cosmos must be at least 764 billion km in diameter.[11]

At around the same time that Galileo first published the findings from his telescopic observations, the King James Bible was coming off the presses in London. English idioms such as, 'fallen from grace', 'all things to all men', 'holier than thou', 'out of the mouths of babes', 'eat, drink and be merry', 'signs of the times' and 'thorn in the flesh' were either coined by or popularized by the King James Bible of 1611. It is a remarkable and remarkably influential book that is profoundly connected to both William Tyndale and the crews of two Apollo missions, whom we shall meet on pp. 210–11.

Fast-forwarding through Cromwell, the execution of Charles I and the English Civil Wars, we arrive in Oxford in 1652 to witness the opening of England's first coffee house. Later that same year, coffee houses began springing up in London. By 1700, the city was home to several hundred.[12] They soon became sober centres for political, philosophical, literary and scientific debate, places to conduct business and to catch up on the latest news and gossip. Among their most avid patrons was the brilliant and irascible Robert Hooke, Curator of Experiments at the newly founded Royal Society in London and one of the greatest experimental scientists of the century. In 1665, Hooke published *Micrographia*, a beautifully illustrated book on microscopy. According to Samuel Pepys, it was 'the most ingenious book that ever I read in my life'.[13] Hooke opened our eyes to the world of the infinitesimally small, including the revolutionary discovery of cells as the building blocks of all living organisms. We will also discover how a bubble-blowing ant came to be drunk on brandy, how a bishop and an apothecary created one of the most remarkable botanical books ever conceived, and how the first female entomologist, Maria Sibylla Merian, living at a time when most believed insects appeared spontaneously from dung and dirt, set off on a perilous journey to the other end of the world – a scientific and artistic mission to describe their secret lives, habitat and metamorphosis.

Excellentis
sima. et glo
riosissima
Atqz sanctissima ui
rgo semper maria.
mater domini nri

1

FROM PILGRIMS TO PRINT

GUTENBERG BIBLE (*c.*1454)

Our age has witnessed the invention of a new form of writing. Now, in a single day, one person can print more text than several scribes were able to produce by hand in a whole year.

VIRGIL POLYDORE, 1499[14]

Before the invention of printing, every book – millions of books – were handwritten. Copying an entire book by hand, especially a long one like the Bible, for example, would take months or even years. When the sun set each day, the scribe continued working by candlelight and, when mistakes were inevitably made, a small penknife was used to scratch away the ink and smooth the parchment, ready for another try. A scribe's work was not easy. It was especially hard on the eyes, hands and back, and scribes throughout history often said as much in colophons and marginalia. Towards the end of the eighth century, one copyist lamented, in what was to become a popular scribal refrain, 'Three fingers write, the whole body labours. Whoever has read this book, pray for me.'[15]

In Europe, this laborious method of producing books did not change until the fifteenth century. Meanwhile, the Chinese had printed books from woodblocks since at least the ninth century. The earliest surviving woodblock or xylographic book, the *Diamond Sutra*, was printed in 868, many centuries before woodblock printing reached Europe. The Chinese also used woodblocks to print paper money, something described in detail by the Venetian merchant-explorer Marco Polo (1254–1324). In the mid-eleventh century, again in China, during the early Song dynasty, Bi Sheng invented moveable type made from baked clay, although his invention was not as widely adopted as woodblock printing. By the early thirteenth century, metal moveable type was being used in Korea. Moveable type would not be adopted in Europe until the mid-fifteenth century.

6 A *trompe l'oeil* border of painted pilgrim badges surround the text and a miniature of Virgin and Child in this page from *The Hours of Engelbert of Nassau*, c.1475–85.

HOLY SOUVENIRS AND THE MAINZ ENTREPRENEUR

We do not know if Johannes Gutenberg's invention was influenced by printing innovations in East Asia. What we do know is that he was able to successfully adapt existing technologies to mass-produce books. Gutenberg found a solution to casting tens of thousands of sorts (letters) from a lead tin alloy, with antimony added to make the type sharper, harder and more durable. It also cools and hardens quickly for speedier production. He also overcame the challenge of ensuring that each piece of type was the same height – even tiny variations could result in uneven printing or, worse still, that some parts of the page would not print at all. It was probably Gutenberg who invented some form of hand mould, an adjustable handheld device for quickly casting those individual pieces of metal type. He also developed a printing press from an existing screw press, the kind then commonly used in the manufacture of paper. The final part of Gutenberg's ingenious printing puzzle was the ink. Traditional water-based inks, the kind used in pens, would not adhere to metal type, so Gutenberg developed a sticky oil-based ink that has more in common with varnish and oil paint. Ink for typographic printing needs to adhere evenly to the surface of the metal type, to print without smudging and, of course, it must not dry too quickly. Modern-day analysis reveals a rather unique chemical profile: Gutenberg's ink contains very high concentrations of copper and lead, in addition to traces of titanium, iron, nickel and zinc.[16]

It appears that the idea of printing with moveable type on a press came to Gutenberg while he was staying in Strasbourg. His hometown of Mainz, in economic decline, was not conducive to his entrepreneurial ambitions, so he had packed up and headed for Strasbourg, which was at the time one of the largest cities in central Europe. In 1438 Gutenberg teamed up with several Strasbourg partners to produce pilgrim badges for the upcoming Aachen pilgrimage (held every seven years). Demand for the badges had increased to the point where local workers were no longer able to cope. Typically restricted to local guilds and hence local artisans, the manufacture of badges was now opened up to outsiders. Gutenberg and company were among them.

Anyone who has read Chaucer's bawdy and brilliant *The Canterbury Tales*, written around 1400, will be familiar with the manifold motives of medieval pilgrims. In addition to the more obvious holy and penitential motivations, for many a pilgrimage was also a rare opportunity to travel – an expression of medieval

7 Gutenberg Bible, *c.*1454. Opening to the book of Genesis.

Incipit liber bresith quē nos genesim

In principio creauit deus celū dicim⁹ et terram. Terra autem erat inanis et vacua: et tenebre erāt sup faciē abissi. et sp̄s dn̄i ferebat̄ sup aquas. Dixitq; deus. Fiat lux. Et facta ē lux. Et vidit deus lucem q̄ esset bona: ⁊ diuisit lucē a tenebris. appellauitq; lucem diem ⁊ tenebras noctem. Factūq; est vespe et mane dies vnus. Dixit q; deus. Fiat firmamentū in medio aquaꝝ: ⁊ diuidat aquas ab aquis. Et fecit deus firmamentū: diuisitq; aquas que erāt sub firmamento ab hijs q̄ erant sup firmamentū. et factū ē ita. Vocauitq; deus firmamentū celū: ⁊ factū ē vespe et mane dies secūd⁹. Dixit vero deus. Congregent̄ aque que sub celo sūt in locū vnū ⁊ appareat arida. Et factū ē ita. Et vocauit deus aridam terram: congregacionesq; aquaꝝ appellauit maria. Et vidit deus q̄ esset bonū. et ait. Germinet terra herbā virentem et facientē semen: ⁊ lignū pomiferū faciēs fructū iuxta genus suū. cui⁹ semen in semetipo sit sup terrā. Et factū ē ita. Et protulit terra herbā virentē ⁊ facientē semē iuxta genus suū: lignūq; faciēs fructū ⁊ habēs vnūqdq; sementē scd̄m speciē suā. Et vidit deus q̄ esset bonū: et factū est vespe et mane dies tercius. Dixitq; autē deus. Fiant luminaria in firmamēto celi. ⁊ diuidāt diem ac noctem: ⁊ sint in signa ⁊ tempora ⁊ dies ⁊ annos. ut luceant in firmamēto celi. ⁊ illuminent terrā. Et factū est ita. Fecitq; deus duo magna luminaria: luminare maius ut preesset diei: ⁊ luminare minus ut preesset nocti: ⁊ stellas. ⁊ posuit eas in firmamēto celi ut lucerēt sup terrā: ⁊ preessent diei ac nocti. ⁊ diuiderent lucē ac tenebras. Et vidit de⁹ q̄ esset bonū: et factū ē vespe ⁊ mane dies quartus. Dixit etiā de⁹. Producāt aque reptile anime viuentis ⁊ volatile super terrā. sub firmamēto celi. Creauitq; deus cete grandia. et omnē aīam viuentē atq; motabilē quā pduxerāt aque ī species suas. ⁊ omne volatile scd̄m gen⁹ suū. Et vidit deus q̄ esset bonū. benedixitq; eis dicens. Crescite ⁊ mltiplicamini. ⁊ replete aquas maris. auesq; mltiplicent̄ sup terrā. Et factū ē vespe ⁊ mane dies quītus. Dixit quoq; deus. Producat terra aīam viuentē in genē suo. iumenta ⁊ reptilia. ⁊ bestias terre scd̄m species suas. Factūq; ē ita. Et fecit de⁹ bestias terre iuxta species suas. iumenta ⁊ omne reptile terre ī genere suo. Et vidit deus q̄ esset bonū. et ait. Faciamus hoīem ad ymaginē ⁊ silitudinē nostrā. ⁊ presit piscibꝫ maris. et volatilibꝫ celi ⁊ bestijs vniuersēq; terre. omīq; reptili qd̄ mouetur ī terra. Et creauit deus hoīem ad ymaginē ⁊ silitudinē suā. ad ymaginē dei creauit illū. masculū ⁊ feminā creauit eos. Benedixitq; illis deus. ⁊ ait. Crescite ⁊ mltiplicamini ⁊ replete terrā. et s̄bicite eā. et dn̄amini piscibꝫ maris. et volatilibꝫ celi. et vniuersis animātibꝫ que mouent̄ sup terrā. Dixitq; de⁹. Ecce dedi vobis omnē herbā afferentē semen sup terrā.

8 St Sebald dressed as a pilgrim and sporting an assortment of pilgrim badges pinned to the upturned brim of his hat, 1487 (detail from altarpiece).

wanderlust in an age that was otherwise profoundly parochial. Pilgrim badges feature in *The Canterbury Tales* with the grifting and unscrupulous Pardoner, a seller of indulgences for the church who made a little money on the side hawking chicken bones and rusty baubles passed off as holy relics and reselling stolen pilgrim badges. Originating in the twelfth century, these inexpensive badges were at their most popular in the fourteenth and fifteenth centuries, with millions of them produced in thousands of designs. They served as souvenirs and as charismatic objects or talismen.

Gutenberg would have done his sums and been keenly aware of just how lucrative the sale of pilgrim badges could be. He had evidently hit upon a new way to mass-produce these lead and pewter badges, and in particular the new mirror pilgrim badge. As pilgrimages became more popular, it became increasingly difficult for pilgrims to approach, let alone touch, the relics at busy pilgrim centres. The mirror pilgrim badge, inset with a convex polished metal or glass mirror, was an ingenious solution to this problem. Pilgrims could simply hold their badges aloft and capture the relics' reflection from afar, thereby absorbing their miraculous powers.

We only know about Gutenberg's foray into pilgrim badge manufacture because of the death, in 1439, of one of his business partners, Andreas Dritzehen. This prompted a lawsuit brought about by Dritzehen's brothers with the aim of either recouping their late brother's investment or being admitted as partners in the business. From court records and witness statements, we learn, for example, that in 1438 Gutenberg partnered with Hanns Riffe and Andreas Heilmann to produce pilgrim badges for the upcoming Aachen pilgrimage. Witnesses mention seeing a 'press', a 'form' and another unidentified device disassembled into four pieces. It appears likely that these devices were related to printing and even type-making. The four-component device that Gutenberg was eager to have disassembled, lest anyone fathom its purpose, might have been a prototype mould for casting pieces of metal type. It is also likely that it was during the process of casting lead alloy pilgrim badges that Gutenberg hit upon the idea of casting individual metal letters from a similar alloy – letters that could be arranged or typeset, inked and printed. As a trained goldsmith, Gutenberg would have been familiar with metalworking, casting techniques and producing punches and matrices for striking coins – this combination of skills would prove invaluable for his most ambitious project.

By the autumn of 1448 at the latest, Gutenberg had returned to Mainz. In October he took out a loan from a relative, Arnold Gelthus. But if Gutenberg were to finance his next business venture, he would need considerably more capital. In 1449 Gutenberg took out a much larger loan, of 800 guilders, from businessman and financier Johann Fust. He borrowed the same amount again from Fust in 1453. To put Gutenberg's loans in perspective, in 1450 a good-sized townhouse cost roughly 500 guilders. With his new printing press and metal type, Gutenberg began to print small items such as single-sheet letters of indulgence for the church, small grammar books and other printed ephemera such as calendars and propaganda. These modest pamphlets and broadsides were quick to typeset and print, and profits from their sale could be reinvested in Gutenberg's primary, considerably more ambitious, endeavour – a printed Bible.

THE GUTENBERG BIBLE

Only fragments of what Gutenberg printed in those early days have survived. Not a single complete grammar book has survived, which is not entirely surprising as schoolbooks were often used to destruction. Gutenberg is best remembered not only as the European inventor of printing with moveable type but also for Europe's first substantial printed book, the so-called Gutenberg Bible – sometimes called

the 42-line Bible, or even the B42 for those in a hurry. It is one of the most exhaustively studied books in history. The font, paper, inks, bindings, illumination, rubrication, marginalia, watermarks, gatherings and quire structure, and even the smallest registration pinholes have all been the subject of meticulous study.

It is something of a quantum leap to go from broadsides and pamphlets to a 1,200-page large-format lectern Bible, but Gutenberg was an ambitious man. The work was a formidable undertaking, requiring an enormous investment of capital and labour. Casting tens of thousands of pieces of metal type by hand would have taken at least six months. Typesetting the Bible's 1,200 pages, the work of six compositors or typesetters, would have taken up to two years, and with twelve printers and their various assistants working at six printing presses, the actual work of printing would also have taken about the same time. During this time, Gutenberg would need to pay his printshop workers their wages, pay upfront for a huge amount of paper imported from Italy,[17] parchment (3,200 skins), printing presses, lead and other metals for the type, materials for ink and so on.

Although the Bible is not dated, we know it was completed no later than 1455. Sheets from the Bible were seen in 1454 by Aeneas Silvius Piccolomini, who at the time was working at the court of Emperor Frederick III, and who would later be elected Pope Pius II. Writing to his friend in Rome, the Spanish cardinal Juan de Carvajal, Aeneas describes his first encounter with Gutenberg's Bible:

> What was written to me about that marvellous man in Frankfurt was undoubtedly true. I have not seen complete copies of his Bible, but I did see a number of quinternions [bound signatures of five folded sheets] of various books [of the Bible], executed in a very neat and legible script, which Your Grace would be able to read without the slightest trouble, and indeed with no need even to use your glasses. Several people told me that 158 copies have been finished, although others say there are 180. I'm not certain of the exact number, but I'm in no doubt that the volumes are complete … Had I known your wishes I should certainly have bought you a copy – some quinternions were actually brought here to the emperor. If I can I will try and get one of the Bibles that are for sale brought here, which I can then purchase on your behalf, but I fear that might not be possible, both because of the length of the journey and because buyers are apparently already lining up to buy the copies even before they are finished.[18]

The 'marvellous man in Frankfurt' is not named. As a successful entrepreneur and evidently skilled in securing funding for his various business ventures, I think we can imagine Gutenberg as a rather charismatic person, and it is not difficult to envisage him attending the Frankfurt Fair, in person, to promote the first substantial product of his brilliant invention – his beautifully printed Bible.

In the time it took a single scribe to copy a large Bible by hand, Gutenberg had printed 180 copies. It marked the beginning of the mass production of books in Europe. Within fifty years of Gutenberg's Bible, the printing press and moveable type had reached every corner of Europe, and millions of books had been printed, perhaps even more than the total of all handwritten books produced in the preceding 1,500 years.[19] Within the span of a single lifetime, typographic printing had transformed the book from something rare and expensive to an affordable, widely available, mass-produced commodity.

The European adoption of print and the subsequent communications revolution it

9 A fifteenth-century stone pilgrim badge mould depicting John Schorne.

spawned were the result of the combination and repurposing of existing technologies rather than any single invention. Crucially, it was also about timing. Population growth, economic expansion and an intellectual climate forever altered by the Italian Renaissance made fifteenth-century Europe an especially fertile time and place for a printing revolution. These factors, together with the increasing availability of paper (a much cheaper alternative to parchment), were able to sustain the rapid mass production of millions of new books.

SURVIVAL

Forty-nine copies of Gutenberg's Bible have survived: thirty-seven printed on paper, and twelve on parchment. Other fragments have survived, albeit indecorously, as binders' waste that was recycled to fortify book bindings. The lives of books, or what historians of the book and book dealers refer to as their provenance, can be as intriguing as the books themselves. The Bodleian Library copy of the Gutenberg Bible has had an especially fascinating journey. Its first owner was Erhard Neninger, the mayor of Heilbronn, a city about 160 km south-east of Mainz. He gifted it to the city's Carmelite monastery in around 1474, where it remained for more than 150 years. During the Thirty Years War, the monastery was captured and dismantled by Swedish forces under Axel Oxenstierna (1583–1654), who, in 1633, became the Bible's next owner. By the eighteenth century, the Bible was in the library of the French cardinal and finance minister of Louis XVI, Étienne-Charles de Loménie de Brienne (1727–94). On 16 February 1794, during the French Revolution, and despite renouncing the priesthood, Loménie de Brienne was arrested and died the same night in prison, probably from a stroke or perhaps even poisoning. In 1793, a year before his death, his copy of the Gutenberg Bible had been sold to the Bodleian Library for £100.

Nowadays, we can count ourselves lucky that we do not have to wait months or even years for our local scribe to copy that must-have book – and for that, we can be thankful to brilliant early East Asian inventors and an ingenious fifteenth-century German entrepreneur.

10 A book of hours with metal badges sewn to the pages, Flanders c.1490.

59

Deuotissima oro ad glo
riosam virginem mariam

Obsecro te
domina
sancta ma
ria mat
dei plenis
sima sum
mi regis
filia mater gloriosissima
mater orphanorum consola
tio desolatorum via erran
tium salus et spes in te spe
rantium. virgo ante par
tum virgo in partu et virgo
post partum. fons miseri
cordie fons salutis et gra

2

ILLUMINATING PLINY

PLINY THE ELDER, *HISTORIA NATURALIS* (1476)

Deus est mortali iuvare mortalem, et haec ad aeternam gloriam via.

(For mortal to aid mortal – this is god; and this is the road to eternal glory.)

PLINY, C.77 CE[20]

A mushroom cloud of dense smoke rose 30 km into the autumn sky, its billowing outlines illuminated by lightning. While the earth shook and columns of smoke climbed higher, hot ash, pumice and molten rock rained down, sending many to seek shelter indoors. Some ran about with pillows tied about their heads. But even those lucky enough to make it to shelter would not escape the impending pyroclastic surge, a broiling maelstrom, a super-heated avalanche of boulders, rubble, dust and poisonous gases that was poised to come barrelling down the steep slopes of Mount Vesuvius at up to 700 kph.

These cataclysmic events took place in Campania, southern Italy, on 24 August 79 CE, and led to the destruction of Pompeii, Herculaneum, Stabiae and Oplontis. One eyewitness to the fateful eruption of Vesuvius was Gaius Plinius Secundus, better known as Pliny the Elder. Born in Novum Comum (modern Como) in northern Italy in 23 CE, Pliny was an insatiably curious and altogether remarkable man. By the time of Vesuvius's eruption, he was admiral of the Roman fleet at Misenum, at the northern end of the Bay of Naples. When not working at his official duties for the empire, he devoted every waking minute to reading, writing and studying. For Pliny, every second of the day was precious, and when he was not reading he was being read to – while eating, bathing or on the road. He studied at night too, for, in his own words, 'to sleep is to lose half of one's allotted time'.[21] His nephew, Pliny the Younger, wrote that his uncle had once rebuked him for walking, a pastime the elder Pliny deemed a terrible waste of time. Better that he should be carried about in a litter, so moving from one place to another was spent

11 *The Last Day of Pompeii*, painting by Karl Bryullov, oil on canvas, 1830–33.

in more intellectually profitable pursuits such as reading.

Pliny the Elder was not only a prolific learner but a prolific writer too. He wrote a history of Rome; a history of the German wars in twenty volumes; multi-volume works on rhetoric and grammar; a two-volume biography of his patron, the Roman statesman Pomponius Secundus; and even a treatise on how to throw a javelin from a horse. But of all his works, only one has survived: his *Historia naturalis* (*Natural History*), completed in around 77 CE. Although not the first, Pliny's *Natural History* is arguably the earliest surviving encyclopaedia.[22] While it hardly resembles a modern encyclopaedia, it is certainly encyclopaedic in its scope and comprises thirty-seven volumes. Pliny claims that it contains an astounding 20,000 facts (there are, in fact, 37,000). Book One, which doubles as an introduction or preface, opens with a letter to his friend and the future emperor Titus, followed by a *summarium*, a kind of table of contents and bibliography rolled into one. The remainder of the *Natural History* is broadly divided thus: astronomy (Book Two); geography (Three to Six); humans and animals (Seven to Eleven); botany (Twelve to Nineteen); medicine (Twenty to Thirty-Two); and mining, precious metals, gems, art and architecture (Thirty-Three to Thirty-Seven).

For the next 1,400 years, Pliny's *Natural History* was an authoritative source on natural history and the ancient world. Its text was plagiarized, epitomized and abridged countless times, proving the major source for many medieval herbals, bestiaries, lapidaries and florilegium. Interest in Pliny's encyclopaedia was reignited in the fourteenth century by Petrarch (1304–74) and, in the following century, it was among the first books to be printed in Italy.

PRINTING PLINY

By the 1470s, Venice was not only one of Europe's most important trade centres, but it was also well on its way to becoming the capital of European printing. And it would be another immigrant, this time from France, who would play a significant role in Venice's meteoric rise. But the story of our present book, the so-called Douce Pliny in the Bodleian Library begins with Ferdinand I, king of Naples (1423–94). Ferrante, as he is more commonly known, was an authoritarian ruler, a formidable politician, and ruthless with his enemies. The historian Jacob Burckhardt wrote of him that 'he liked to have his opponents near to him, either in well-guarded prisons, or dead and embalmed'.[23] But he was also a keen and generous patron of the arts. In 1474 he commissioned Cristoforo

Landino (1424–98), a leading humanist scholar and champion of the Italian vernacular, to translate Pliny's *Natural History* from Latin into the *lingua fiorentina*, the Tuscan dialect. Completed by the autumn of 1475, the translation was to be a gift for Charles the Bold on the engagement of Ferrante's son Federico, prince of Taranto, to Charles's only child, Mary of Burgundy. After the wedding was called off, the manuscript book remained with Ferrante. But all was not lost. It was decided to put the translation to another use – it would be printed. Pliny's *Natural History* had first been printed in 1469 by Johannes de Spira, the first to establish a printshop in Venice, but that *editio princeps* was published in the original Latin. This new edition would be the first printed vernacular translation of Pliny.

No doubt, the timing felt right. Fluency in Latin was in decline, and thanks to Dante and a new enthusiasm for *dolce stil novo*, interest in reading and writing in the vernacular was on the rise. This shift, plus a burgeoning interest in the Latin classics, points to Pliny's *Natural History* as a sound choice for a book that would satisfy intellectual and artistic curiosities and still make a profit. In the dedication, addressed to Ferdinand the king of Naples, Landino explicitly states the motive for publishing a vernacular translation: 'knowing that many people do not understand Latin, you wished to bear them again in mind in this matter by providing Pliny's Latin work turned into Tuscan'.[24] A vernacular translation also fulfilled Pliny's original desire to see his work reach an audience beyond academics and intellectuals, as his *Natural History* was 'written for the masses, for the horde of farmers and artisans and, finally, for those who have time to devote to these pursuits'.[25]

Printing such a large edition in Florence was out of the question, so Filippo Strozzi and his brother Girolamo arranged for the Frenchman Nicolaus Jenson in Venice to print it. By the mid-1470s, Jenson was already on his way to becoming the greatest printer in Venice, if not the whole of Europe. The print-run of about 1,025 copies was large for the 1470s. Most of the copies were printed on paper, but a very small number were printed on the considerably more expensive parchment (treated animal skins). Those printed on parchment were destined to be deluxe copies, decorated by hand and gifted to dignitaries or sold to the rich at a considerable premium. Printing so many copies of a large folio edition measuring about 41.5 × 28 cm and running to 826 pages was also an incredibly expensive undertaking. The cost of the paper alone, about a quarter of a million sheets, ran to the enormous sum of 731 ducats, and perhaps another 400 ducats were paid to Jenson for the actual printing.[26] This was a large sum to invest, even for someone as wealthy as Strozzi, and it appears that the venture was underwritten by Ferdinand.[27] The price for an unbound and undecorated copy was set at 7 ducats (or florins).

In 1479 Filippo Strozzi, perhaps in celebration of the successful publishing venture, had one of the parchment copies sent to the famed Florentine illuminators, Monte and Gherardo di Giovanni di Miniato (or del Fora). The work was completed by 1483 at a cost, for the illumination and binding, of 120 florins. It is this copy that we now call the Douce Pliny, named after Francis Douce who bequeathed it to the Bodleian Library in 1834.

Opening the Douce Pliny is like lifting the lid of a treasure chest. It is a luxuriously beautiful book. Its stiff parchment, crisply printed type and hand-decoration, with colours as bright and vibrant as though they were painted yesterday, are just magnificent. Book One opens with a marvellous border laced with typically classical motifs, a dense latticework of vines, flowers and gems, punctuated with putti and traced with gold leaf. The text opens with a large letter D, in which is painted an anachronistically medieval Pliny seated at a lectern with an armillary sphere in his left hand. At the bottom left is a portrait of Ferrante, and facing him from the opposite border are Filippo Strozzi and his young son Alfonso. Recumbent lambs beneath banderols inscribed with Strozzi's motto *mitis esto* (be gentle) are painted either side of a larger central roundel emblazoned with the three crescents of the Strozzi coat of arms, supported by yet more putti and crowned by a falcon with wings outstretched.

The major decorated initials in the book have a narrative or story-telling function (hence the term 'historiated' to describe them), and the lavish borders are richly populated with both classical and Christian motifs and symbolism. But these elements also serve a further practical purpose as navigational aids, helping readers find their way around the book's more than 800 pages. Each of the thirty-seven books opens with a border piece and a large historiated initial; for example, the illuminated initial E (fol. 21r) depicts the orbs of heaven with the planets revolving around Earth at the centre of the cosmos. It marks the opening of Book Two, Pliny's account of the world and the heavens. Smaller and plainer three-line initials are used throughout the book to mark chapter or section openings. These make finding one's way around the book – printed long before pagination was widely adopted – pretty effortless.

12 Opening to Pliny's *Natural History* in the illuminated Douce Pliny printed by Nicolaus Jenson in 1476.

LIBRO PRIMO DELLA NATVRALE HISTORIA DI .C. PLINIO SECONDO TRADOCTA IN LINGVA FIORENTINA PER CHRISTOPHORO LANDINO FIORENTINO AL SERENISSIMO FERDINANDO RE DI NAPOLI.

PREFATIONE

DITERMINAI O GIOCONDISSIMO
imperadore con epiſtola forſe di troppa licētia
narrarti elibri della hiſtoria naturale: opera no
uella alle muſe romane: nata apreſſo di me nel
lultima genitura. Sia adunq; queſta prefatiōe
ueriſſima di te mētre che gia inuecchia nel grā
diſſimo tuo padre: per che uſando el uerſo di
Catullo mio compatriota tu ſoleui pure ſtima
re qualche choſa le mie ciācie. Tu conoſci que
ſta caſtrenſe & militare parola. Et lui chome tu
ſai mutando le prime ſyllabe ſi fece alquanto
piu duro che non uolea eſſere ſtimato da tuoi
familiari & ſerui. Per queſto adunq; ditermi
nai ſcriuerti: & āchora per che le noſtre choſe appariſchino & ſieno manifeſte p queſta
mia audacia maxime dolēdoti tu che pel paſſato non lhabbi facto in una altra noſtra
procace epiſtola. Et accio che tutti glhuomini ſappino quanto di pari lomperio techo
uiua: Tu elquale hai triomphato & ſe ſtato cenſore & ſei uolte cōſolo & participe del
la tribunitia poteſta: Se ſtato prefecto del pretorio: ilche hai facto piu nobile che tutti
glaltri magiſtrati: perche per piacere a tuo padre & allordine equeſtre lacceptaſti: Et
tutte queſte coſe per riſpecto della republica hai facto: Et me chome nel contubernio
caſtrenſe tractaſti? Et certo niēte ha mutato inte lamplitudine & grandezza della tua
fortuna: ſe non che tanto piu poſſi & uogla giouare: quāto quella e maggiore. Adūq;
bēche a tutti glaltri huomini ſia aperta la uia a impetrare ogni choſa da te uenerādoti:
Niente di meno ſolo laudacia fa che io piu familiarmente te honori. Queſta audacia
adunq; imputerai a te medeſimo: & a te medeſimo nel noſtro fallo perdonerai. Io mi
ſtroppicciai la faccia: & niente di meno neſſuno proficto ho facto: perche per unaltra
uia mappariſti grande: & di lontano mi rimuoui con le faccelline del tuo ingegno. Et
certo in nexuno piu ffolgora quella: laquale piu ueramente e decta in te che in altri for
za deloquentia. In te e quella facundia che alla tribunitia poteſta ſi conuiene: Con q̄ta
riſonantia tuoni tu le laude paterne? Cō quanta (non ſanza amore) dimoſtri quelle di
tuo fratello? Quanto ſe excellente & ſublime nella poetica faculta? O gran fecondita
danimo. Certo hai trouato inche modo poſſi imitare tuo fratello. Ma queſte choſe
chi potrebbe ſanza paura conſiderare: hauendo a uenire al giudicio dellongegno
tuo: maxime eſſendo quello dame prouocato? Certamente non ſono in ſimile
conditione quegli che publicano alchuno libro: & quegli che ate glintitolano. Impero
che ſe io lo publicaſſi & non lo intitolaſſi ate: potrei dire perche leggi tu queſte choſe o
imperadore? lequali ſono ſcripte albaſſo uulgo & alla turba de glagricultori & de glar
tefici & a quegli che cōſumano elloro otio negli ſtudii? Perche adunq; ti fa tu giudice:

The Douce Pliny is not, in any sense, a subtle book. Not only was it the greatest compendium of classical knowledge ever produced in antiquity, but this edition and this specific, unique deluxe copy was a showpiece. It was not a book intended for reading next to the fireplace on a wet Sunday afternoon. It was a status symbol taken down from its shelf or lifted from its trunk to impress. It was a kind of Renaissance coffee table book fit for royalty – albeit before both coffee and coffee tables, of course.

SAVING POMPONIANUS

Pliny's last days were marked by insatiable curiosity and self-sacrifice. It was his sister, Plinia, mother of Pliny the Younger, who alerted him to the plume of smoke rising from the vicinity of Vesuvius. His curiosity piqued, Pliny decided that this strange phenomenon warranted closer inspection. Just as he was about to set off, he received an emergency communiqué from his friend Rectina who was stranded on the opposite side of the bay. Pliny's mission now changed from one of scientific curiosity to a full-blown rescue mission. He set sail from his home in Misenum with several large *quadriremes* (ships). As conditions worsened, rather than turning back Pliny insisted that they press on, famously exclaiming, 'fortune favours the brave; steer to where Pomponianus is'.[28] They eventually docked at Stabiae, several kilometres south of Pompeii, where they found Pliny's friend Pomponianus waiting for them. However, the favourable winds that had helped them on their outbound journey hampered their return, so they headed for Pomponianus's villa. The port town of Stabiae might have been spared the avalanche that befell Herculaneum, but ash and pumice, in places several metres deep, had already buried most structures and led to the collapse of many others, crushing those who had not already perished from asphyxiation. On the walk back to the ships, Pliny, who was probably asthmatic, was overcome by the fumes and died on the beach at Stabiae.

LEGACY

Not everyone was a fan of Pliny's *Natural History*. Between 1492 and 1509, the Italian physician Niccolò Leoniceno (1428–1524) published a series of tracts attacking it for its corrupt texts and translations, and Pliny personally for his credulity and factual errors. One modern encyclopaedia of classical literature is brutal in its characterization of Pliny, describing him as 'catastrophically indiscriminate … and an aspirant to style

13 A plain printed copy of Pliny's *Natural History*, printed in Venice by Nicolaus Jenson in 1476.

LIBRO PRIMO DELLA NATVRALE HISTORIA DI.C. PLINIO SECONDO TRADOCTA IN LINGVA FIOREN TINA PER CHRISTOPHORO LANDINO FIORENTI NO AL SERENISSIMO FERDINANDO RE DI NAPOLI.

PREFATIONE.

d

ITERMINAI O GIOCONDISSIMO
imperadore con epistola forse di troppa licẽtia
narrarti elibri della historia naturale: opera no
uella alle muse romane: nata apresso di me nel
lultima genitura. Sia adunq; questa prefatiõe
uerissima di te mẽtre che gia inuecchia nel grã
dissimo tuo padre: per che usando el uerso di
Catullo mio compatriota tu soleui pure stima
re qualche chosa le mie ciãcie. Tu conosci que
sta castrense & militare parola. Et lui chome tu
sai mutando le prime syllabe si fece alquanto
piu duro che non uolea essere stimato da tuoi
familiari & serui. Per questo adunq; ditermi
nai scriuerti: & ãchora per che le nostre chose apparischino & sieno manifeste p questa
mia audacia maxime dolẽdoti tu che pel passato non lhabbi facto in una altra nostra
procace epistola. Et accio che tutti glhuomini sappino quanto di pari lomperio techo
uiua: Tu elquale hai triomphato & se stato censore & sei uolte cõsolo & participe del
la tribunitia potesta: Se stato prefecto del pretorio: ilche hai facto piu nobile che tutti
glaltri magistrati: perche per piacere a tuo padre & allordine equestre lacceptasti: Et
tutte queste cose per rispecto della republica hai facto: Et me chome nel contubernio
castrense tractasti? Et certo niẽte ha mutato inte lamplitudine & grandezza della tua
fortuna: se non che tanto piu possi & uogla giouare: quãto quella e maggiore. Adũq;
bẽche a tutti glaltri huomini sia aperta la uia a impetrare ogni chosa da te uenerãdoti:
Niente di meno solo laudacia fa che io piu familiarmente te honori. Questa audacia
adunq; imputerai a te medesimo: & a te medesimo nel nostro fallo perdonerai. Io mi
stroppicciai la faccia: & niente di meno nessuno proficto ho facto: perche per unaltra
uia mapparisti grande: & di lontano mi rimuoui con le faccelline del tuo ingegno. Et
certo in nexuno piu ffolgora quella: laquale piu ueramente e decta in te che in altri for
za deloquentia. In te e quella facundia che alla tribunitia potesta si conuiene: Con q̃ta
risonantia tuoni tu le laude paterne? Cõ quanta (non sanza amore) dimostri quelle di
tuo fratello? Quanto se excellente & sublime nella poetica faculta? O gran fecondita
danimo. Certo hai trouato inche modo possi imitare tuo fratello. Ma queste chose
chi potrebbe sanza paura considerare: hauendo a uenire al giudicio dellongegno
tuo: maxime essendo quello dame prouocato? Certamente non sono in simile
conditione quegli che publicano alchuno libro: & quegli che ate glintitolano. Impero
che se io lo publicassi & non lo intitolassi ate: potrei dire perche leggi tu queste chose o
imperadore? lequali sono scriptẽ albasso uulgo & alla turba de glagricultori & de glar
tefici & a quegli che cõsumano elloro otio negli studii? Perche adunq; ti fa tu giudice:
concio sia che quando io scriueuo questa opera: non thaueuo posto nella tauola doue
sono descripti egiudici: Et eri di tanta excellentia: che non stimauo che tu ti degnassi
scendere si basso? Preterea quando bene non fussi in si excelso grado: nientedimeno gli
scriptori comunemente fuggono el giudicio de docti. Questo fa Cicerone: elquale e
di tanta eloquentia: che puo sottomettere longegno al giuocho della fortuna: & quel

who could hardly frame a coherent sentence'.[29] Buried among more pedestrian facts and figures are the Monocoli of the Umbrella-foot tribe, a one-legged people who, according to Pliny, lie on their backs and use their enormous feet (foot!) as parasols (Book 7.2). Incidentally, these one-footed fantasies reappeared nineteen centuries later as 'dufflepuds' in C.S. Lewis's *The Voyage of the Dawn Treader* (1952). Pliny also reports that diamonds can be shattered with the blood of billy goats (Book 20.1), and writes of the dreaded Mantichora, an ancient monster with the face and ears of a man, blue eyes, blood-red skin, three rows of teeth, the body of a lion, a tail like a scorpion's and a voice resembling the combined sounds of a flute and trumpet – oh, and 'particularly fond of human flesh' (Book 8.30). One wonders whether to run in terror or die laughing.

At times, Pliny was indeed uncritical, even credulous. Sometimes he mixed things up, was mistaken or just got things wrong. Not only was he not infallible, but he was writing 2,000 years ago. Is it fair to censure first-century Pliny when he records that, if bitten by a rabid dog, one should burn a handful of the offending dog's hair and apply the ash to the wound – the origin of the colloquial 'hair of the dog' (Book 29.32) – when the germ theory of disease was not fully articulated until the nineteenth and twentieth centuries? Can we blame him for not understanding why, on a spherical Earth, people in the Southern hemisphere didn't fall off (Book 2.65) – when, for the subsequent fifteen centuries we continued to believe that Earth was at the centre of the universe and that the stars and planets, embedded in crystalline spheres, were turned by God or angels?

The *Natural History* is a treasure trove of facts, methods, attitudes and histories – some of which are not to be found elsewhere – and the Douce Pliny is its most fabulous incarnation, a tangible and unequivocal reminder of Pliny's rich and enduring legacy. But even more valuable is that the *Natural History* has bequeathed to us a remarkably rich, immersive and authentic snapshot (albeit a Roman imperial one) of the world Pliny inhabited. Pliny's colourful anecdotes, facts and fictions, monsters and myths capture the first-century zeitgeist, illuminating and bringing into focus the prevailing intellectual climate, and the worlds and cultures not of some alien species but of our very own ancestors.

14 Opening to Book 2 of Pliny's *Natural History*, 1476. The larger historiated initials are used to indicate the opening of a book; smaller, three-line initials mark section or chapter openings.

following pages

15 Historiated initials from the Douce Pliny, 1476.

LIBRO SECONDO DELLA HISTORIA NATVRALE DI.C.PLINIO SECONDO TRADOCTA DI LINGVA LATINA IN FIORENTINA PER CHRISTOPHORO LANDINO FIORENTINO AL SERENISSIMO FERDINANDO RE DI NAPOLI.

SEL MONDO HA TERMINI ET SE E VNO: CAPITOLO PRIMO.

L MONDO ET QVESTO ELQVALE PER altro nome Anoi piacie chiamare Cielo : elquale intorno gyrando tutte lechose chuopre: E giusta chosa credere che sia deita etherna & infinita : Ne mai generata: Ne mai da douere perire. Ricerchar̃ lechose extrĩseche di chostui ne sapptiene alhuomo: ne comprendere lepuo la congectura delhũana mente. Sacro e & etherno & sãza misura. Tutto nel tutto: Anzi esso e tutto & e infinito : ma simile al finito . Di tutte lechose e certo & simile a lincerto. Difuori & dentro ogni chosa ĩ se Abbraccia. Lui medesimo e opera della natura : & e essa natura. Furore sãza fallo mosse alchuni A pẽsare la misura sua: & dipoi Ardire experla. Furono etiam mossi da furore quegli equali prendendo occasione di qui innumerabili mondi essere affermorono: Onde altrettante nature delle chose fussi necessario credere. Et pure se in una natura tutti si posassino: Sarãno constrecti credere che altrettãti sieno esoli: Altretante lelune & laltre immense & innumerabili stelle similmente sieno multiplicate. Ilperche rimanghono occupati nella medesima inuestigatione : non hauendo per questo trouato el fine che disiderano. Et se pure uoglamo attribuire alla natura: laquale e artefice delluniuerso che essa habbi prodocto lechose in infinito: q̃to e piu facile intenderlo in uno mondo solo: maxime essendo quello si grande opera: Furore e per certo: Furore non piccholo Vscire di quello : Et chome se gia lechose dentro allui poste anchora anoi incerte ci sieno note Inuestigare quelle difuori: Stimando che chi non sa lamisura dise possi conseguire quella dalchuna altra chosa. O che lamente humana possi uedere quello che ilmondo inse non cape.

DELLA FORMA DEL MONDO. CAPITOLO. II.

I L nome in prima & dipoi il consenso di tutti glhuomini equali dicono elmõdo orbe cioe tondo: Dimostrano laforma del mõdo essere ridocta in tondo pfecto. Ne mãcono glargomenti aprouare questo medesimo: perche tale figura da tutte le sue parti richade in se medesima: & da se medesima puo essere sostentata: & in se si chiude & contiene: ne dalchuna commissura o cõgiunctura ha dibisogno: ne fine o principio in alchuna sua parte sente. Preterea al moto elquale ha affare elmondo chome pocho disotto dimostrerremo: Tale figura e aptissima. Et finalmente glocchi ne danno uero giudicio: Conciosia che ilconuexo & ilmezo della forma spericha da ogni parte siuede: Ilche in altra figura non puo addiuenire che nella sperica cioe tonda.

DEL MOTO SVO. CAPITOLO. III.

E L nascimẽto & loccaso del sole manifestamente Cidimostrano : che in spatio di xxiiii. hore Questa sperica machina fa tutta la sua circulare reuolutione: laquale ethernalmente senza alchuno riposo & con celerita inenarrabile Gyra. Ne si puo facilmẽte intẽdere se elsuono: elquale nascie dellassiduo uoltare ditanta machina e imẽso: & per questa chagione uincendo elsenso dellaudito non altrimenti si possa udire che

3

HISTORY IN YOUR HANDS

SCHEDEL, *NUREMBERG CHRONICLE* (1493)

The knowledge of past events is the sovereign corrective of human nature.

POLYBIUS, second century BCE[30]

The desire to record or chronicle past and present events existed long before the advent of writing. Oral transmission, through stories, plays, poetry and song, was one way in which history was preserved and passed on to future generations. Some of these survived long enough to eventually be transcribed from the collective memory into writing. The great creation stories of many cultures predate their written adaptations by thousands of years. The oldest surviving work in Greek, Homer's *Iliad*, was likewise part of a far more ancient oral tradition. An important part of many ancient histories was the annal, often little more than a list of monarchs and the dates of their reigns – something that eventually evolved into more detailed and expansive chronicles. In Western history, the Egyptian Royal Annals is the oldest known chronicle to have survived and was probably written between 2470 and 2450 BCE. It tells the story of Egypt's first dynasties, including tales of military conquest and maritime ventures, and even mentions the start of copper smelting in Egypt by about 2700 BCE.

It was not until late antiquity that the chronicle genre really began to take off. A watershed in the compilation of chronicles came in the first decades of the fourth century with a chronicle compiled by the Greek historian and Christian apologist Eusebius of Caesarea (*c*.265–339 CE).[31] In compiling his *Chronicle*, Eusebius consulted many ancient sources – Chaldean, Assyrian, Egyptian, Greek and Roman – distilling them into a universal history from Adam until his own time and the reign of Constantine the Great. In the second book of his *Chronicle*, Eusebius introduced a novel way of presenting his chronologies

16 Arrival of the Antichrist, *Nuremberg Chronicle*, 1493.

PERSARUM	INITIUM CONSULUM	ROMANOR	MACEDONUM
II	ARMODIUS ET ARISTOGITON	XXVIII	XXXIIII
III	HIPPARCUM TYRANNUM INTER	XXVIIII	XXXV
	FECERUNT ET LAENA MERETRIX		
	AMICA EORUM CUM TORMEN		
IIII	TIS COGERETUR UT SOCIOS	XXX	XXXVI
∞D V	PRODERET LINGUAM SUAM MOR	XXXI	XXXVII
LXVI OLYMP	DICUS AMPUTAUIT		
VI	TEMPLUM IN HIEROSOLYMIS	XXXII	XXXVIII
VII	CONSUMMATUR PROFETAN	XXXIII	XXXVIIII
VIII	TIB APUD IUDAEOS AGGAEO ET	XXXIIII	XL
VIIII	ZACHARIA	XXXV	XLI
LXVII OLYMP			
X	PULSIS URBE REGIB UIX USQ AD		XLII
	XU LAPIDEM ROMA TENEBAT IMPE		
	RIUM ROMANOR REGES UII A RO		
	MULO USQ AD TARQUINIUM SUPER		
XI	BUM IMPERAUERUNT AN CCXL SIUE		XLIII
	UT QUIBUSDAM PLACET CCXLIII ROMAE		
	POST EXACTOS REGES PRIMUM CO		
	SULES A BRUTO ESSE COEPERUNT DE		
XII	INDE TRIBUNI PLEBIS AC DICTATO		XLIIII
	RES ET RURSUM CONSULES REMP		
	OBTINUERUNT PER ANNOS FERME		
	CCCCLXIIII USQ AD IULIUM CAESA		
	REM QUI PRIMUS SINGULARE ARRI		
	PUIT IMPERIUM OLYMPIADE CLXXXIIII		
XIII	XUIII MARE OBTINUERUNT AEGINETAE AN		XLU
	XX USQ AD TRANSITUM XERXIS		
LXVIII OLYMP	UALERIUS BRUTI COLLEGA ADEO PAU		
XIIII	PER MORTUUS UT SUMPTU PUBLICO		XLUI
∞DX XU	SEPELIRETUR		XLUII

UII REGES FUERUNT USQ AD TARQUINIUM SUPERBUM ANN CCXLIII ITEM A BRUTO PRIMO CONSULE OPTINUERUNT CONSULES ET TRIBB PLEBIS USQ AD IULIUM CAESAREM ANN CCCCXLIIII

UALERIUS BRUTI CONS COLLEGA ITA PAUPER FUIT UT PUBLICO SUMPTU SEPELIRETUR

XVI xlviii
XVII xlviiii

lxviiii olymp.

XVIII CENSU ROMAE AGITATO INVENTA | L
SUNT HOMINUM CXX MILIA   MACEDONUM 10
NONO ANNO POST EXACTOS REGES ALEXANDER XLIII
NOVA DIGNITAS EST CREATA DICTA
TURA SCILICET ET MAGISTER EQUI
TUM QUI DICTATORI OBSEQUERE
XVIIII TUR DICTATOR PRIMUS LARCIUS I
XX MAGISTER EQUITUM SPURIUS II
XXI CASSIUS FUIT III

Nono anno post reges dictator primus Largius fuit et magister equitum primus Purius Cassius qui dictatori obsequeretur factus est

lxx olymp.

XXII HELLANICUS HISTORIOGRAFUS IIII
ET DEMOCRITUS PHILOSOPHUS ET
XXIII HERACLITUS COGNOMENTO TENE V
BROSUS ET ANAXAGORAS PHYSICI
XXIIII CLARI HABENTUR VI

Democritus Heraclitus tenebrosus Anaxagoras philosophi

XXV PYTHAGORAS PHILOSOPHUS MORI
TUR UULSI CORIOLOS PERDIDERAT VIII

Pythagoras philosophus moritur

lxxi olymp.

XXVI AESCHYLUS TRAGOEDIARUM SCRI VIIII
BTOR AGNOSCITUR
XXVII LATINI CONTRA ROMANOS REBEL VIIII
LAVERUNT
XXVIII ROMA E POPULUS A PATRIB. FACTA X
SEDITIONE DISCEDIT
XXVIIII MARCIUS QUI CORIOLOS CEPERAT XI
INTERVENTU MATRIS UICTURIAE ET
UXORIS UOLUMNIAE AB OBPUGNA

previous pages

17 Jerome's version of the *Chronicle* of Eusebius, 440 CE.

opposite 18 The Peterborough Chronicle (Chronicle of History from the Creation), *c*.1121–31.

as parallel timelines set across the page in columns. To do this, he exploited the newly popularized book format of the codex, which had been so quickly and enthusiastically adopted by early Christians.[32] With its discrete pages, the codex was ideally suited to the columnar layout, the design of which permitted a visual narrative and highlighted places where different chronological traditions intersected. Eusebius had started a new historiographical tradition, and his *Chronicle* soon became a model and a foundational source for countless chronicles throughout the entire Middle Ages, in both the Byzantine east and the Latin west. Universal, national and local chronicles flourished during this time.[33]

The medieval tradition of chronicle writing begins in seventh-century Visigothic Spain with the historian and encyclopaedist Isidore of Seville (*c*.560–636 CE). This also marked the beginning of a new sub-genre known as the epitome chronicle, a still-universal but much-abridged adaptation. Medieval chronicles brought together countless sources, some of which have since been lost. For example, the Anglo-Saxon Chronicle, compiled in the ninth century during the reign of Alfred the Great, is the most important source for our understanding of Anglo-Saxon England. The Peterborough Chronicle, a version of the Anglo-Saxon Chronicle copied in the early twelfth century, is held at the Bodleian Library.

The first printed chronicles appeared in the 1470s, of which the most popular was *Fasciculus temporum* (literally, 'a bundle of times'), compiled by Werner Rolevinck, a Carthusian monk in Cologne. The first edition appeared in 1474. For the most famous of all printed chronicles, we turn south-east to Germany's largest self-governing city, the free imperial city of Nuremberg.

THE NUREMBERG CHRONICLE

It is no surprise that early printing spread first via major trade centres such as Cologne, Augsburg and Nuremberg. Not only were these cities home to wealthy patrons and entrepreneurs who had the means to finance printing projects, but they also possessed a literate, reading populace. Printing had begun early in Nuremberg. Its first press was established in the city in about 1470, just fifteen years after Gutenberg, in Mainz, had produced his first printed Bible. Nuremberg would soon be host to Europe's first scientific press, when Regiomontanus (1436–76), the brilliant mathematician and astronomer, set up his printshop in the city after relocating there in 1471. The city soon became a major centre for the production of astronomical and scientific

Brittene igland is ehta hund mila lang.
⁊ twa hund brad. ⁊ her sind on þis
iglande fif geþeode. englisc. ⁊ brit
tisc. ⁊ wilsc. ⁊ scyttisc. ⁊ pyhtisc. ⁊
boc leden. Erest weron bugend þises
landes brittes. þa coman of armenia. ⁊ gesætan
suðewearde bryttene ærost. Þa gelamp hit þ pyh
tas coman suþan of scithian. mid langum scipum
na manegum. ⁊ þa coman ærost on norþ ybernian
up. ⁊ þær bædo scottas þ hi ðer moston wunian. ac
hi noldan heom lyfan. forðan hi cwædon þa scottas.
we eow magon þeah hwaðere ræd gelæron. We witan
oþer egland her be easton. þer ge magon eardian gif
ge willað. ⁊ gif hwa eow wiðstent. we eow fultumiað. þ
ge hit magon gegangan. Ða ferdon þa pihtas. ⁊ ge
ferdon þis land norþanweard. ⁊ suþanweard hit hef
don bryttas. swa we ær cwedon. And þa pyhtas heom abæ
don wif æt scottum. on þa gerad þ hi gecuron heora
kyne cynn aa on þa wif healfa. þ hi heoldon swa lange
syððan. ⁊ þa gelamp hit imbe geara rina. þ scotta
sum dæl gewat of ybernian on bryttene. ⁊ þes lan
des sum dæl geeodon. ⁊ wes heora heratoga reoda ge
haten. from þam heo sind genemnode dælreodi. Six
tigum wintrum ær þam þe crist wære acenned. Gaius iulius
romana kasere mid hund ehtatigum scipum gesohte
bryttene. Þer he wes ærost gewenced mid grimmum
gefeohte. ⁊ micelne dæl his heres forlædde. ⁊ þa he

instruments, as well as one of Europe's most important centres in the international book trade, and was also a burgeoning hub for the arts and scholarship, establishing itself as the heart of the German Renaissance and northern humanism. Nuremberg's success rested on its geographically central location within the Holy Roman Empire and its position at the intersection of north–south and west–east trade routes. It was also home to, after Gutenberg's Bible, the best-known book of the fifteenth century, the *Nuremberg Chronicle*. But before opening the pages of that storied book, let us pause to meet its author.

Hartmann Schedel (1440–1514) was a German physician, humanist and book lover. He began studying law in Leipzig, but in 1463 moved to Padua to study medicine, where he was awarded his doctorate three years later. After serving as a physician in Nördlingen and then Amberg, Schedel returned to his hometown of Nuremberg, where he would live the rest of his life. Here he continued his work as a physician but increasingly devoted more time to scholarly pursuits, amassing a considerable library of some 370 manuscripts and 670 printed books – one of the largest private libraries of its day. Besides the library, a large part of which has survived, Schedel is best remembered for his *Liber chronicarum*, known in German as *Schedelsche Weltchronik* and in English as the *Nuremberg Chronicle*.

The *Nuremberg Chronicle* appeared first in a Latin edition printed in 1493 (the same year that Columbus returned to Spain from the Americas), followed later in the same year in a German translation by George Alt (*c*.1450–1510). It is one of the most remarkable printed books of the century. A large format folio edition, it measures 49 × 32 cm, runs to more than 600 pages, and is filled with 1,809 illustrations. It was printed in a large edition of more than 2,000 copies – a big print-run for the fifteenth century. Wilhelm Pleydenwurff and Michael Wolgemut, local artists and printmakers (the latter was Albrecht Dürer's former teacher), were commissioned to produce 645 woodcuts. Many of them were used multiple times to illustrate diverse peoples and places. For example, the woodcut for the city of Mainz (fol. 39v), which bears no resemblance to the actual city and is instead a generic or archetypal medieval cityscape, was also used to illustrate Naples, Aquileia, Bologna, Lyon and Heraklion on the island of Crete. Similarly, a woodcut of Pope Leo II (fol. 156v) was used ten times, and the woodcut for the famed Council of Nicaea held in 325 CE was also used to illustrate the councils of Rome, the Lateran Council convened by Pope Martin I in 649 CE and

the councils of Constantinople (380–81 CE) and Basel–Ferrara–Florence (1431–39), among others.

The project of compiling a universal chronicle was commissioned by two wealthy Nuremberg patricians and entrepreneurs, Sebald Schreyer (also a churchwarden) and his brother-in-law Sebastian Kammermeister. The production and writing of the chronicle was Schedel's job. His broad interests and learning, and his ready access to a large personal library, made him ideally suited for the Herculean task. When it came to printing and promotion for such an ambitious book, printed in so many copies, there was only one serious option for the job. Anton Koberger, one of the first to establish a printshop in Nuremberg, had in the intervening decades turned his business

19 Construction of Noah's Ark from the *Nuremberg Chronicle*, 1493.

into a printing empire. By the last decade of the fifteenth century, when he came to print the *Nuremberg Chronicle*, he was the owner of one of Europe's largest printing firms. Not only did Koberger have the capacity to print the chronicle, but through his decades of printing and publishing he had become highly skilled in all aspects of the book trade, including international sales and distribution. A bookseller's advertisement, which has survived because Schedel pasted it into his personal copy of the chronicle, reads, in part:

> Speed now, book, and make yourself
> known wherever the winds blow free.
> Never before has your like been printed.
> A thousand hands will grasp you with
> eager desire
> And read you with great attention.
> Each page adorned with glittering
> illustrations.[34]

When it comes to books printed in the fifteenth century, we often know very little about the details of their production. In most instances, we are left to guess about the size of an edition or, in some cases, even who was responsible for printing it. But with the *Nuremberg Chronicle*, not only have hundreds of copies survived until the present day, but contracts related to the book's production and even manuscript layouts for the design of the book have also survived. A contract drawn up in 1491 between the book's financiers (Schreyer and Kammermeister) and the artists commissioned to produce the woodcut illustrations stipulated that the finished woodcuts should be supplied with sketched layouts for both the Latin and German editions. The surviving layouts, now in the Nuremberg City Library, show how meticulously the book was planned.

HISTORY IN YOUR HANDS

The broadside advertisement pasted into Schedel's copy of the *Nuremberg Chronicle*, mentioned above, explains why it was a must-have book: 'I venture to promise you, reader, so great delight in reading it that you will think you are not reading a series of stories, but looking at them with your own eyes.' Indeed, to contemporary readers, it must have felt as though they held the entire history of the world in their hands. And they must have felt, too, that they were living in momentous times. According to the *Nuremberg Chronicle*, readers were living in the prophesied end times of the Six Ages of the World, a schema proposed by St Augustine (354–430 CE), who suggested that each age spanned about 1,000 years.

The chronicle was published in Latin

and German. There are minor but notable differences between the two editions, designed to accommodate different audiences. In the Latin edition, for example, it reads *de hoc etia[m] ovidi[us] meminit* (Ovid also mentions this),[35] but in the German edition the translation becomes 'Ovid, the poet …' – a useful qualification for those not raised on Latin grammars and who might well have been unfamiliar with the ancient Roman poet.

Although the *Nuremberg Chronicle* claims to be a universal history, it must be remembered that it is limited geographically to Europe and the Holy Land. Much of the text is biblical paraphrase, and its view of history is emphatically Christianized. According to the chronicle, all of history is part of God's providential plan. Secular and religious narratives are wound into a single timeline, culminating in the Apocalypse and the end of the world and of history itself. The introduction to the seventh age (following the sixth and final age of man) opens with considerable space devoted to the prophesied Antichrist. A full-page woodcut (fol. 261v) describes a chaotic scene of preachers and false prophets competing for an audience. The accompanying text paraphrases much from the book of Revelation about the coming of the Antichrist, explaining that 'the entire earth will be overrun and reduced to naught by general plunder and murder' (fol. 263). In this respect, the *Nuremberg Chronicle* is eschatological propaganda designed to prepare the faithful for an imminent Judgement Day so that they might prepare themselves to survive it.

The chronicle also proved influential in perpetuating the long-standing antisemitic canard of blood libel. It repeats the baseless accusation that in 1144 the local Jewish community in Norwich, England, who had only recently settled there, ritually slaughtered and crucified a young boy named William. In the aftermath, several hitherto unsolved child murders were subsequently ascribed to Jewish perpetrators. The increasing hostility and anti-Jewish polemic that these stories fomented led to the eventual expulsion of Jews from England in 1290.[36]

What must have impressed readers even more than the book's size and pretended scope were its illustrations. The *Nuremberg Chronicle* is the most profusely illustrated book of the fifteenth century. It was a large and expensive book. A plain, unbound copy cost about 3 guilders – a bound and hand-coloured copy would set you back almost three times that. Although the *Chronicle* sold reasonably well both in Germany and abroad, a ledger from 1509 reveals that there were still almost six hundred copies unsold (from an estimated 2,100 copies), evidence perhaps that its initial print-run had been somewhat optimistic.

The size and price would certainly have been a major factor influencing sales. However, perhaps even more significant was the appearance soon after of an unauthorized edition. No copyright laws existed at the time, so unauthorized reprints were commonplace. Johann Schönsperger, in nearby Augsburg, quickly got to work producing a considerably smaller German quarto edition (29 × 20 cm) that he published in September 1496, quickly followed by a Latin edition in February of the following year. The fact that he then published a reprint of the German edition in 1500 demonstrates that his smaller format edition proved popular. The success of Schönsperger's smaller and much cheaper edition might explain why, a decade later, there were still hundreds of unsold copies of Schedel's original chronicle.

The *Nuremberg Chronicle* was one of the last great chronicles. For more than a thousand years, the chronicle genre, an essentially uncritical accounting of chronologically ordered events, was the preferred way to write history. Christendom's conception of history was Whiggish – history was not arbitrary and aimless, but was characterized as a progressive journey towards a preordained conclusion. This Christianized history seldom demanded deeper examination into causes and motives because it was simply the unfolding of God's immutable plan.

Although still deeply religious, the humanists of the Italian Renaissance began to look at history differently – not only in reconsidering how history should be written, but with an eye to its political and propagandistic potential. The chronicle was gradually superseded by new historiographical traditions that were sometimes more literarily ambitious and dressed in the classical Latin of Cicero or Livy rather than the pedestrianly bastardized Latin of medieval clerks. Those same humanist scholars also began, despite their reverence for them, to reappraise the histories of antiquity (including antique luminaries such as Herodotus and Livy), in light of new philological and archaeological evidence. They also – and Petrarch springs first to mind – laid the groundwork for a new periodization of history, dispensing with the Six Ages of the World in favour of an even broader tripartite division of Western history into ancient, medieval and modern. Despite its obvious flaws, this has proven remarkably enduring.

20 Days four, five and six of Creation, from the 'pirated' *Chronicle* by Schönsperger (Latin edition, 1497), with woodcuts considerably smaller than those in the original *Nuremberg Chronicle* of 1493.

sed tunc ⁊ animaliũ ⁊ nostris vsibus idonea cum ab eo secedens mari magis magisq̃ aspectũ venit. tũnc fertilis tunc fecunda. Qđ hic a Moyse apertissime demonstratur. Cum eã simul atq̃ apparet ⁊ herbarũ ⁊ frutictum ⁊ arborum parentem facit recte post illam aquarum congregationem terram inducit statim viridem ⁊ florescentem. In medio autem mũdi tanq̃ centrum posuit. venis metallorum videlicet auro. argento ere. cupro. stanno. plumbo. ferro (quod omnia donat) dotauit. cunctisq̃ herbarum generibus summa oblectatione in viridi maturitate illico vestiuit. Herbeq̃ semina. arbores fructus suauissimos produxerunt. Ferunt q̃ eodem die paradisum ab eo factum id est ortum fecundissimum ⁊ amenissimum. omni genere lingni arborumq̃. Quem mũ omni amenitate fontiũ. ⁊ terre virentiũ. lignorumq̃ fructum vberrimum producentiũ conseruit.

Qvarto die dixit deus. Fiant luminaria in firmamento celi. et diuidant diem ⁊ noctem. Et sint in signa ⁊ tẽpora. ⁊ dies et annos. vt luceant in firmamento celi ⁊ illuminent terram. Et factum est ita. Fecitq̃ deus duo luminaria magna. luminare maius. vt preesset diei. et luminare minũs vt preesset nocti ⁊ stellas. vt diuiderent lucem et tenebras. Moyses primo celestium meminit. que posuit deus in firmamento vt lucerent in celo. ⁊ terram illuminarent. solem videlicet lunam ⁊ stellas. quibus ipsa superior mundi ꝑs ornatur. vti terra ornatur his que in ea sunt metallis. plantis animantibus. Cum enim de natura firmamenti dixerat testabat vt de operibus siderum. deq̃ eorum officio dissereret. declarans in quem vsum fundata. ⁊ cui muneri delegata a deo fuerint. Celestium enim corporum due in vniuersum manifeste operationes motus ⁊ illuminatio. motus duplex statuitur Alter mundi totius quo celum ⁊ ether viginti quattuor horis. per totum spacium vniuersi ꝑfecto ambitu circumuoluuntur. Alter siderũ proprius multiplex ⁊ vari⁹. Inter quos principalis motus solis. qui spacio duodecim mẽsium zodiaci signa omnia circuit. ille diem facit. vnde ⁊ diurnus dicitur. hic autem annum Reliqui siderum motus varijs temporum interuallis peraguntur. Recte igitur ⁊ breuiter nos omnium admonuit. Moyses cũ dixit posita sidera in firmamento in dies annos ⁊ tẽpora. Indicauit preterea expresse reliquã operationem siderum. Que est illuminatio. cũ dixit statuta illa vt lucerent in celo ⁊ terram illuminarent. in hec igitur ministeria ⁊ lune et solis ⁊ stellarum sunt corpora distributa. Sol q̃ qui oritur in die. licet sit vnus (vnde solem esse appellatum. Cicero vult videri) ꝙ obscuratis sideribus solus appareat. Tamen verum ⁊ ꝑfecte plenitudinis lumen est. ⁊ a calore potissimo. ⁊ vulgore clarissimo. Quamuis enim stelle innumerabiles micare ac radiare videantur tamen quia non sunt plena ac solida lumina. nec caloris perferunt quicq̃. nec tenebras multitudine sua vincunt. Duo igitur principalia inueniuntur. que diuersam ⁊ contrariam sibi habent potestatem calor et humor. que mirabiliter deus ad sustentanda et gignenda oĩa excogitauit. altissime hic pertractande essent q̃stiones. ⁊ que sibi singule iustum volumen exposcerent. quo pacto hec sidera sint in firmamento. an vti partes eius nobiliores. an vt animalia in suis speris. in aqua pisces. iumenta i terris. congressum hic item locus cum Genethliacis sibi exposcere diuinandi per astra. ⁊ prenoscendi futuros euentus. scientiam hinc confirmantibus ꝙ Moyses sidera insigna posita a deo dixerit. Querendum hic etiam de natura siderum. de motu. de principatu. de lũe maculis. deq̃ omni siderali scientia. Verum quã q̃ sint pulcra ⁊ digna cognitu. Audiemus fortassis Horationum illud, sed nunc non erat hic locus.

Qvinto die dixit deus. ꝓducãt aque reptile anime viuentis. ⁊ volatile super terrã sub firmamẽto celi. Creauitq̃ deus cete grandia. ⁊ oẽm animã viuentẽ atq̃ motabilem quas produxerãt aque in species suas. ⁊ oẽ volatile scđm genus suũ. Videns qđ esset bonũ benedixit ei dicens. Crescite ⁊ multiplicamini ⁊ replete aquas maris. auesq̃ multiplicent̃ sup terrã. Ornauit igit̃ eo die deus aerẽ ⁊ aquam. volatilia dans aeri. natalia aquis. q̃ reptilia dicunt̃. cum impetu quodã se rapiunt. Cete eñ grandia ⁊ belluas. maioraq̃ terrestrib⁹ aĩalibus ex habundãtia humoris monstrifica in mari reperiunt̃. Et quicquid in vlla ꝑte nature nascit̃. ⁊ in mari eẽ vulgi opinio fert. Manifesta iam que sequunt̃ de animaliũ productiõe. post plantas eñ ea sũt mixta que sentiũt ⁊ mouent̃. quãq̃ in plantis stupidũ sensũ adscribant pitagorici. Hec autẽ animantia que citra oĩẽ controuersiã motu sensuq̃ participant. ⁊ hic a Moyse ⁊ in Timeo in volatilia. ⁊ in aquis degentia ⁊ terrestria distinguunt̃. Veniamus igit̃ ad moysen q̃ postq̃ de celestib⁹ dixit terrestriũ animaliũ meminit ordine cõgruẽti. q[illegible] aq̃s vel terrã vel aerẽ inhabitant. Si tamen inhabitare aerẽ volucres dici possunt. Relinquam⁹ hic disputatõẽ. quo pacto corpora aĩaliũ ex elemẽtis. aut q̃đ sint indite a deo naturis rerũ seminarie rationes. sitne itẽ vita brutoꝝ de sinu educta materie. an diuino potius principio oĩs vita proueniat. vt cõstantissime asserit. Plotinus. cui sententie fortasse videbit̃ hoc loco propheta suffragari. Cũ postq̃ dixit. producant aque reptile aĩe viuentis adiecit postea creauit deus oẽm aĩaz viuẽtẽ. vbi nõ id dũtaxat q̃si piã obseruaret ꝙ ⁊ aq̃ ꝓducãt deo iubẽte. ⁊ deinde etiã de⁹ ꝓducat. verꝫ ⁊ illud qđ vbi de dei ope agit̃ scriptũ ẽ. creauit de⁹ aĩaz viuentẽ vbi aũt de aq̃s. non aĩaz. sed reptile aĩe viuẽtis q̃si aq̃s vehiculũ. Inter aĩalia terre tria mẽorat Moyses q̃ in seq̃nti die insinuat. Plima aũt ⁊ maxia in indico mari aĩalia Eq̃b⁹ balene quaternũ iugerꝫ. Et i mari bellue circa solsticia maxie visunt̃. Tũc illi eruũt turbines. tũc imbres. tunc deiecte montiũ iugis ꝓcelle ab imo vertũt maria. pulsatasq̃ ex ꝓfũdo belluas cũ fluctibus voluũt. auiũ q̃ grãdissime ⁊ pene bestiarũ generis structio cameli affrici vel ethiopici altitudinem equitis insidentis equo excedunt. celeritatem vincunt Multo mirabilius de naturis auium ⁊ piscium ratio experiendi quotidie in varijs locis datur.

Sexta die dixit deus. Producat terra animam viuentem. iumenta. ⁊ reptilia ⁊ bestias terre iuxta species suas. Et vidit deus quod esset bonũ. ait. Faciamus hominem ad imaginem ⁊ similitudinem nostram. Et presit piscibus maris et volatilibus celi. ⁊ bestijs vniuerse terre. Et creauit deus hominem ad imaginem ⁊ similitudinem suam. Ornatis superioribus mundi partibus tandẽ sexta die terram generibus animalium ornauit. Inter animalia terre tria memorat moyses. iumenta reptilia ⁊ bestias. In q̃bus differẽtias brutorum irrationabilium in commune nobis insinuat Sunt enim bestie que perfecta

4

LUCA AND LEONARDO

PACIOLI, *DE DIVINA PROPORTIONE* (1509)

The chief forms of beauty are order and symmetry and definiteness, which the mathematical sciences demonstrate in a special degree.

ARISTOTLE, fourth century BCE[37]

We see and use them every day, and yet most of us seldom give them much thought. They tell us whether we are financially rich or poor, how old we are, how many days there are until our next vacation or the distance to the closest petrol station or even the Moon. They are also used to estimate the mass of the Higgs boson and the quantum mechanical wave properties of orbiting electrons within atoms. All these things, from the prosaically pedestrian to the perplexingly profound, are described by numbers. The graphic symbols of those numbers (numerals), along with systems of counting, are human inventions.

No one knows precisely when humans began counting. In Africa, incised bones, some dating to about 35,000 BCE, appear to record quantities. In the Middle East, archaeological digs have unearthed scores of small clay tokens. Those date to as early as 8000 BCE and might have been used as counters at markets to denote different kinds of produce. In South America, *quipu* (knotted strings) were used as counting devices by the Inca. It is difficult to imagine our lives without them, and yet in the Pirahá language of the indigenous Pirahã of Amazonas in Brazil, there are simply no words for numbers. Anthropologist Caleb Everett, in his book about the invention and history of numbers, explains that numbers do not appear to be innate: 'Mathematical concepts are not wired into the human condition. They are learned, acquired through cultural and linguistic transmission.'[38]

It is no accident that the decimal or base-10 system is the world's most widespread counting system. That our ten (*decem* in Latin) fingers make convenient counters was undoubtedly

21 Portrait of Fra Luca Pacioli. Typically attributed to Jacopo de' Barbari, c.1500.

a prehistoric epiphany. It is also why, in many languages, the word for five comes from the word for hand. The ancient Sumerians and Babylonians, however, used base-60. No one is entirely sure why they adopted the sexagesimal system, but its legacy is ubiquitous – in 60-second minutes and 60-minute hours. In Europe, the widespread use of roman numerals (also base-10), which appear to have evolved from earlier Etruscan tally-mark numerals, persisted well into the fifteenth century. Hindu–Arabic numerals were a significant advance. Originating in India, they were introduced into Europe by Persian and Arab mathematicians in the eleventh and twelfth centuries, and subsequently enthusiastically recommended by Fibonacci in the early thirteenth century.

LUCA PACIOLI

Part of the European Renaissance of the fourteenth and fifteenth centuries was a renaissance in mathematics, during which the works of ancient and medieval authors alike, from Euclid and Archimedes to al-Khwārizmī and Fibonacci, were re-evaluated. At the same time, the mathematization of science, necessitated by advances in astronomy, cartography and surveying, was gaining momentum. One of the central figures in this mathematical renaissance was Luca Pacioli. Born sometime between the autumn of 1446 and the summer of 1447 in Borgo Santo Sepolcro in Tuscany, Luca received a humanist grammar school education, including instruction in Latin and possibly Greek, in the town's only school. He was tutored separately in *abaco* mathematics – arithmetic and algebra for commerce – perhaps by the artist and mathematician Piero della Francesca (1415–92).

In 1464, while still a teenager, Pacioli headed north along the Adriatic coast to Venice, where he was an apprentice to Antonio Rompiasi, a Venetian leather merchant. He tutored Rompiasi's three sons, and studied mathematics under Domenico Bragadino at the Scuola di Rialto. By 1470 he had finished writing his first *abaco* book. That same year he spent months in Rome with the humanist architect, author and consummate Renaissance man, Leon Battista Alberti (1404–72). In the more magnanimous humanist tradition, Alberti believed that one of life's greatest virtues was to produce work that benefited the greatest number of people – an ideal exemplified in Pacioli's own pedagogy and publishing.

After Rome, Pacioli returned home to Borgo Santo Sepolcro, and by the autumn of 1475, at the latest, he had been ordained as a Franciscan friar. Thereafter, he began his university education at Perugia, the closest to his

22 Leonardo da Vinci's drawings of regular, semiregular and convex polygons. From Codex Atlanticus.

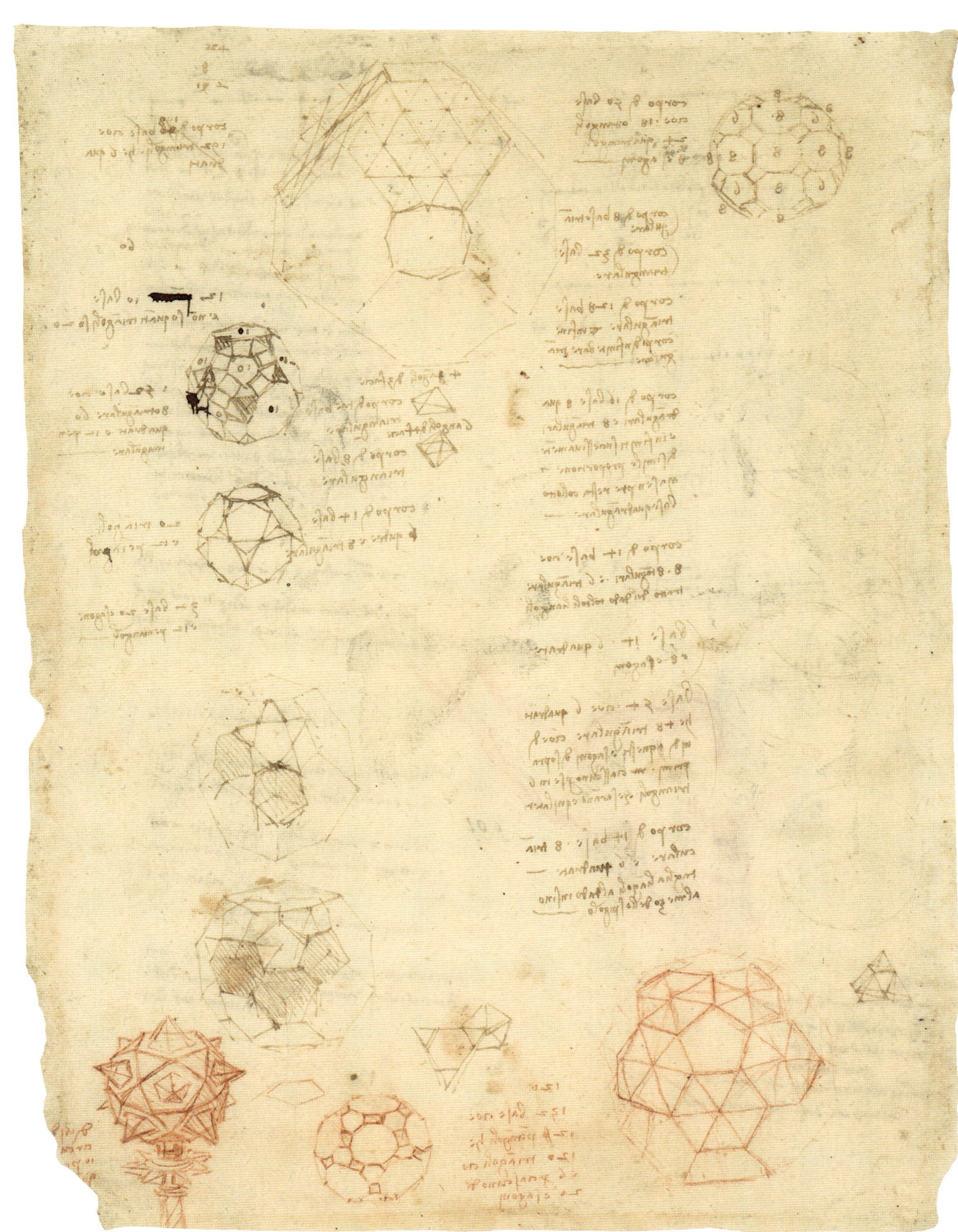

hometown, where he studied theology – all the while supporting himself by teaching *abaco* on the side. Back in Venice in 1494, he published *Summa de arithmetica*, a 600-page book of mathematics that contained the first printed exposition of double-entry bookkeeping, earning him the moniker, the 'father of accounting'. Pacioli was about fifty when he got his big break. In 1496, he was invited to teach mathematics at the court of Ludovico Sforza (also known as Ludovico il Moro) in Milan. It was here that Pacioli found a close friend and collaborator in Leonardo da Vinci (1452–1519), who had worked at the Milan court as a painter and engineer since 1482. It is not unreasonable to suppose that Leonardo had a hand in bringing Pacioli to the Sforza family court.

DIVINE PROPORTIONS

In Milan, sharing an apartment with Leonardo da Vinci, Pacioli completed his *De divina proportione* (*The Divine Proportion*). Early in 1498, deluxe illuminated copies written on parchment were prepared for Pacioli's patrons. Two of them have survived – one was presented to the Florentine statesman Piero Soderini, and another gifted to Galeazzo Sanseverino, beloved son-in-law of Ludovico Sforza and his wife Beatrice.[39] These presentation copies were accompanied by illustrations and wooden models of polyhedra (three-dimensional geometrical figures). There is nothing at this time to suggest that Pacioli planned to have his book printed. But a decade later, he headed to Venice to oversee the first printed edition (1509). It was printed by Paganino Paganini, whom Pacioli had used back in 1494 to print his *Summa*.

Pacioli's *De divina proportione* is broadly divided into three sections or books. The first, 'Compendio divina proportione', deals with the golden ratio or 'divine proportion'; the second, 'Tractato del'architectura', is a treatise on geometry in architecture, with many references to Vitruvius (see pp. 67–78); while the third part is a vernacular translation of Piero della Francesca's *Libellus de quinque corporibus regolaribus*, a book about geometry and the construction of regular solids, illustrated with scores of diagrams in the margins. This third part is the most controversial, because nowhere is Piero credited as the work's author. In a brief biography of Piero della Francesca published in 1550, Giorgio Vasari lambasts Pacioli for his unabashed plagiarism, writing of him that he had 'wickedly and maliciously sought to remove his teacher Piero's name', and that in doing so he had, in a splendid turn of phrase, 'covered his ass's hide with the glorious skin of a lion'. More recently, it has been suggested that Pacioli

23 Miniature of Pacioli presenting a copy of his *De divina proportione* to the duke of Milan. From a manuscript presentation copy of *De divina proportione*, 1498.

EX.^mo P. LVDOVICO. M. SF. AN. MEDIOLANEN. DVCI.
INCLYTO. PACIS. ET. BELLI. ORNAMENTO. FR.
LVCE EX BVRGO S.^ti SEPVLCRI. OR. MI. SACRE.
THEO. PROFES. DE DIVINA. PROPORT. EPISTOLA.

ssendo Ex.° D.
adi viiii de Febra
ro de nostra sa
lute gliánni o
1498. corrend°
nelinspugnabil
arce. delincly
ta uostra cita
de Milano di
gnissi[illegible] luogo de sua solita resid[illegible]tia ala r
presentia di quella constituto. in[illegible]udabi
le e scientifico [illegible]llo da molti de ogni gra
do celeberrimi. e sapientissimi ac[illegible]ompagna
ta. si religiosi como seculari: deliquali a[illegible]
due la sua magnifica corte habunda: I[illegible]
cui numero. oltra le R.^me S. de uescoui. pro
tonotarii: e abbati [illegible]on del nostro sacro
seraphico ordine. [illegible] padre. e sublime. o
theologo. Maestro Gometio. col dignissim°

M. Gometius.

Queſta lettera .M. ſe caua del tondo e del ſuo quadro le gambe ſuttili uogliáo eſſer per mezo de le groſſe comme la ſeniſtra del. A. le extreme gambe uogliano eſſer al quanto dentro al quadro le medie fra quelle e le interſecationi de li diametri lor groſſeze . groſſe e ſutili ſereſereſcano a quel le del. A. cõme di ſopra in figura aperto poi comprendere.

24 Constructed M from Luca Pacioli's *De divina proportione*, 1509.

might have authored or at least contributed to the treatise.[40]

Pacioli's title, *The Divine Proportion*, refers to what is nowadays commonly known as the golden ratio or golden section. According to *The Concise Oxford Dictionary of Mathematics*, 'a line segment is divided in golden section if the ratio of the whole length to the larger part is equal to the ratio of the larger part to the smaller part'.[41] To three decimal places, the golden ratio is 1.618 and is often denoted by the Greek letter φ (phi). For those preferring pictures over algebra, the golden ratio can be seen in action in the 'golden rectangle' whose sides are in the golden ratio. This is easily drawn with just a straight edge and compass. The golden rectangle is fascinating in that it exhibits a form of self-similarity – if you add or remove a square from either end, the resulting rectangle is also in the golden ratio! Although Euclid did not discover it, his *Elements*, written in about 300 BCE, include the first extant description of the golden ratio, which he calls the 'division in extreme and mean ratio'[42] – an appellation destined never to catch on. The golden ratio features little in medieval mathematics texts but resurfaces in the work of Fibonacci in the early thirteenth century. By Pacioli's time, interest in the golden ratio (a term not coined until the nineteenth century) was undergoing a full-blown renaissance.

LEONARDO'S INEFFABLE LEFT HAND

Beyond the title, Pacioli's *De divina proportione* is best known for its magnificent series of fifty-nine woodcut illustrations grouped together at the end of the book. The series begins with the famous five Platonic solids. In his dialogue *Timaeus*, Plato (427–347 BCE) describes five possible convex regular polyhedra or regular solids: the tetrahedron, cube, octahedron, dodecahedron and icosahedron. These Platonic solids are a special case of polyhedra – each has regular congruent polygonal faces and identical vertices. Expressed in simpler terms, all the faces are identical and all corners are of the same shape. Take, for example, the simplest of the Platonic solids, the tetrahedron (a triangular pyramid). Its four faces are identical equilateral triangles that meet in four identical vertex corners.

The dimensions of the two Platonic solids with the most faces – the dodecahedron and icosahedron (twelve and twenty faces, respectively) – are intimately related to the golden ratio. In the dodecahedron, with its twelve regular pentagons as faces, we see this in action if we draw internal lines connecting the vertices. The ratios of the unequal sides of the resulting isosceles triangles are in the golden ratio! The dodecahedron is also remarkable in that the other four Platonic solids can be derived from it. This fact delighted Pacioli, and he used it to advance a religious or divine analogue, writing that it 'sustains the existence of all the others'.

In the dedication to *De divina proportione*, Pacioli credits Leonardo da Vinci as the artist of the polyhedra drawings. These are the only drawings by Leonardo to have been published in print during his lifetime. At around the time Leonardo and Luca were living together in Milan, and when Pacioli was completing his manuscript of *De divina proportione*, Leonardo was drawing geometrical figures, including sketches of the five Platonic solids, in his small notebook. In his usual mirror writing, he noted the respective number of faces underneath each figure.

The polyhedra in *De divina proportione* are really the product of exceptional pedagogy, mathematics and artistry. What is particularly novel about them, besides their obvious artistic merit, is how Leonardo and Pacioli chose to present the various polyhedra in two configurations: in enclosed or solid forms (*solidus*), and as wire-frames or unenclosed skeletal forms (*vacua*). These two arrangements of the various polyhedra better illustrated their three-dimensionality and their overall construction; it highlighted the congruity of their faces, and permitted a view of surfaces that would otherwise have remained hidden. The book's enormously generous outer margins are another aid to learning. This is not a book made to sit pretty and undisturbed on a high shelf, but one that has intentionally broad margins designed to facilitate engagement with the text through note-taking and workings.

GOLDEN NONSENSE

Pacioli was truly awestruck by mathematical wonders like the golden ratio – and indeed by mathematics in general. Through his expert exposition and the splendid illustrations prepared by his brilliant friend Leonardo, interest in the golden ratio has captured the popular imagination ever since. It has confounded, fascinated and beguiled generations of people across countless disciplines – from biology and biomechanics to physiology and psychology, and the arts. But its popularity has also led to exaggerated and sometimes patently false claims. Even otherwise rational commentators have been taken in by the sensationalism of 'golden numberism',[43] in repeating, for example, that the ancient Greeks incorporated the golden section into their architecture, including the Parthenon – claims easily debunked by anyone with a tape measure and some common sense.

Similarly, we learn that Leonardo da Vinci and other Renaissance artists made frequent use of the golden ratio in their art. Such claims fall prey to even the slightest scrutiny. The same goes for the Egyptian pyramids. That the Egyptians built them using the golden ratio makes for entertaining TV shows and sells books, but it has no foundation in reality. Grossly exaggerated claims of the golden ratio manifested in nature and natural phenomena also abound. The nautilus, a kind of mollusc, is trotted out ad nauseam as evidence of the golden ratio in nature. While they are indeed marvels of nature, with their growth following a logarithmic spiral, one only has to measure them to see that typically their shape is not determined by the golden ratio.[44] The golden ratio is related to objects exhibiting fivefold symmetry (such as the pentagon), and fivefold symmetry occurs frequently in nature; for example, many animal viruses are icosahedral. But the golden ratio is just one of many ratios that appears in nature – sometimes. Most exaggerated claims of the golden ratio appearing in art and nature are usually cases of special pleading, highlighting its appearance and ignoring its absence.

NUMBERS ALL THE WAY DOWN

In 1516, taking up an invitation from King Francis I, Leonardo retired to France. The following year Pacioli died, aged seventy, probably in his hometown of Borgo Santo Sepolcro. Their remarkable friendship mutually inspired their intellectual and creative endeavours, leaving behind a rich and magnificent legacy in numbers and art. For Pacioli, mathematics was not an esoteric or philosophical abstraction, but had extraordinary practical applications in all aspects of life, from commerce to cosmology. But it also served and highlighted a yet higher purpose – one connected to his humanist ideals and, most importantly, to his faith. For Pacioli, 'mathematics was not simply the mother of science and art, it was the language in which God created the world'.[45]

The ancient Greek philosopher Pythagoras, who lived in the sixth century BCE, believed that nature is essentially mathematics, that numbers underpin reality itself. Plato took that a step further when he probed the ontological status of numbers. In his Theory of Forms, he introduced numbers as a class of immaterial or abstract objects in the realm of Forms. The great medieval encyclopaedist Isidore of Seville stressed the foundational nature of numbers when he wrote in the early seventh century, 'Remove numbers from all things, and everything perishes'.[46] Numbers are indelibly written into the fabric of our existence. And whether we take the extreme Platonic position and see numbers existing independently from reality, or we simply view them as the nominalists do, as essentially invented and descriptive, what we cannot deny is that the world we inhabit is not only described by numbers but is inspired by them too.

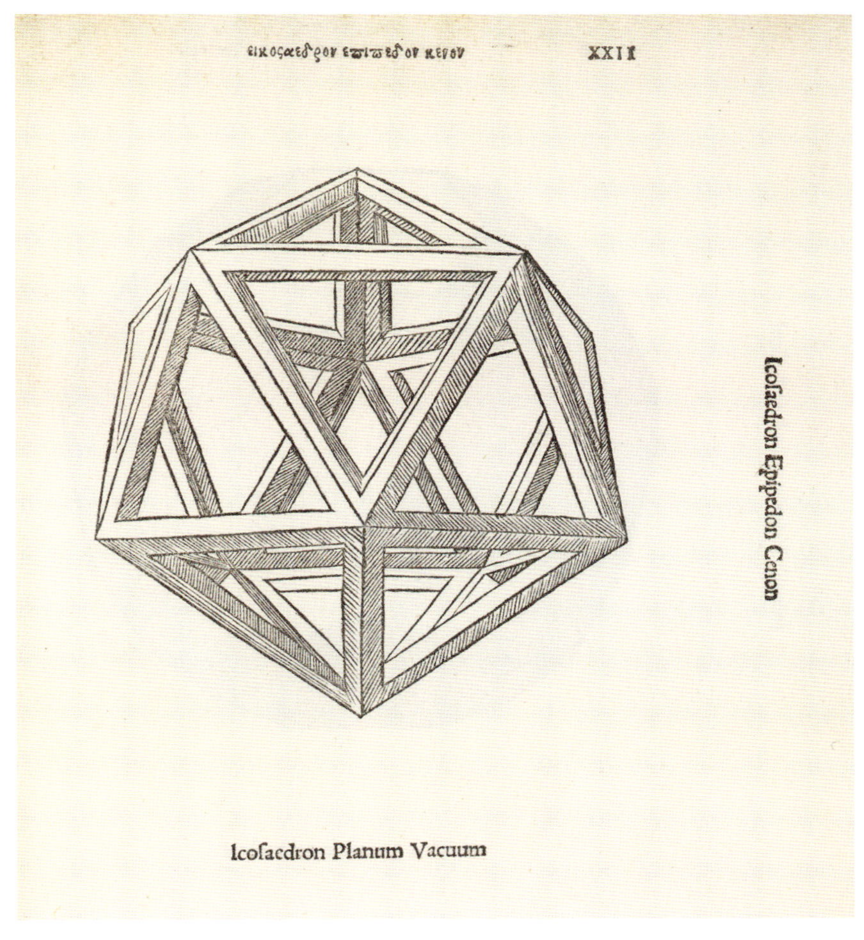

25 Wire-frame version (*vacua*) of a regular icosahedron after Leonardo da Vinci. From Luca Pacioli's *De divina proportione*, 1509.

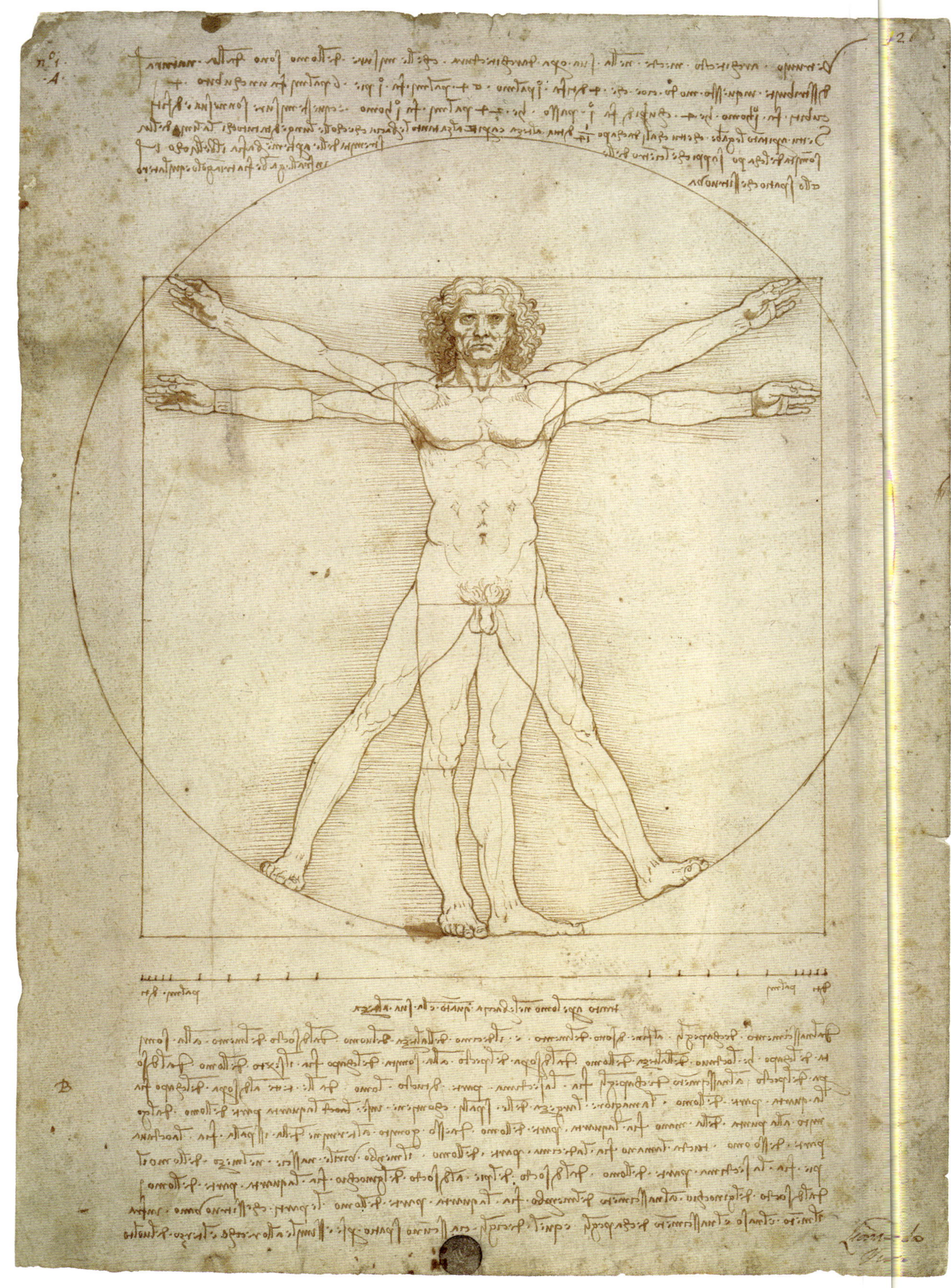

5

CATAPULTS AND CORNICES

VITRUVIUS, *DE ARCHITECTURA* (1521)

If the boy seems slow of wit, you should make an auctioneer of him or an architect.

MARTIAL, between 86 and 98 CE[47]

Contrary to popular belief, only a small number of our prehistoric ancestors lived in caves. Although insulated from extremes of temperature and affording protection from the elements, caves were, in most locales, few and far between. And they were sometimes home to bears and big cats, who were probably not keen to cohabit with our Neanderthal and *Homo sapiens* forebears. Most, then, lived in small temporary or mobile shelters and tipis. But around 10,000 BCE, the beginning of the Neolithic period, the way humans lived began to be transformed. Loosely speaking, this time corresponds with the beginnings of architecture, when humans began to build their environments and construct more permanent, fixed dwellings. It also broadly coincides with a shift away from hunter-gatherer communities to plant and animal domestication and farming economies. Once humans began to abandon their nomadic lifestyles, some of those small, agglomerated networks of former hunter-gatherers became the inhabitants of the first cities.

Among the oldest surviving permanent settlements are the ruins of what is colloquially known as Göbekli Tepe (Potbelly Hill), a fortified complex in south-east Turkey, constructed around 10,000 BCE. In Mesopotamia, baked mud bricks were used in construction. They were even stacked in hundreds of thousands to form ziggurats, scattered throughout what is now Iran and Iraq. From about 2600 BCE, the Egyptians used millions of limestone and granite blocks to construct enormous pyramids that serve as both monuments and tombs, the largest measuring almost 150 m tall. In northern China's Shaanxi province are the ancient

26 Study of the proportions of the human body, known as the *Vitruvian Man*, by Leonardo da Vinci, c.1490.

ruins of Shimao, a massive fortified network of stone buildings dating to about 2000 BCE and built on a large 400-hectare site, the largest late Neolithic settlement in China. From the third century BCE, the city of Petra was a major hub on the trans-Arabian 'incense route', a commercial network that connected the producers of spices and aromatics on the Arabian Peninsula to the Mediterranean coast. Built by the Nabateans around 300 BCE, the sculptured tombs and temples of Petra, in what is now south-west Jordan, were carved out of the local pink sandstone cliffs.

DE ARCHITECTURA

In January 1417, while scouring the shelves of a monastery library, the humanist scholar and obsessive book hunter Poggio Bracciolini famously discovered a complete manuscript of Lucretius's didactic poem *De rerum natura* (*On the Nature of Things*). What is less well known is that, shortly before the Lucretian find, Poggio had also chanced upon a dusty and long-forgotten manuscript copy of *De architectura libri decem* (*The Ten Books on Architecture*), written by the Roman architect and engineer Vitruvius. It is the only substantial architectural treatise to have survived from antiquity. Vitruvius probably composed it around 25 BCE, shortly after the defeat of Mark Antony and Cleopatra at the hands of Octavian, to whom, as Emperor Augustus, *De architectura* is dedicated.

Described as a 'technical handbook with literary ambitions',[48] *De architectura* is divided into ten main sections or 'books' (originally ten *volumen* or scrolls), which include the origins of architecture, architectural theory and practice; the status, training and behaviour expected of an architect; and the classical architectural orders of Doric, Ionic and Corinthian (though he does not use the term 'order' to describe them). Also covered are civil engineering and town planning; water supply and hydraulic engineering; building materials; the construction of sundials, water clocks and mosaic floors; and a formula for concrete (volcanic ash, lime and seawater). In addition, there are countless design principles and practical prescriptions, including that libraries should face east to benefit from morning sunlight, which will limit humidity that would otherwise damage books (Book 6.4.1); that streets should be planned obliquely to winds to prevent them from becoming virtual wind tunnels (1.6); that the corner columns in a temple building, which appear a little narrower, should be made wider 'by one-fiftieth of their diameter' to compensate for this optical illusion (3.3.11); how to plan and construct the *hypocaustum* (10.2), a kind of central heating;

and that the lead in lead water pipes is toxic – the first time this fact is recorded.

However, *De architectura* is much more than an architectural handbook. Vitruvius is also keen to elevate both the practice of architecture and the social status of the architect. It annoys him that Olympic athletes should be feted and live luxuriously on generous pensions, while writers – and indeed architects – remain sorely underpaid and undervalued (9.praef.1–2). Writing a century or so later, the Roman poet Martial recommends architecture for children 'slow of wit' (*Epigrams*, 5.56). Aware that architects are not particularly well respected, Vitruvius insists that they receive a broad liberal arts education encompassing everything from music theory, medicine and philosophy to law, mathematics and geometry. Not only should a better education solicit greater respect, but it would have practical advantages too. For example, the study of law would prove useful in the construction of 'party walls' and in property or land disputes, knowledge of the harmonic proportions from music could be useful in aspects of architectural design, and proficiency in astronomy was crucial, for 'anyone who lacks this knowledge cannot understand the principle of a sundial' (1.1.10).

Hardly anything is known about Vitruvius besides the scant details he discloses throughout the course of his ten books. He served in the Roman army and was put in charge of designing and building fortifications, siege engines and artillery machines for Julius Caesar (1.praef.2). According to the first-century Roman civil engineer Sextus Julius Frontinus, Vitruvius had also worked as *curator aquarum* (head of waterworks) for Rome, and in that role introduced new standard sizes for water pipes. Head of waterworks might not sound like much, but in Rome it was a very prestigious position.

VITRUVIAN MAN

As buildings are constructed for use by humans, it makes sense that their dimensions and proportions are somehow related to the size of the people who inhabit them, work in them or visit them. The dimensions of a typical doorway are an obvious example of this practical, common-sense relationship. Ceiling heights, the height of a counter, the pitch and tread of staircases and steps – all are designed to accommodate typical human beings.

In Book Three, devoted to the building of temples, Vitruvius introduces us to the ancient idea – later enthusiastically appropriated and repopularized during the Renaissance – that the human body is a microcosm of the larger macrocosmic universe. Leonardo da Vinci's friend, the Sienese architect Francesco di Giorgio, believed that 'all the arts and all the world's rules are derived from a well-composed and proportioned human body'.[49] Similarly, Leonardo himself noted that the 'body is an analogy for the world'.[50]

Vitruvius describes anthropomorphically derived proportions formalized into a geometrical diagram – a human figure imposed on a circle and square. If Vitruvius ever actually drew the primordial Vitruvian Man that he described in his third scroll, it has long since been lost. But fast-forward 2,000 years to about 1490, and we might discreetly peer over the shoulder of a brilliant young artist in Milan who, with a copy of Vitruvius's *De architectura* opened to Book Three, is carefully drawing a nude male figure sporting eight superimposed limbs inscribed in a circle and square. Today, Leonardo da Vinci's *Vitruvian Man* is one of the most famous images in the world.

DID VITRUVIUS DRAW?

By the 1480s, woodcut illustrations had become quite common in printed books, so why was the *editio princeps* (first printed edition) of Vitruvius's *De architectura* published without them? This begs a further question – did Vitruvius, when he set reed pen to papyrus or parchment in the first century BCE, supplement his text with drawings? Some parts of *De architectura* are hard to follow without reference to drawings and diagrams. Vitruvius admits as much, and on no fewer than nine occasions he assures his readers that he will supply drawings for the purpose of clarification. In Book One, when discussing the orientation of streets and buildings with respect to the direction of winds, he promises to supply figures at the end of the book:

> For the readier understanding of these topics, since I have treated them with brevity, it has seemed best to me to give two figures, or, as the Greeks say, σχήματα [*schemata*], at the end of this book: one designed to show the precise quarters from which the winds arise; the other, how by turning the directions of the rows of houses and the streets away from their full force, we may avoid unhealthy blasts.[51]

No ancient manuscript of *De architectura* has survived, and therefore we have no ancient Vitruvian drawings – if ever they existed. The earliest surviving Vitruvian manuscript belongs to the first quarter of the ninth century. It contains just a single simple drawing of the aforementioned winds, drawn in brown ink.

27 Vitruvian Man from Cesariano's Italian translation of *De architectura libri decem*, 1521.

ꝟS

e: Con le qual hano uſato: An-
quali ſono aſequiti magne &

emeo ſi uedeno ſapientiſſimamente
ncipale : & capi legionarii de le altre
ernotato : & coſi infinite altre ratio
& piu ſubtile ſono quelle de la Archi-
igneo diuiſo como li noſtri Archite-
ano de uno ben proportionato ho-
o la longitudine del dicto brazo : Et
a particula anchora in duodece altre
a Minuto : che conſta de .12. minime
ano chiamate nulle : Poi .12. minuti
puncto etiam fu facto cō .12. Atomi :
e duodece licet il brazo ſeu menſura
ndo queſto e formato perfectamente
lcuni chiamano trabucho : & li noſtri
e mai perho ſono commutate le præ
mmetria & chi a pertice : & chi a Bu-
nare la ſymmetria onziale : da la qua
dubio coſa manifeſta . Ma cum ſia
rpo humano bene affigurato : perho
deformare uno corpo humano . ma
ſtre : Acio ſi ſapia in qual modo ocu-
are præcipue piu per il decore & pro-
circūſtāte : ſi como hāo curato operare
a per in potentia ne per auaritia : ma
miſſo molti graui errori : & quaſi in
e ſymmetrie non paiano formare uno
le la Eurythmia : acio poſſa dimōſtra-
ne . Et e coſa ſcienda in ueritate : che
ire q̄ſta ſymmetria ꝓportionata per le
di Architectura . Et iudicio meo : mi
ido : aut Ciuitate : aut tuto uno ma-
roportionati & diligentemente ſym-
arie profeſſione operare li Architecti
inare Pſeudi Architecti : ſeu profeſ-
ilmente deli aurifici & altri tractabi-
li ſculptori : chi operāo di quadrato
coſe cha di eſſere ſtatuarii nel ſigilla-
rie proportionate : ſono piu atractiue
gratiſſime quanto meglio ſono ſta fa
onſtituite a dimonſtrare . De le quale
oderni pictori : non ſolum le hano fa
re aquiſtare le perpetue laude & nō eſ
græco & di molti auctori ſi como di
i adoctorarſi perfectamēte inſpecu-
ltre piu ſubtile & electe ſymmetrie cō
quaſi nulla ſaperein comparatione di
a ſuo piacere laborando hano cō ep
a la cōparatione de epſi antiqui : Si
to il Gobo : & Auguſtino Buſto Me-
olti altri che floreno p le loro opere
olanenſi . Compagni noſtri : Como
axima & diligēte pratica uniuerſale di
ardo Triuiliano non mancho Bar
o florenti & le loro opere nō ſolū in
. Hora Vitruuio hauendo dimonſtra
la præſente figura . Et primamente
he primo faci una linea Catheta ſeu
o ſignarai le littere . A . in cima & .B.
mēte : ſi da la dextra & ſi da la ſiniſtra
radualmente ſi potra diſtinguere da
ra . A . ſuper ſummum uerticem capi
de le mane da . G . ad . θ . tute quelle
laterale Cathete : ſi como uedi con-
da . K . ad . L . per la quale interſectio
e per extenſa linea equilibrata . facen
emi di queſta ſono le littere . . N . da
. A . ad . M . & da . A . ad . N . Simil-
entri ſerano le littere . S . P . Q . R .
pra lo baſſo plano : acio poſſa pro-
e queſta regula ti uoglio explicare ſi
e regularmente ho uoluto operare.

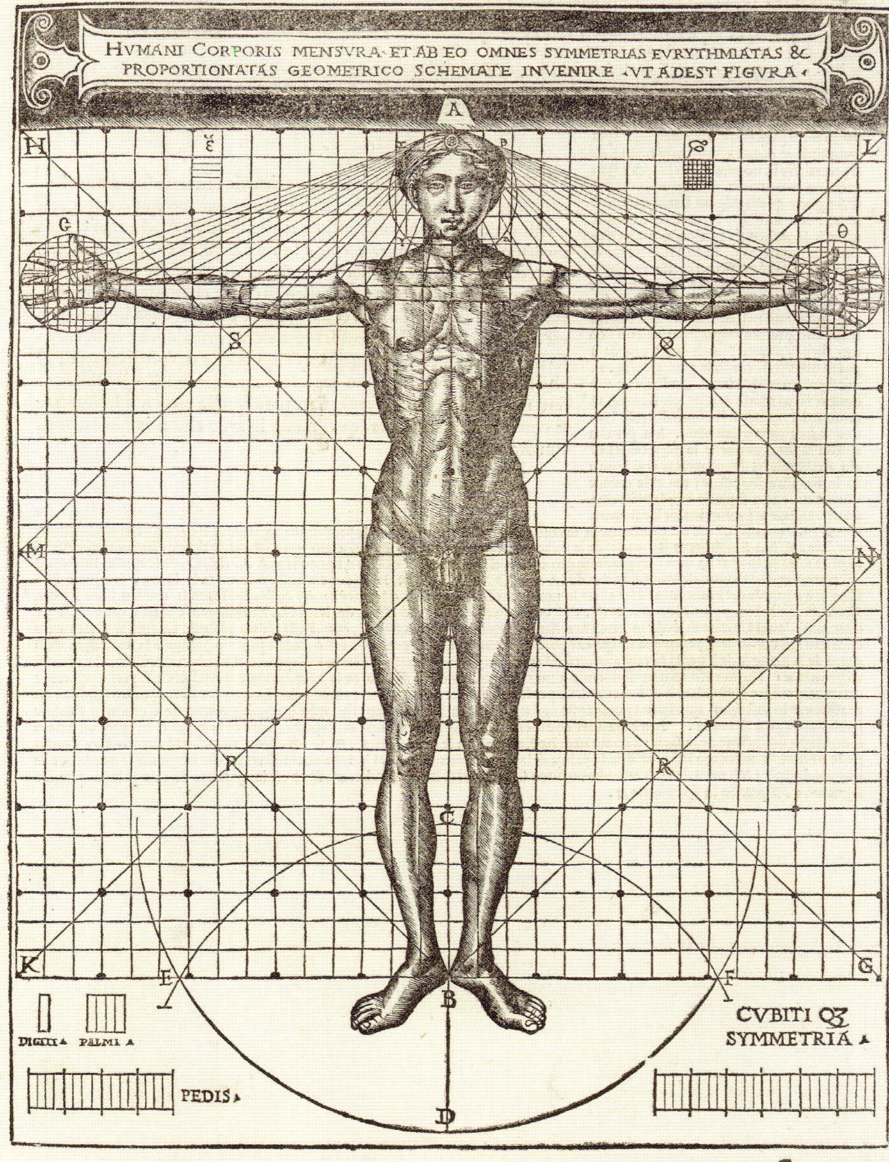

Some later medieval manuscript copies of *De architectura* are accompanied by a few more diagrams and drawings, but it does not appear that they were copied from an older common source. Of course, it is possible that Vitruvius never got around to completing his promised drawings. The medieval scribes who supplied them did so either because they were rectifying what they believed to be lacunae, or simply because they deemed their drawings useful in clarifying the text.[52]

CESARIANO AND THE ITALIAN VITRUVIUS

In print, the first illustrated edition of *De architectura* was edited and produced by Friar Giovanni Giocondo, a painter, architect and scholar who later collaborated with Raphael on St Peter's Basilica in Rome. Printed in 1511 and illustrated with 136 woodcuts, Giocondo's edition (the fourth overall) proved successful enough to warrant a second, much smaller, octavo or 'pocket-size' edition, printed in Florence.

Around the time that Giocondo's edition was going to press in Venice, the Milanese architect Cesare Cesariano (1475–1543) partnered with Aloisio Pirovano and Agostino Gallo to publish an Italian translation of *De architectura*, the very first into a vernacular or modern tongue. Little is known about Cesariano, but in his formative years in Milan he brushed shoulders with the likes of Donato Bramante and Leonardo da Vinci, learning the rudiments of architecture from the former and drawing and hydraulics from the latter. However, after his mother-in-law threatened to poison him, he was forced to flee Milan. For about the next sixteen years he sojourned throughout the Italian peninsula, but spent most of his time studying and working in Ferrara, where he began work on his translation. He returned to Milan and his mother-in-law at the beginning of 151[illegible], when he began to work as a military engineer to Maximilian Sforza, duke of Milan.

Translating *De architectura* was a formidable challenge, owing to Vitruvius's sometimes inscrutable Latin and his frequent use of hybrid Greek and Latin terms that had no ready Italian counterparts.[53] Cesariano's ambitious plans also included more than a hundred original illustrations and a comprehensive commentary that was five times longer than the text. It was a monumental undertaking – and one that very nearly failed.

By 1521 Cesariano's partners (perhaps 'patrons' or 'sponsors' more accurately describes their role) had grown impatient. They seized Cesariano's text and illustrations and handed them over to two humanist scholars, Benedetto Giovio and Mauro Bono, who completed the work (part of Book Nine and all of Book Ten). Cesariano's name does not appear on the title page. The colophon (fol. 183r) mentions the 'magnificent and noble' sponsors of the project, Aloisio Pirovano and Agostino Gallo, but again the actual author of the translation and commentary and of the one hundred or so woodcut illustrations is absent. In fact, Cesariano's name appears only on the very last page in a paragraph buried beneath the *Tabula de li errori* (erratum).

Cesariano was justifiably furious, and he promptly sued his partners. As soon as printing in Como was completed, the entire print-run was confiscated while the magistrates deliberated on the case. By May 1523 the case was settled in Cesariano's favour, and he was able to secure 150 copies of the 438 the court awarded him – out of a total of 1,312 printed. He was not fully compensated until 1529. According to the art historian Giorgio Vasari (1511–74), a younger contemporary of Cesariano, the hijacking of his magnum opus and the subsequent bitter lawsuit led to a disenchantment so profound that he 'became so strange that he would work no more; and, having grown almost savage, he died more like a beast than like a human being'.[54]

THE VITRUVIAN LEGACY

Cesariano's translation and commentary were met with mixed reviews. The painter and architect Giovanni Battista Caporali was anything but magnanimous in his review of Cesariano's work, and yet somehow found his translation and woodcuts perfectly suitable to plagiarize for his own edition, published in 1536. Cesariano's work paved the way for countless other vernacular translations and commentaries, reignited a zeal for classical Graeco-Roman architecture, and forged a path for the likes of Andrea Palladio (1508–80), the most distinguished of Renaissance architects. Palladio's influence rapidly spread across continents and time through the publication of his own architectural treatise, *I quattro libri dell'architettura* (*The Four Books on Architecture*), first published in 1570. In the eighteenth and nineteenth centuries, the American architect and statesman Thomas Jefferson (1743–1826) referred to Palladio's *Four Books* as his architectural bible. Palladio's influence – and therefore Vitruvius's – is evident in the vigorous neo-classicism of monumental civic buildings like Jefferson's Rotunda at the University of Virginia (1826), and William Thornton's designs for the United States Capitol (1793). In early seventeenth-century England,

Palladianism – Europe's take on Palladio's neoclassicism – was championed by Inigo Jones (1573–1652).

Palladio was well aware of the debt owed to Vitruvius, referring to him in the preface to his *Four Books* as his *maestro e guida*, but he was by no means uncritical. He understood that Vitruvius's idealized anthropomorphically derived proportions, although yielding beautiful designs, were sometimes impractical and structurally unstable. Palladio, like the best of the Renaissance humanists, saw in classical antiquity not a model to uncritically ape, but a firm foundation upon which to build and improve. And nowhere is this better exemplified than in the concept of *aemulatio,* 'the act of improving and building upon another's creative production'.[55]

In Book One of *De architectura*, Vitruvius introduced what is now known as the Vitruvian virtues or triad: *firmitas*, *utilitas* and *venustas.* This has been translated as 'strength, utility and beauty', or sometimes 'soundness, utility and attractiveness' – constituting a checklist of fundamental attributes for any and all buildings. And although Vitruvius's influence has waned, especially since the rise of twentieth-century modernist architecture, born of new materials such as glass, steel and reinforced concrete, Vitruvian precepts continue to inspire irrespective of time, place and fashion.

28 The text of the Italian translation surrounds the central block of the original Latin. Cesariano's Italian translation of *De architectura libri decem*, 1521.

following pages

left 29 William Thornton and Benjamin Henry Latrobe's neoclassical United States Capitol, Washington, DC. North wing, vestibule with colonnade section. Drawing by Benjamin Henry Latrobe (1764–1820).

right 30 The architectural 'orders' from Cesariano's Italian translation of *De architectura libri decem*, 1521.

IDEA GEOMETRICAE ARCHITECTONICAE AB ICHNOGRAPHIA SVMPTA. VT PERAMVSSINEAS POSSINT PER ORTHOGRAPHIAM AC SCAENOGRAPHIAM PERDVCERE OMNES QVASCVNQVAE LINEAS. NON SOLVM AD CIRCINI CENTRVM. SED QVAE A TRIGONO ET QVADRATO AVT ALIO QVOVISMODO PERVENIVNT POSSINT SVVM HABERE RESPONSVM. TVM PER EVRYTHMIAM PROPORTIONATAM QVANTVM ETIAM P SYMMETRIAE QVANTITATEM ORDINARIAM AC PER OPERIS DECORATIONEM OSTENDERE. VTI ETIAM HEC QVAE A GERMANICO MORE PERVENIVNT DISTRIBVENTVR PENE QVEMADMODVM SACRA CATHEDRALIS AEDES MEDIOLANI PATET. ETC. P. M. C. C. A. P. VI. Q. C. AC AF. D.

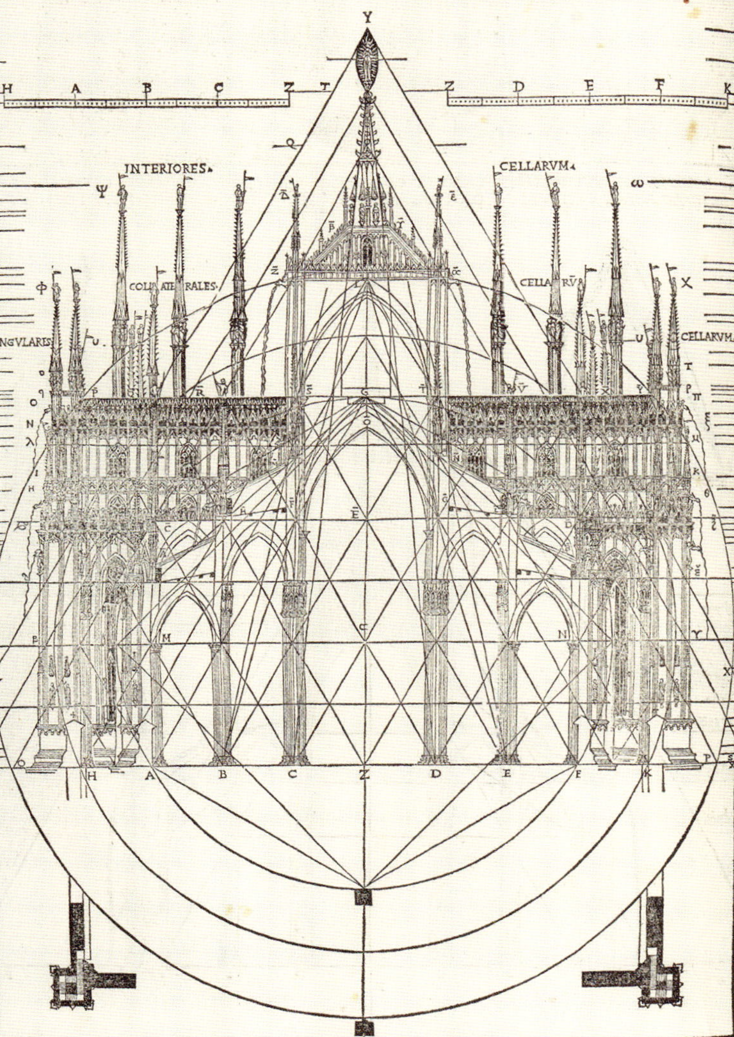

¶ Questa Scenographale figura e conforma ala Supradata Ichnographia & Orthographia. Ma questa & da li Circuli & quadrati & Trianguli excipe le regule: li cui membri & ornamenti cosi de la intestina corporeatura & si de la extrinseca circũcurrentia ho indicato li ordini con le presente littere latine & græce: & con le uirgule che sono posite al extreme de queste due linea erecte cio e: da la base. V. R. S. X. In sino sopra. H. Y. Et dalaltra dextra. K. Le cui commensuratione cõmodulate: da. H. Z. uel da. Z. K. sono parte seu braze. 24. cõ le quale potrai il tuto symmetriare & in magiore aut minore forma persigurare: nõ solum qste ma tute le figuratione & corporeature architectonice & caduna generatione de altre cose de corpi regulari o transregulari che siano nel mũdo (aut fiendi) pur che sapi cõmodulare & intendere il diuidere p eurythmiata symmetria. si como in arithmetica si dice il partire per galea: per che da epsa procede & se intende quasi tuta epsa: scientia: Tuto il resto di questa Theoricale figura consiste hauere inteso la predicta Ichnographia & Orthographia.

¶ Queste idest predicte Ideæ. di Ichnographia: Orthographia: & Scenographia: sono nate de cogitatione & de inuentione. Et ben de cio si uede essere il uero per che la natura non ha demonstrato ne dimonstra tale cose. Vnde uolere considerare & cogitare & inuenire qualche noua cosa: bisogna che lo intellecto nostro sia ben apto & disposito: per che certamente uidemo che nulla cosa e piu diuina & piu apta di quello: si como uole Aristotele in libro de anima. cum ait intellectus est q diuinum impassibile & incorruptibile &c. Ma cum sia talhora chel patisse fragilita & si corumpe de facile licet chel sia abstrato & incorporeo: qsto procede quãdo lanima patisse con il corpo per li alterati sensi: aut quando el si admischia con qualche fantasia & a quelle attende: de facto in la sua interiore cogitatione luno studio de inuentione per uno altro e corupto insiema con lo acto speculatiuo: & cosi nullo bono effecto si produce. aduncha bisogna che lo intellecto & la fantasia purrificata laborano in un medemo effecto diligentissimamente. epsi uoleno inuenire lo optato suo. Et cosi sucedara cio che dice Aristotele si q anima intelligit quando uult: sed nõ sentit quando uult quia obiectũ intellectus. s. ulis est anima: E perho da questo obiecto se extrahe il senso particulare & uene la cogitatione como dice Vitruuio: Et queste cose procedeno da li nobili animi qli fano como li ueri Inamorati che semp sono pertinaci & hano lo animo peruigilante &c. ¶ La uoluptate cosi si expone: Esse eam que diffinitur per modum elatæ læticiæ opinione psentis magni boni: in qua Epicurus summum bonum constituit. In quacunq aliqua delectatione animũ demulcet. & in uoluptatibus quas maxie uellemus: Ma la curiosita sempre fa [illegible] ento lo animo tanto in le cose che ase quanto etiam che a se non apertaneno: ma pur el e una prompta affectatione per essere parato ali bisogni de li effecti occurenti per se & p altri. ¶ Queste sono le terminatiõe de le dispositione cioe li termini & modi quali si soleno tenere in le corporature: uel ædificatione. Et cosi dice. ¶ Ma la Eurythmia e una uenusta specie idest pulcherima effigie ben formata che p distinctione de li numeri fa apparere la cosa bella con delectatione. Et perho dice Vitruuio che la Eurythmia e una uenusta specie & cõmodo aspecto in le cõpositione de li mẽbri. Ma questo ha dicto non solum per la apertinentia de li membri & corpi Architectonici ma de ogni altri & declara in qual modo ella si effice & como gia molto habiamo declarato di sopra per le conrespondentie de le quantita coniuncte & disiuncte: & poi reasummendole insiema formano tuto il suo numero persymmetriato. Ma per explicare questo præponeremo per exemplo cognito: uerbi gratria Sia dato uno numero ut puta de integra quantita de Cento questo si lo diuiderai seu smembrarai in due parte conueniente serano cinquanta idest. 50. p parte: si in quatro parte serano uinticinque p pte (iuncte isiema psto) due uolte cinquãta farano cẽto: si como quatro uolte uinticinque farano cẽto. Similiter si lo diuiderai in cinque parte: ueran uinte: per parte: si in dece parte sũmendo insiema cinque uolte uiginti fara tanto quanto le dece uolte dece che fano cento: Et sic de singulis maioribus uel minoribus quantitatibus & particulis aptis ad hanc coniunctionem: & disiunctionem consimilem &c. ¶ Ma per simili pdicti numeri cognosco anchora non potersi expedire la uerita de la symmetria quando ne conuen diuidere una cõsimile quantita in la infrascripta proportione. Imperoche le sue remanente particule non sono apti suplementi. Adunca aceptarai li cõsimili numeri de magiore aut minore quantita aggregatiua como e il senario numero del quale se dira nel libro tertio: Aut como e ut puta il numero uigesimo octauo: quale ha li soi membri proportionati ala conrespondentia de tuta la sua integrita: Il che la medieta dil dicto numero si e quatordece: il quarto de epso uintiocto si e septe quale superadiuncto a quatordece fa uintiuno: Il septimo de uintiocto: si e quatro: qual superadato al uintiuno: fa uinticinque. Il quatuordecimo de uintiocto: si e due: qual supraiũcto a uinticique fa uigintisepte: po finalmẽte Il uigesimo octauo de uintiocto si e uno: idest: uno. si supraponerai al uigesimoseptio fara uintiocto totalmẽte. Et cosi di qsta Eurythmia si pfice la uera symmetria quando epsi membri & particule conrespondeno ala sua summa cõmodamente & conuenientemente. Ma si de magiore satisfatione uolesti studerai Euclide dal libro decimo insino al quinto decimo: Et si questa symmetria uoi Expeditamente intendere opera & pratica la Agrimensura. con li dati numeri & epsi pedi uel brazi Symmetriati seu distincti ciascuni in dodece parte &

Queste son nate de cogitatione & de Inuentione. La cogitatiõe e una cura plena di studio. & de industria. & de uigilantia cum uoluptate dil preposito effecto. Ma la inuentione e de le obscure questione una explicatione: & ratione de la noua cosa cõ mobile uigore reperta. Queste sono le terminatione de le dispositione: Ma la Eurythmia e una uenusta specie: & cõmodo aspecto i le cõpositione de li mẽbri: Questo si effice quando li membri del opera son conuenienti: cioe quilli del altitudine a la latitudine: & de la latitudine ala longitudine: & che tute correspondeno a la summa de la sua symmetria. Item la symmetria e uno conueniente consenso de li membri de quella opera: & de le parte separate ala specie de la uniuersa figura: un responso de la rata parte. Si como in un corpo di homo: dal cubito: dal pede: dal palmo: dali digiti: Et da le altre particule. La Symmetria si e la qualita de la Eurythmia. Et cosi e in le perfectione de le opere: Et primamente si como e in le sacreæde. in le crassitudine de le Columne: aut del Triglypho. o uero anchora lo Embatere del foramine de la Balista: che li Græci περιτρητον: uocitano: anchora como lo interscalmio de le naue qua le διφηχιακη si dice. Similmente de tute le altre opere da li membri se troua la ratiocinatione de la Symmetriã: Ma il Decore e uno emendato aspecto de la composita opera cum auctoritate de le cose probate. Questo si perfice per statione quale græcamente θεματισμος si dice. o uero per consuetudine o per natura. Per Statione quãdo a Ioue con il fulgure dal Cœlo: Et al Sole: & a la Luna li ædificii & le Hypetræ soto lo Aere son constituite. Per che la specie de quisti Dei & lo effecto in lo aperto & lucente mundo noi anchora presenti li uidemo. Ma a Minerua & Marte. & a Hercule le Aede dorice seran facte. Per che a quisti Dei per la uirtu senza deliciæ sta bene gli sia constituito li ædificii.

COLVMNARVM EX SEX GENERIBVS CAPITVLORV: BASIV & SPIRAR ALIOR QVOQZ GENERV CAPITVLOR QVOR A VITRVVIO SYMMETRIAE PERSCRIPTAE SVT AFFIGVRATIONES.

li Epistylii Zophori & corone & sic de singulis: Li capitelli de queste sono quasi di tanta uenustate: quanto li Corinthii: & sono facti in uarii modi: ma quasi perho con pocha comentatione de symmetrie diferente ut dictum est da li Corinthii: La uarietate de li quali & de altri capitelli imitati da le symmetrie de le campane & uasi: si como e signata la dictione ℞. & Si como da molti Romani aedificii ho exemplato alcuni quiui etiam per dimonstrarte di quello dice Vitruuio in la praesente lectione li ho affigurati.

Ma il tertio quale Corynthio si dice ha imitatione de uirginale gracilitate: per che le uirgine per la tenereza de la aetate con piu subtili membri figurati receueno li effecti piu uenusti in lo ornato. Ma la prima inuentione di epso capitello essere facta cosi se memora: una uirgine Ci

¶ Ma il tertio che Corynthio si dice &c. Vitruuio quiui describe la inuentione del capitello Corinthyo con breuita del historia. ¶ Matura a le nuptie: idest epsa uirgine era Matura ad essere maritata: seu da ponerla in la religione. per che in qui-

6

A WEDDING AND FOUR FUNERALS

BOOK OF HOURS (1525)

But when ye pray, use not vain repetitions, as the heathen do: for they think that they shall be heard for their much speaking.

MATTHEW 6:7

A rendezvous with our next remarkable book demands a rather incredible journey from Como, where *De architectura* was printed, to Paris. In our century, a flight from Como to Paris takes just 90 minutes. How you chose to make the journey during the early decades of the sixteenth century, though, would have depended largely on your constitution and your purse. You could undertake a 900 km journey overland by mule or horse (as done by Leonardo da Vinci when retiring to France in 1516), crossing the Alps and heading north-west via Switzerland – or you could set out in the opposite direction to Genoa and board a trade ship on a rather circuitous voyage through the Mediterranean, north along the Atlantic coasts of the kingdoms of Spain and Portugal, then south-easterly along the Seine, and finally disembark in the heart of Paris, in the shadow of Notre-Dame. If you were fortunate enough to have survived Alpine snowstorms and bandits, or to avoid pirates and scurvy, then, by saddle, sandals or sea, you would have arrived about a month later and probably considerably the worse for wear in Europe's biggest city.

By the early sixteenth century, Paris was second only to Venice as a book-publishing centre. It had grown into a burgeoning international trading hub, and it is here, in the university quarter – on the rue Saint-Jean-de-Beauvais, to be precise – that we meet with a very different kind of book, both smaller and more personal. The book of hours (*horae*, after the Latin for hours) first appeared in the early thirteenth century, and was descended from the clerical breviary and the psalter used by lay women and men. It was an anthology of prayers, penitential psalms, Gospel lessons

31 The duke of Berry, in blue, seated. From the *Très Riches Heures*, illuminated by the Limbourg brothers, c.1412–16.

SVBSOLANVS
LA VILLE CITE
BELEVILE
BANIOLET
PROPINCOVRT
LABASTILLE
PORTE S ANTHOINE
SEPTETRIONES
LE PONT AR CANS

32 Hand-coloured woodcut plan of Paris by Truschet & Hoyau, c.1550.

and hymns, with each copy personalized by the addition of a near infinite variety of supplementary materials chosen by their patrons to suit individual tastes and personal devotional needs.

A book of hours invariably opened with a calendar of the ecclesiastical year, in which the more important festivals (Easter, the Annunciation, the Nativity and so on) were often highlighted in red, hence the expression 'red letter days'. The heart of the book was the Hours of the Virgin, from which the book takes its name, comprising prayers and devotions that were to be recited at the eight canonical hours throughout the day (matins, lauds, prime, terce, sext, none, vespers and compline). Books of hours were among the most popular books of the fourteenth and fifteenth centuries, and are often described as late medieval bestsellers. Although they served principally to guide meditative private devotion, copies owned by nobility were sometimes covered in jewels and filled with lavish illuminations, making them conspicuous status symbols that could even be taken to church as a sign of one's worldly affluence and otherworldly piety.

Among the most celebrated examples of medieval illuminated books of hours is the *Très Riches Heures* (fig. 31), magnificently illustrated by the famed Limbourg brothers.

33 *The Hours of Engelbert of Nassau*, Flemish, 1475–85.

It was commissioned by their patron the duke of Berry. Brother to King Charles V of France, he was a prolific and wealthy collector of all things rare, beautiful and exotic, including no fewer than fifteen books of hours, a leopard, a camel, 1,500 hunting dogs and countless other exquisite and expensive *objets d'art*. In a tragic twist of fate, and before the manuscript could be completed, all three Limbourg brothers (still in their twenties) – and their patron the duke – died in 1416.

PRINTED HOURS

The advent of print in the mid-fifteenth century precipitated a steep and substantial decline in the price of books. By the 1480s, according to the *zornale* (ledger) of Venetian bookseller Francesco de Madiis, a plain printed book of hours was sold for 8 soldi. This was the equivalent of about two chickens, two kilos of cherries or approximately half a day's wage for an unskilled labourer.[56] Both manuscript and printed books of hours existed on a broad spectrum, from small printed and unbound copies on cheap-grade or 'grey' paper and even 'mass produced' shop-copy manuscripts, right through to jewel-encrusted bindings, gilded initials and exquisitely painted miniatures.

The earliest known printed book of hours appeared in 1471, from the press of Augsburg's

133

Deus
in adiutoriu
meum inten
de. Domine ad adiu
uandum me festina
Gloria patri et filio
et spiritui sancto

first printer, Günther Zainer. This small (15 × 10 cm) German-language *Gebetbuch* (prayer book) contains no illustrations or decoration but for a few red-and-blue painted initials and some underlining in red. The second printed book of hours, and the first to appear in Italy, came from the press of Theobald Schenckbecher in Rome in about 1473 and was, uncharacteristically for fifteenth-century books of hours, printed in a roman font.[57] Between these tentative first efforts in the early 1470s and the end of the century, more than 420 editions of books of hours were published.

However, it was impossible to replicate the lavishly coloured and painted manuscript books of hours in print. In fact, it would be several hundred years before such a thing was feasible. Instead, printed books of hours were commonly decorated with woodcuts that could, if one had the means, be completed or coloured in by an illuminator. The brothers Gilles and Germain Hardouyn, both printers and illuminators in Paris, successfully served both ends of the market – with the production of deluxe editions printed on parchment and illuminated by hand for their affluent clientele, and a much larger run of regular or 'mass-market' copies printed on paper and sold inexpensively to the broader public. Antoine Vérard, Simon Vostre, Philippe Pigouchet and Thielman Kerver led the way in the production of printed books of hours, so that by the last decade of the fifteenth century Paris had risen to become the pre-eminent centre for their production. Vérard alone, one of the city's foremost publishers of vernacular and illustrated books, printed more than eighty editions of books of hours between 1485 and his death in 1512.

34 Decorated title page from the Colines and Tory book of hours, 1525.

COLINES AND TORY

If you were walking along the rue Saint-Jean-de-Beauvais in the early months of 1525, you might bump into Simon de Colines's assistants carting freshly printed pages to Geoffroy Tory's bookshop just around the corner on rue Saint-Jacques, home to innumerable other printers, booksellers, scribes and illuminators. These quires (folded and unbound pages) belong to a rather special book of hours printed by Simon de Colines in collaboration with Geoffroy Tory, both luminaries of early French Renaissance printing and typography.

Simon de Colines (*c.*1485–1546) was one of the foremost printer-publishers of his time and among the most accomplished punchcutters and type designers of all time. During a career spanning twenty-six years, he produced more than 750 editions. Colines got his break in 1520 when, upon the death of Henri Estienne, he took over management of his print shop.

HORAE, in laudem beatiss. semper
virginis MARIAE secundum con
suetudinem curiæ Romanæ. vbi or-
thográphia, puncta, & accentus suis
locis habentur.

HORAE, in laudem beatiss. semper virginis
MARIAE, secundum consuetudinem ec-
clesiæ Romanæ.

AVE GRATIA PLENA, DOMI-
NVS TECVM. BENEDICTA
TV IN MVLIERIBVS.

Ad matutinum Versus.

DOmine labia mea aperies. ℟. Et
os meum annunciabit laudẽ tuã.
℣. Deus in adiutoriũ meũ intẽde
℟. Dñe ad adiuuãdũ me festina.
Gloria patri, & filio, & spiritui sã
cto. Sicut erat in principio, & nunc, & semper,

D.iiij.

cem, vt & corda nostra mandatis tuis dedita, & hostium sublata formidine, tẽpora sint tua protectione tranquilla. Oratio.

VRe igne sancti spiritus renes nostros, & cor nostrũ domine, vt tibi casto corpore seruiamus, & mundo corde placeamus. Oratio.

FIdelium deus omnium cõditor & redemptor, animabus famulorũ famularumq; tuarum, remissionem cunctorum tribue peccatorũ, vt indulgẽtiam, quam semper optauerũt, pijs supplicationibus cõsequantur. Oro.

ACtiones nostras quæsimus domine aspirando præueni, & adiuuando prosequere, vt cuncta nostra oratio, & operatio à te semper incipiat, & per te cœpta finiatur. oro

OMnipotens sempiterne deus, qui viuorum dominaris simul & mortuorũ, omniumq; misereris, quos tuos fide & opere futuros esse prænoscis, te suppliciter exoramus, vt pro quib9 effũdere preces decreuimus, quosq; vel præsens seculum adhuc in carne retinet, vel futurũ iam exutos corpore suscepit, intercedẽtibus omnibus sanctis tuis pietatis tuæ clemẽtia omnium delictorum suorum veniam consequantur, Per dominum. ℣ Domine exaudi orationem meam. ℟ Et clamor meus ad te veniat. ℣ Benedicamus domino. ℟ Deo gratias. ℣ Fidelium animæ defunctorum per misericordiam dei requiescant in pace. ℟ Amen.

¶ Sequitur officium pro defunctis. Ad vesperas añ. Placebo domino. Psalmus.

DIlexi quoniã exaudiet dominus vocem orationis meæ.
Quia inclinauit aurem suam mihi: & in diebus meis inuocabo.
Circundederũt me dolores mortis: & pericula inferni inuenerunt me.
Tribulationẽ & dolorem inueni: & nomen do-

O.iiij.

A year or two later he married Estienne's widow, Guyonne Viart, becoming stepfather to six children including Robert Estienne (then aged seventeen). Geoffroy Tory (*c*.1480–1533), publisher, bookseller, author, professor and typographer, is perhaps best known for *Champ fleury*, his treatise on letterforms that was printed by Colines in 1529, and for his contribution to French orthography – for example, the use of ç and é.

Prior to their work on books of hours, Colines and Tory had collaborated on the publication of a book written by Tory upon the tragic death of his daughter Agnès, shortly before her tenth birthday. She appears to have been a precocious child, and Tory had delighted in teaching her Latin, Greek, music and art. His *Epitaphia*, a eulogy in verse, was printed by Colines in 1523. It is from this time that Tory adopted the *pot cassé* (broken urn) as his printer's device, representing the frailty of human existence.

The 1525 book of hours printed by Colines, and financed, art-directed and published by Tory, is noteworthy in several respects. At this time the fashion for books of hours was a dense and dark page, with heavy borders and Gothic types. By contrast, the border designs in the 1525 book of hours are drawn in outline and make for a much lighter page. The subjects of the borders are different too. Rather than the typical biblical or pastoral scenes, they are filled with acanthus leaves, vines and vases, putti and pedestals – quintessentially classical (and pagan) motifs, which were now leitmotifs of the Italian Renaissance. Tory's illustrations serve more than a merely decorative function, however. Major illustrations, appearing in chronological sequence, mark the openings of key sections. An annunciation scene introduces the Hours of the Virgin and a scene of a prostrate King David marks the beginning of the Penitential Psalms, while the final opener is a chilling hellscape in which Death walks over the bodies of the damned.

For the most part, Tory limits the more explicit classical motifs to the borders. However, in the Crucifixion scene, those motifs enter the scene itself. Surrounding the centrepiece illustration of Jesus on the cross are panels illustrating Virgil's cryptic quatrain *sic vos non vobis* ([we labour] not for ourselves but for others) with scenes of bees, birds, sheep and oxen – living their lives in the service of others, a lesson in selflessness and sacrifice as exemplified in the Crucifixion. Besides the twelve woodcut scenes, painted *trompe l'oeil* initials serve to introduce each of the canonical hours; smaller red-printed initials and other selective red printing function as headings or for

previous pages

left 35 Annunciation scene from the Colines and Tory book of hours, 1525.

right 36 A chilling Hellscape in which Death walks over the bodies of the damned, from the Colines and Tory book of hours, 1525.

opposite 37 Crucifixion scene from the Colines and Tory book of hours, 1525.

ndis clamaui ad te domine:do-
audi vocem meam.
ures tuæ intendentes in vocem
ex.
bseruaueris domine : domine

opitiatio est: & propter legem
domine.
mea in verbo eius: sperauit a
mino.
utina vsq; ad noctem speret Is-

inum misericordia: & copiosa
ptio.
Israel ex omnibus iniquitati-
iem æternam dona eis domi-
rpetua luceat eis. ℣. Domine
n meam. ℟. Et clamor meus
Oratio.
nter apostolicos sacerdotes fa
nos pontificali seu sacerdotali
ignitate vigere: præsta quæsi-
quoque perpetuo aggregentur
Oratio.
eus omnium conditor & redē-
abus famulorū, famularumq;
missionem cunctorum tribue
ndulgentiam quam semper o-
upplicationibus cōsequantur,
as deus, Per omnia secula secu
quiescant in pace. Amen.

nctæ crucis. Ad matutinū ℣.

SIC VOS NON VOBIS MELLIFICATIS APES.

QVOS ALII MERVERE FERO; PATIOR QVI LABORES.

SIC VOS NON VOBIS NIDIFICATIS AVES.

SIC VOS NON VOBIS VELLERA FERTIS OVES.

SIC VOS NON VOBIS FERTIS ARATRA BOVES.

DOmine labia mea aperies. ℟. Et os meū annunciabit laudem tuā. ℣. Deus in adiutoriū meū intēde ℟. Domine ad adiuuādū me festiña. Gloria patri, & filio, & spiritui sancto. Sicut erat in principio, & nunc, & semper, & in secula seculorum. Amen. añ. Salue

‡

emphasis. These features join forces to establish a consistent typographic hierarchy, making it easy for readers to find their way around the book without the need for pagination.

In most copies of the Colines and Tory book of hours, including the Bodleian's, the title page bears only the five short lines of the book's full title. However, in one of the copies now held at the Bibliothèque nationale de France, the title page was painted by illuminator and bookseller Étienne Colaud who, incidentally, lived on the rue de la Draperie in front of the cathedral on Île de la Cité, a stone's throw from the shops of Colines and Tory across the Petit Pont. The scene depicts a contemporary printing press with a press operator in the foreground, an assistant with a pair of ink balls at the ready and, on the right, a compositor seated at a type-case, upon which stands the exemplar manuscript, serving as his guide to typesetting (fig. 34). In this same copy, another nice surprise awaits readers at the end of the book – a charming uncoloured double-page fold-out woodcut, illustrating the Triumph of the Virgin, wherein Mary is depicted in a chariot drawn by unicorns, led by Faith, Hope and Charity.

Visually, the Colines and Tory book is a radical departure from the Gothic *horror vacui* (fear of empty spaces) exemplified in turn-of-the-century books of hours printed by the likes of Kerver and Pigouchet. In the fifteenth century, only a handful of religious books were printed with roman types. The 1525 book of hours sets a new standard for the printing of prayer books, using a fine roman type designed by Colines.

The Colines and Tory book of hours, then, marks a significant milestone in the design of books, and the abandonment of the Gothic aesthetic – including Gothic fonts – in favour of a Renaissance or neoclassical aesthetic and the broader adoption of roman types throughout most of Europe. This graphic and typographic sea-change was dramatically summarized by William Ivins Jr, when he wrote that 'the day of the gothic book in France was over, attacked and killed in its deepest citadel, the prayer book'.[58]

THE FINAL HOURS

In Europe, books of hours were the most popular book of the late Middle Ages. For about 300 years, perhaps with the exception of mass-produced Latin grammars, more books of hours were made than any other kind of book. They were often expensive luxury items, commissioned by aristocrats and the otherwise wealthy, but the advent of printing saw the mass production of affordable versions, launched in the 1480s. This, and the vernacularization of prayer books, fuelled their growing popularity. Yet, by the mid-sixteenth century, the genre was poised for a precipitous decline. The very printers behind its incredible success might well have contributed to its demise. In a bid to upstage the competitors, unscrupulous printers incorporated fabricated prayers and pardons into their books of hours. For example, in a book of hours printed in 1510, on commission for the London publisher William Bretton, the famed Parisian printer of books of hours Thielman Kerver included a prayer vouchsafed by Pope Alexander VI. It promised devout precants '5,000 years of pardon for deadly sins and 20 years for venial sins' – an impressive indulgence, and yet a cynical fabrication designed to sell more copies![59] It was partly in response to these kinds of practices that the Catholic Church, already keen to standardize the liturgy, censured the use of books of hours through the Council of Trent (1545–63).

Protestant reformers were also critical of books of hours, arguing that their use promoted hollow, ritualistic devotion whereby their readers, according to the firebrand reformer Guillaume Farel (1489–1565), 'rattle their lips' in the recitation of Latin prayers they scarcely understand.[60] And Martin Luther wrote in his quintessential colloquialisms that they 'drub into the minds of simple people such un-Christian tomfoolery about prayers to God and his saints'. He suggests that books of hours needed a 'thorough reformation if not total extermination'.[61] What had begun with the Council of Trent was formalized in 1571, when Pope Pius V announced an officially sanctioned Latin Hours, effectively prohibiting or suppressing the use of other unofficial versions. But their decline had already begun. Market saturation, the transformation of religious life, evolving devotional practices and competition from other kinds of religious books contributed to their dwindling popularity.

Books of hours served a variety of purposes, depending on the time, place and needs of those who read them. Primarily, they were archives of prayer,[62] but they also document modes of medieval and early modern piety. Their growing popularity from the late Middle Ages also reflects rising literacy among the laity. They also serve as a record of evolving artistic tastes and traditions. In some respects, the work of Colines and Tory can be considered the culmination of a graphic revolution launched by Petrarch's disdain for Gothic script, famously disparaging it in a letter to Boccaccio as, 'that pompous and fancy lettering … destined for something other than reading'.[63]

following pages

38 A typical late fifteenth-century printed book of hours, *Horae ad usum Sarum* (Salisbury). Johann Philippi for Thielman Kerver in Paris, 1497.

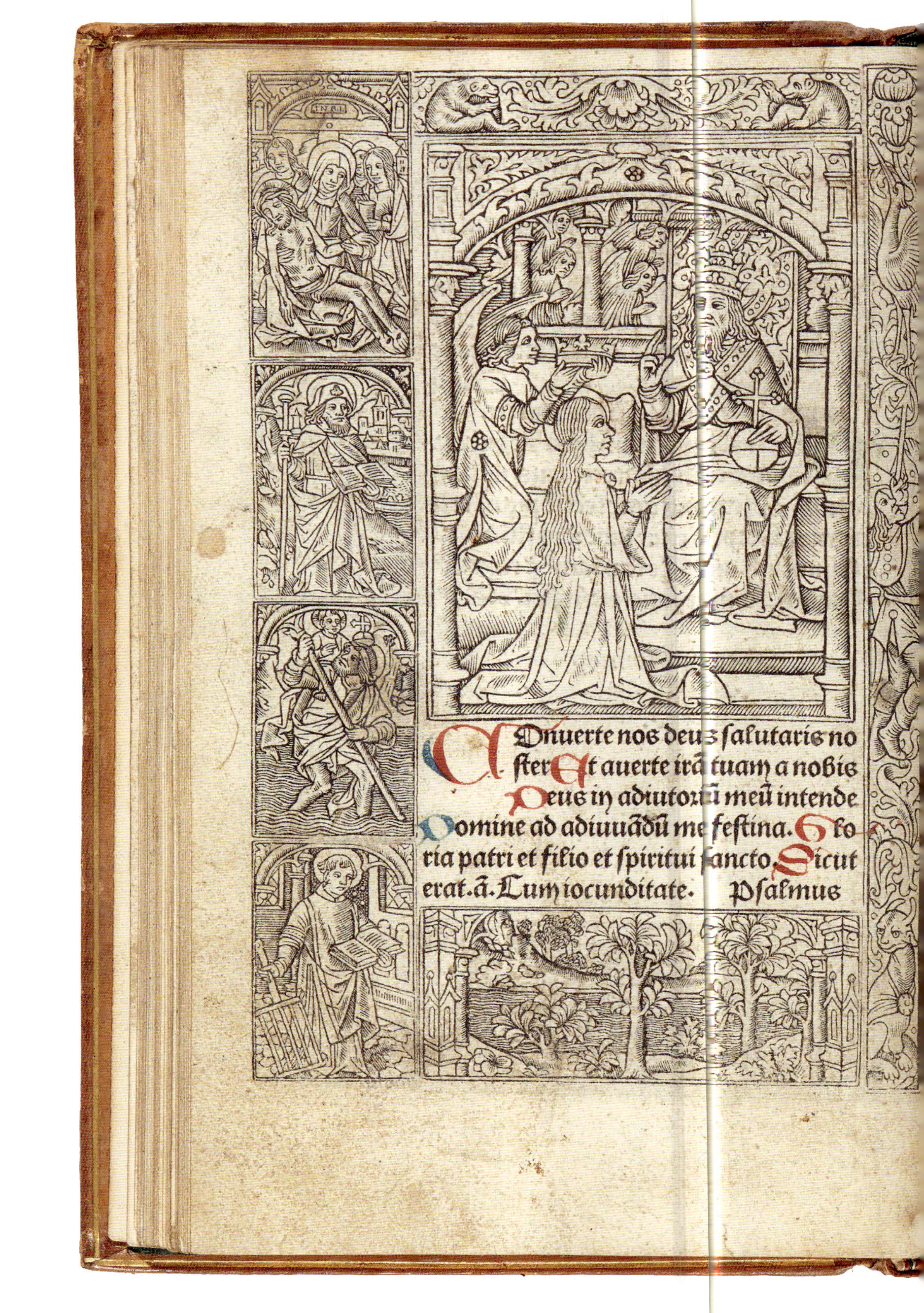

COnuerte nos deus salutaris no
ster. Et auerte irã tuam a nobis
Deus in adiutoriũ meũ intende
Domine ad adiuuãdũ me festina. Glo
ria patri et filio et spiritui sancto. Sicut
erat. ã. Cum iocunditate. Psalmus

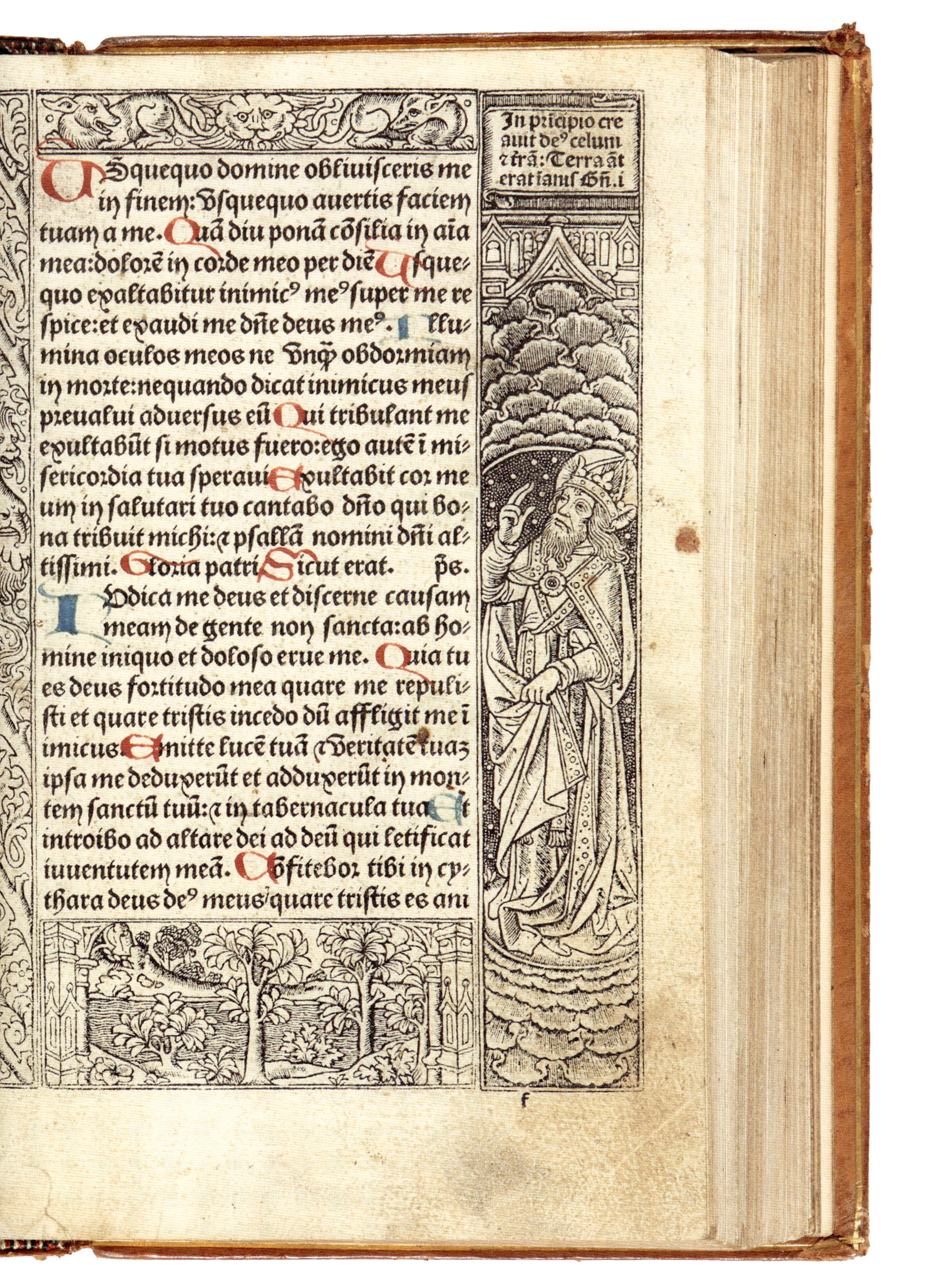

Usquequo domine obliuisceris me
in finem: Usquequo auertis faciem
tuam a me. Quã diu ponã cõsilia in aĩa
mea: dolorẽ in corde meo per diẽ. Usquequo exaltabitur inimic⁹ me⁹ super me re
spice: et exaudi me dñe deus me⁹. Illu-
mina oculos meos ne unq̃ obdormiam
in morte: nequando dicat inimicus meus
preualui aduersus eũ. Qui tribulant me
exultabũt si motus fuero: ego autẽ i misericordia tua speraui. Exultabit cor me
um in salutari tuo cantabo dño qui bo
na tribuit michi: ꝛ psallã nomini dñi al-
tissimi. Gloria patri. Sicut erat. ps.
Iudica me deus et discerne causam
meam de gente non sancta: ab ho-
mine iniquo et doloso erue me. Quia tu
es deus fortitudo mea quare me repuli-
sti et quare tristis incedo dũ affligit me i
imicus. Emitte lucẽ tuã ꝛ ueritatẽ tuaꝫ
ipsa me deduxerũt et adduxerũt in mon-
tem sanctũ tuũ: ꝛ in tabernacula tua. Et
introibo ad altare dei ad deũ qui letificat
iuuentutem meã. Confitebor tibi in cy-
thara deus de⁹ meus quare tristis es ani

In pricipio cre
auit de⁹ celum
ꝛ trã: Terra aũt
erat ĩanis Gñ. i

f

7

NORTHERN RENAISSANCE

DÜRER, *ON MEASUREMENT* (1538)

The eye, which is called the window of the soul, is the principal means by which the central sense can most completely and abundantly appreciate the infinite works of nature.

Leonardo da Vinci, c.1492[64]

On the island of Borneo, off the coast of Indonesia, buried deep inside mountains blanketed in dense rainforest, are clues to our distant prehistory. For tens of thousands of years, a remote and labyrinthine network of caves has been home to a remarkable secret. Forty-thousand years ago, long before humans invented metal tools or writing or thought to build cities or plant crops, the inhabitants of this remote South East Asian island painted pictures on cave walls. These caves are among hundreds of similar sites around the world, some of which contain paintings thought to be 65,000 years old, and might have been made by Neanderthals. From red-ochre handprints and stencils to human figures and animals, to abstract symbols and patterns, these earliest signs of graphic communication – or art – furnish insights into the lives and minds of our Stone Age ancestors.

How art got from cave walls to canvas is a long story, inextricably connected to our evolving perceptions of the world around us and existential questions related to our place and purpose within it. But for brevity's sake, we must fast-forward to the fifteenth century CE, by which time art had become rather sophisticated. In fact, the early decades of the 1400s mark one of the most crucial turning points in the history of art.

Look closely at many ancient and medieval paintings, and you will see that, despite skilful techniques of composition and rendering of colour, light and shadow, the illusion of depth is often unconvincing. In fifteenth-century Italy, a solution to this long-standing problem was discovered. North of the Alps, one of the early proponents of this new method of linear perspective was a brilliant German artist by the name of Albrecht Dürer.

39 *The Ancient of Days* (God as geometer). Frontispiece to William Blake's *Europe: A Prophecy*, copy D, 1794.

DÜRER

One of eighteen children, Albrecht Dürer was born on 21 May 1471 in the German city of Nuremberg, then part of the Holy Roman Empire. Nuremberg was a thriving international trade centre and led Europe in the manufacture of scientific and navigational instruments, weapons and countless kinds of metal goods. It was also just a short distance from the city of Mainz, where just a couple of decades before, Johannes Gutenberg had developed printing with moveable type. And in the very year Dürer was born, his godfather Anton Koberger (see pp. 51–2) gave up goldsmithing to pursue a career in printing and publishing, establishing Nuremberg's first printshop. At first, Dürer apprenticed with his father, a goldsmith, but it soon became apparent that his talents lay in art rather than goldsmithery, and in 1486, aged fifteen, he began an apprenticeship with Nuremberg's leading artist, Michael Wolgemut.

In Wolgemut's studio, Dürer was exposed to many ways of producing art, from paintings and woodcut prints to sculpture and stained glass. Three years later, in 1489, he set out on his own as a journeyman, mostly working as a printmaker, traveling throughout Germany, the Netherlands, Basel and then on to Strasbourg. In the spring of 1494, Dürer returned to Nuremberg for an arranged marriage to Agnes Frey (1475–1539) in the summer. No sooner had their honeymoon ended than he was back on the road. This time he headed to Venice, a booming cosmopolitan city of immigrants, and the centre of a vast international trading empire. Dürer loved Venice, and the Venetians were quick to recognize his prodigious talent. In 1506 while in Venice, he wrote to his best friend, Willibald Pirckheimer: 'Here I am [treated as] a gentleman, at home as a parasite.' Earlier in the same letter, Dürer expressed his hope to 'ride to Bologna to learn the secrets of the art of perspective, which a man there is willing to teach me'.[65] If Dürer's earlier trips had been to study how art was made, then his later trip to Italy was to learn more about art theory.

Although it appears they never met, there are striking parallels between Dürer and his Italian contemporary Leonardo da Vinci. They both possessed preternatural artistic abilities as well as exceptionally fertile and inquisitive minds. However, unlike Leonardo, who published nothing during his lifetime, Dürer embraced print. More than any artist before him, he exploited this relatively new technology to produce standalone 'poster' prints, such as *Knight, Death and the Devil* (1513), *Melencolia* (1514) and the

40 Albrecht Dürer's Four Horsemen from his *Apocalypse* series, 1511.

m et ocu
i nisi in
dextera se
cruisset li-
ttuor seni
singuli ci
ramento
cantabāt
s domine
cius quo-
in sangui
ulo ꝛ nati
sacerdo-
vidi et au
circumitu
rat nume-
oce magna
ccipere vir
fortitudi
ictionem.
super ter-
que in eo
ono et ag
t potestas
malia dice
ores cecide
iuentem in

The original drawing is in the King's collection at Buckingham House.

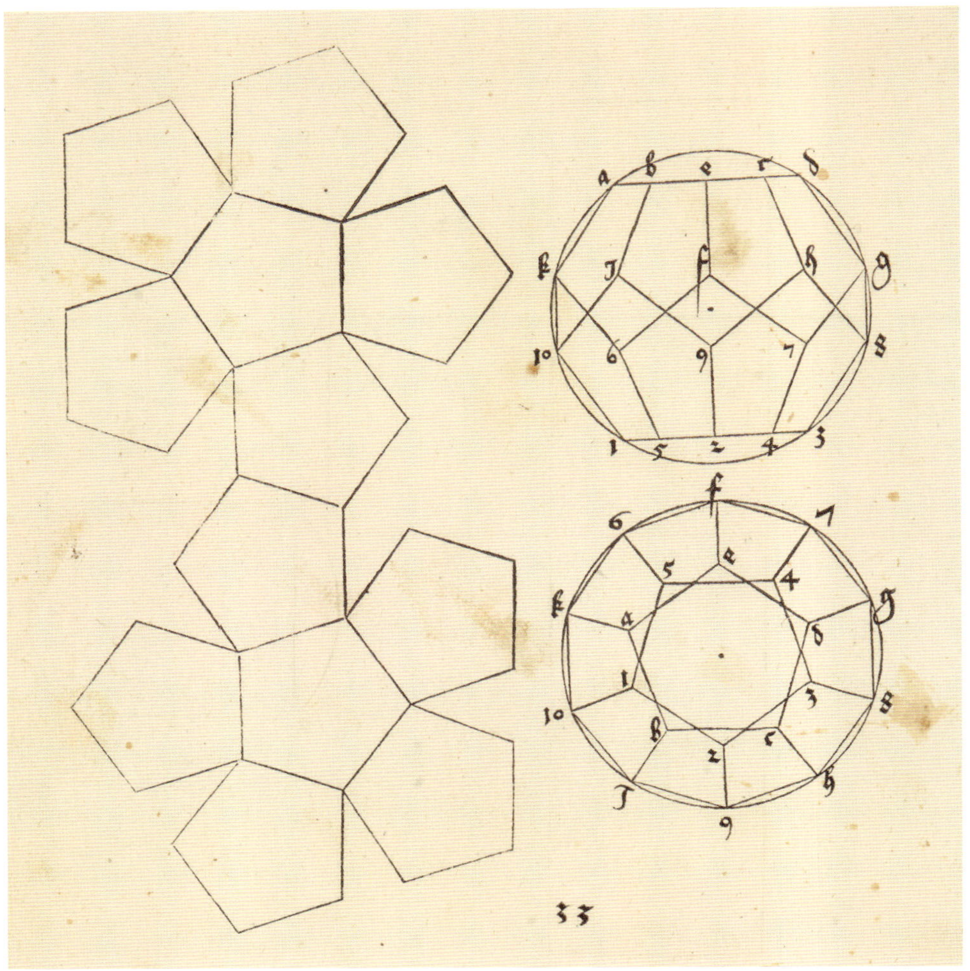

41 Polyhedral nets for a regular dodecahedron, one of the Platonic solids. From Albrecht Dürer's *Underweysung der Messung* (*On Measurement*), second edition, 1538.

Rhinoceros (1515), plus collections of prints published as books, including his acclaimed *Apocalypse* series, published in 1498. Later in life, Dürer again turned to print to publish his ideas about art theory and practice. His first book was a practical how-to guide for artists and artisans, published in 1525 and called *Underweysung der Messung* (*On Measurement*). When Dürer died in April 1528, he had been working on a revised and expanded second edition. The second edition was put together from Dürer's own notes and drawings. The work was directed by his widow, Agnes, and published posthumously in 1538.

ON MEASUREMENT

Dürer was convinced that artists, however talented or technically astute they might be, could not hope to produce good art without first establishing a sound foundation. *On Measurement* was that foundation – and it was written not in the Latin of academia but in the German vernacular, the everyday language of artists and artisans. In the introduction, Dürer is clear about his aims:

> It has until now been the custom in our Germany to put a great number of talented young men to the task of artistic painting without real foundation other than what they learned by daily usage. They have therefore grown up in ignorance like an unpruned tree … For this reason, I have decided to provide to all those who are eager to become artists a starting point and a source for learning about measurement with rulers and compass.[66]

On Measurement is organized into four main sections, or Books. The first two cover the basics of linear geometry. Dürer assures his readers that if they are already familiar with Euclid, then they can safely skip ahead. Book Three deals with the geometry of solids – three-dimensional spaces and linear perspective – and concludes with the design of architectural columns and sundials, as well as a practical treatise on lettering.

The fourth and final book is devoted to more complex geometrical solids, such as polyhedra, and introduces the five very special Platonic solids. Without diving into the details (as Dürer does), the introduction to geometry roughly follows Euclid's *Elements*, but with practical examples of how this newfound knowledge might be useful in the real world. For example, Dürer devotes considerable space to the geometric construction and drawing, with a compass, of many kinds of spirals – these would be useful in painting and engraving and for architects designing, say, an Ionic column with a spiral or scroll-shaped ornament at the capital, for example. Dürer then moves on to solid geometry and reproduces, for the first time in print, unfolded plans or 'nets' of polyhedral solids – all five Platonic solids and several of the Archimedean solids.[67] By producing these nets, readers could trace them, cut them out and fold them into actual three-dimensional paper models. What better way to teach polyhedral geometry! Dürer then explains that he has introduced these solids as a stepping stone to his next lesson: 'Having demonstrated how to construct various types of solids, I also wish to teach you how to render them in a painting.'[68]

A NEW PERSPECTIVE

When we look at the world, objects that are further away appear smaller because they take up less space in our field of view. When drawing a scene, we know that the larger the object we draw, the closer it appears to the viewer. But how much larger? If you were to draw, say, two friends of the same height, one standing just 2 m from you, the second at 2 km, then how much smaller should your second friend appear on paper? A useful answer to this question was a long time coming.

Alhazen's *Kitab al-Manazir* (*Book of Optics*), written in the early eleventh century, established that the way we see can be described in terms of straight visual rays entering the eye, and that the sum of those rays can be visualized as a cone with its vertex converging on the eye. This crucial concept paved the way for the Florentine painter-architect Filippo Brunelleschi's invention of linear perspective drawing in the early fifteenth century. His ideas were codified by the humanist scholar and polymath Leon Battista Alberti. Alberti's ingenious idea, published in his *De pictura* (*On Painting*) of 1435–36, was to think of a picture as a cross section of Alhazen's visual cone. Leonardo da Vinci illustrated a practical application of this conceptualization in his notebooks, where he describes using a sheet of glass to trace a scene. Thus, the glass, held at a fixed distance from the eye, reproduces the planar cross-section of the visual cone or pyramid.

In the final pages of *On Measurement*, Dürer introduces methods of linear perspective drawing. He begins with a cube from the previous section on regular solids, and shows how it can be drawn in perspective. He even describes how the same methods can be used to construct perspectival shadows projected from a chosen light source. The book concludes with four devices, or 'machines', for perspective drawing – these are really shortcut methods to his previously described purely geometrical approaches. In the woodcut depicting a lute (fig. 42), a cord is attached to a plumb-line threaded through a hook attached to the back wall. At the front end, the cord is attached to a wooden pointer. In this way, the cord represents a ray of light passing from the subject (the lute), through the picture plane (the wooden frame), to the eye of the viewer. The device requires two operators: one moves the string to various coordinates on the surface of the lute, while the other plots those coordinates on the picture plane (the canvas or a sheet of

42 A drawing device requiring two operators: one moves the string to various coordinates on the surface of the lute, while the other plots those coordinates on the picture plane. From Dürer's *Underweysung der Messung*, second edition, 1538.

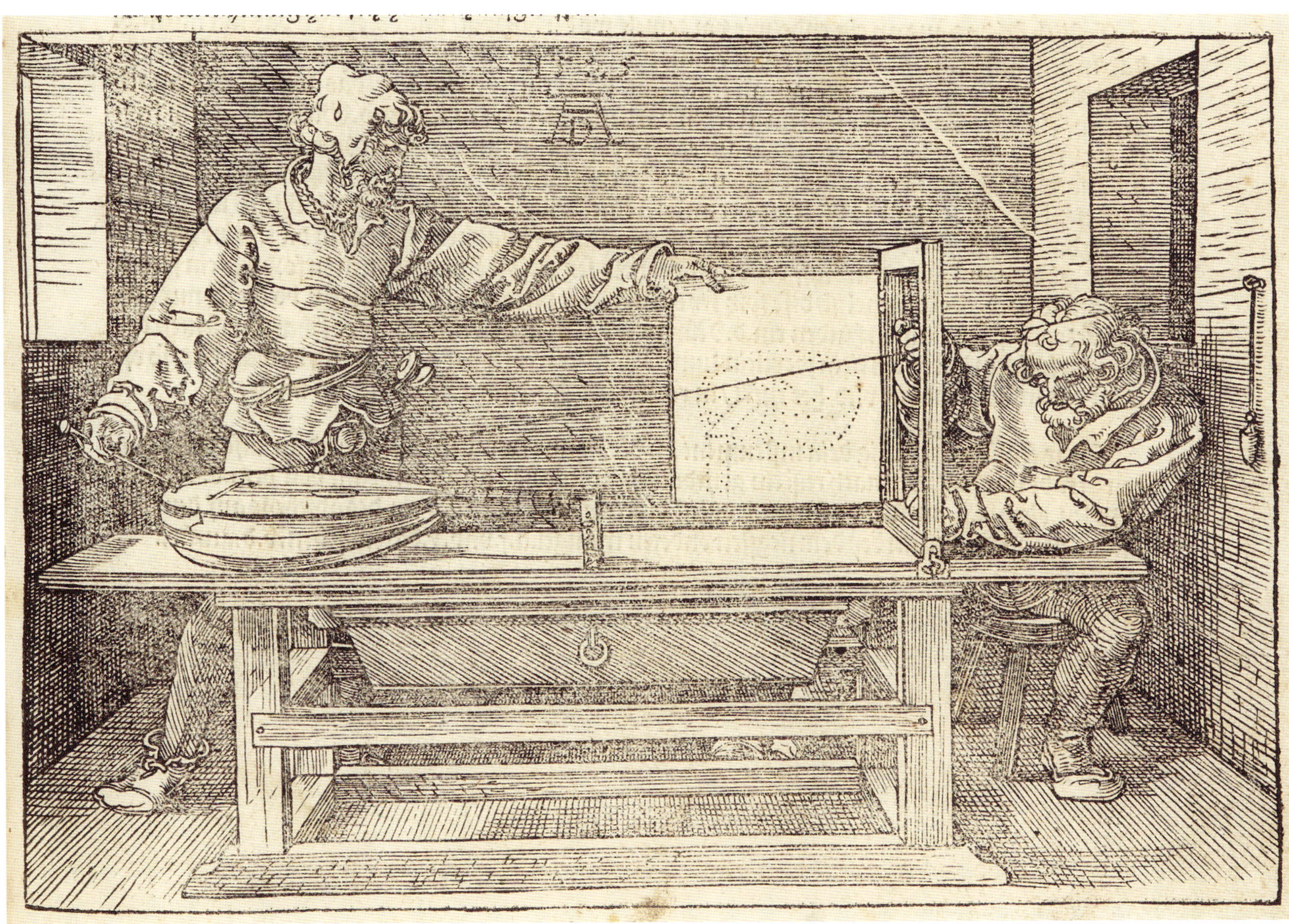

Item noch ein anderen brauch zu Conterfeten/dardurch man eyn ytlichs Corpus mag grösser oder kleyner abconterfeten wie vil man wil/deshalben nutzlicher dañ mit dem glas darumb das es freier ist/ Darzu soll man haben ein ram mit einem gitter von starckem schwartzen zwirn gemacht/die lucken oder fierungen eine vngeferlich zweyer finger breyt/ Darnach soll man haben ein absehen oben zugespitzt/ also gemacht/das man es höher oder niderer richten mag/das bedeut das aug mit dem. o. Darnach leg hinaus in zimlicher weitten dz corpus so du conterfeten wilt/ rucks vnd peugs nach deinem willen/vñ gee alweg hindersich vnd hab dein aug zu dem absehen.o. negst daran/vnd besich das Corpus wie es dir gefall/ vñ ob es recht nach deinem willen lig/ Darnach stell dz gitter oder ram zwischen dem Corpus vnd deinem absehen also/ wilt du wenig lucken oder fierungen begreiffen/so ruck es dest neher zu dem Corpus/darnach besich wie vil dz corpus im gitter lucken begreuf nach leng vñ breyten/ darnach reiß ein gitter gros oder klein auf ein bappir oder tafel darein du conterfeten wilt/ vnd sich hin vber dein aug.o. des spitz am absehen auf das Corpus/vnd was du in yder fierung des gitters findest/das drag in dein gitter das du auf dem bappir hast das ist gut vnd gerecht/ Wilt du aber für das spitzig absehen ein löchle machen/dardurch du sihest ist eben so gut/solcher meynung hab ich hernach ein form aufgerissen.

Item ob einer von einem kleinen bild/einen grossen risen an ein hohen thuren wand wolt malen/ solt man dann so vil bappir zusamen leumen/das gros genug würde zu einem gitter/wer verdrossen vnd vngebrauchsam/darumb mach kein gros gitter von bappir/sonder schneyd groß quadraten auß bappir als gros die fierungen in deinem gitter solten seyn worden/darnach mach eyn fierung nach der andern auß/wie daforn angezeygt ist/verzeychen die firungen wie sie nach einander gehören/darnach leg sie zusamen wie ein kartenspil/vnd so du an die mauren kumbst/magstu eyn plat nach dem andern auß machen/vñ darffst den risen nicht wie sonst not ist gantz verzeychnen.

Zu dem freuntlichen leser.

Zum ende dises buchs/ So bekent der erber man Albrecht Dürer mit seyner eygene handschrifft/zu der zeit/als er noch hie im leben/das er seinem schreiben so er in disem buch an den erbern nnd weysen Bilibaldum Pirckheymer gethan/ein ende wil geben/vud mit der zeit/so im gott das leben verlihe die bücher weil er von menschlicher proportion/vnd andern darzu gehörig geschriben/im truck lassen außgeen/wie es dann von jme selbs/vor seinem absterben mit vleiß ist geschehen. Auch nachmals auß genugsamer verlegung Agnes Dürerin seiner nachgelaßne wittib/in guth latein gepracht/auf das solchs jres haußwirts kunst vnd arbeyt auch andern/welchen teutschē sprach vnbekandt/zu nutze möcht reychen. Hierumb soll menigklich gewarnet sein/dises buch in keinen wege nach zutrucken bey peen vnd straff/so verlichne von Kayserlicher Maiestat/freyheyten anzeygen/darnach mag sich ein yetlicher richten/ Gott dem herren sey lobe vnnd eer ewigklich Amen.

Gedruckt Zu Nürenberg durch Hieronymum Formschneyder.
Anno. M. D. XXXVIII.

paper). The fourth device (fig. 43) comprises a frame divided into a lattice or grid with evenly spaced threads running horizontally and perpendicularly, something Alberti claimed to have invented, and which he called 'the veil'.[69] The resulting grid and coordinates can then be transferred to paper, and then all that is left to do is to connect the dots.

It should be noted that the mechanical drawing aids Dürer illustrates are hardly intended as self-assembly models for real-world use. Instead, they are intended as pedagogical devices that illustrate the mechanics of perspective – taking perspective from a theory or mathematical abstraction to a concrete theatre of props.

CONSTRUCTED ALPHABETS

If art can be improved with geometry, then why not letters too? Dürer was not the first to propose geometrically constructed alphabets. The brilliant mathematician Luca Pacioli was the first to publish them in print in his *De divina proportione* of 1509 (see pp. 57–65). However, Dürer's was the first such treatise published outside of Italy. In it, he explains that his lettering models, for Roman and Gothic alphabets, will prove especially useful for 'architects, painters, and others'. Those 'others' would include anyone using lettering in their work, from engravers working in metal to someone embroidering initials onto a tapestry or an item of clothing. Dürer is not suggesting that the inventors of these letterforms have actually designed them according to strict geometric principles, but that such a system ensures that even those with no formal training in calligraphy or lettering can, by following some simple guidelines, produce a good alphabet with nothing more than a compass and a straight edge. Dürer also shares a simple and practical rule of thumb to compensate for foreshortening in letters – for example, when an inscription is high above ground level, then the letters should be elongated, in the same way that we elongate painted road markings today (fig. 45).

DÜRER'S LEGACY

Dürer lived at a time when educated Europeans saw classical antiquity as a cultural golden age that had been extinguished by barbarians and eclipsed by a 1,000-year Petrarchan Dark Age – an all too familiar Renaissance trope that Dürer repeats in his introduction to *On Measurement*. As a Renaissance man and humanist, Dürer saw it as his duty to use his artistic talents and intellect in the service of the restoration of a long-lost classical heritage. And today, Dürer is considered the leading light of the Northern

previous pages

43 Devices as aids to drawing. From Dürer's *Underweysung der Messung*, second edition, 1538.

opposite 44 Geometrical constructions of a roman alphabet. From Dürer's *Underweysung der Messung*, second edition, 1538.

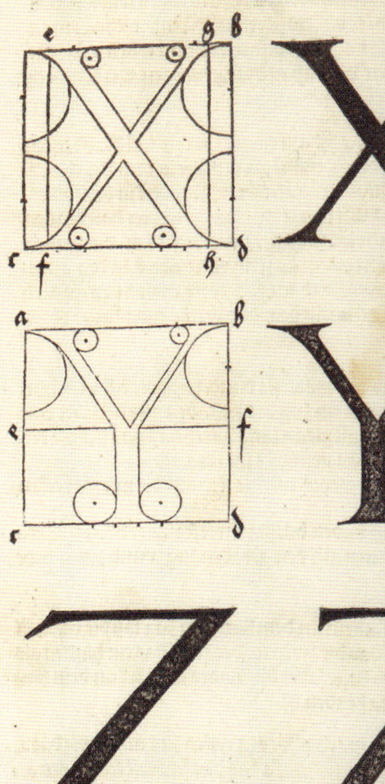

Renaissance. But this transalpine renaissance was not simply a replanting of the Italian flag in northern soil. He travelled, read, sought out the best artists and art theorists, assimilated the best of what he encountered, and in the process fashioned a uniquely northern renaissance. His fame was accelerated by his enthusiastic adoption of print, both for his art (more than 300 of his woodcut designs have survived) and in art theory, including *On Measurement*.

Many great artists are only feted posthumously, but Dürer attained fame during his lifetime. He was celebrated not only at home in Germany but also on the Italian peninsula and beyond. On both sides of the Alps, he was compared to the greatest painters, both contemporary and from antiquity – what better compliment could there be for a humanist, an artist and a Renaissance man? The Nuremberg jurist and diplomat Christoph von Scheurl (1481–1542) called Dürer 'the foremost painter of this century', adding that he was greeted in Italy like Apelles, the legendary painter of ancient Greece. Erasmus claimed of Dürer that he was superior to Apelles. Even the renowned art historian, artist and proud Florentine Giorgio Vasari, who was notorious for dismissing artists from the 'wrong side' of the Alps, praised Dürer's skill and acknowledged that even the great Italian artists imitated him. By the end of the sixteenth century collectors were still scrambling to acquire anything connected to Dürer, with one commentator contending that 'Dürer's manuscripts and paintings, his smallest pieces of paper, are worshipped like relics nowadays … you have to pay just to look at them'.[70]

Albrecht Dürer's simple tomb in Johannisfriedhof in Nuremberg can still be seen today. On a weathered sandstone gravestone is a simple bronze plaque with a Latin epitaph composed by his closest friend, Willibald Pirckheimer: '*Quiquid Alberti Dureri mortale fuit, sub hoc conditur tumulo*' (Whatever was mortal of Albrecht Dürer is covered by this tomb).

45 A practical rule of thumb to compensate for foreshortening in letters – in the same way that we elongate painted road markings today. From Dürer's *Underweysung der Messung*, second edition, 1538.

Es begibt sich offt das man schrift an die seulen/thürn/oder an hohen mauren macht/darumb welcher an ein thuren schreiben will das man die oberst zeil der bustaben als wol gesech zu lesen als die vnderst/der mach sie oben grösser dann vnden/durch ein solchen weg/stell dein gesicht so weit von dem thurn/vnd in der höch wie du wilt/dis sey ein punct.c.vnnd nym für dich den weg des triangels.a.b.c.der.16.figur des lini büchleins/vnnd las das.a.b.sein die thuren höhe oder wandt darauf du schreiben wilt. Nun teyl in das zirkeltrum.b.e.mit puncten gleich weittē der zeylen darein du schreiben wilt/vnd als dann far aus des gesichts punckten.c.mit geraden linien durch all puncten des zirkeltrums.b.e.biß an die auffrecht thurē höe oder want.a.b. Darnach far mit parlinien auß disen puncten auf des thurns want vber zwerch. Zwischē die selben linen must du dein schrift setzen/da wirt dir anzeygt wie vil die obern bustaben grösser werden dañ die vnderen/vñ so du aber ein kurtze lini nach der langen.a.b.gleich mesich wilt teylen/so reiß all linien gerad in den puncten.c vñ schneid sie mit einer aufrechtē parlini.f.g.gegen dem püncten.c.ab/so wirt.f.g.gleich geteylt wie a.b.mit der sie ein paralel ist. Diß ist zu brauchen im für oder hindersetzen zu ergrössern oder kleiner machen. Also sind all lini nach anderen zu teylen in gleichen oder vngleichen dingen/vñ in den teylen die man nit nennen kan/vnd solche teylung hat nit alleyn stat in den bustaben/sunder in allen anderen dingen/vnd in sonders so man einen hohen thuren in allen gaden mit bildwercken zieren will/also das die obern bild gleich den vnderen scheinen kan durch disen weg geschehen/wie das hernach aufgerissen ist.

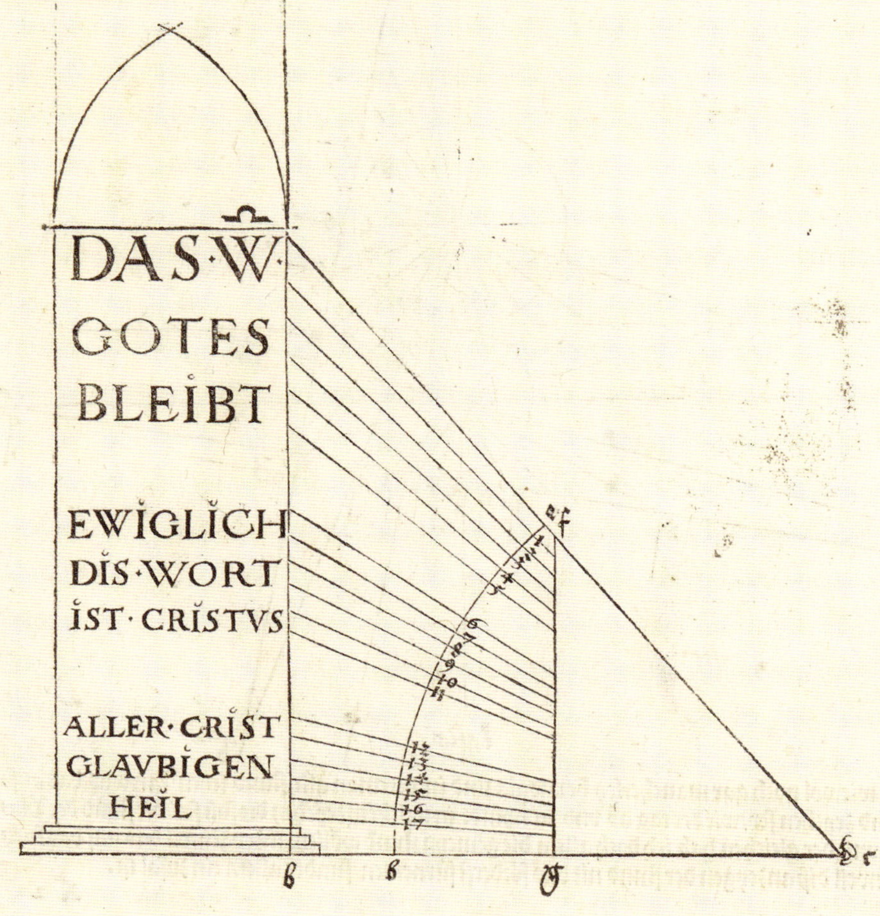

Tauri be war for kuttyng of y nekke & sone the mone be in hym

Arie be warre for cuttyng in the hed & visage a [illegible] y capital veyne [illegible]

Gemini be war for kuttyng of y armes & the [illegible] & for y veynes [illegible]

Canc' be war for kuttyng in the brest & y body for hertyng of the stomake & longs and be war of the harte

Leo be war for kuttyng [illegible]

Virgo kytte no wounde in the wombe ne the lowyne plac in y signe

Libra be war for kuttyng of y wombe the navele & y lowe plag no butok [illegible] that [illegible]

Scorpio be war for kuttyng in the gendryng [illegible] for [illegible] with the [illegible] mone [illegible]

Sagittari be warre for kuttyng in y thy [illegible] kutte no wonne in [illegible] in [illegible] sone

Capricorne be warre for kuttyng in the knees [illegible] of the vainess in the pl.

Aquarius be war for kuttyng in the calves of y legges & veynes

Pisces be war [illegible] kuttyng ne [illegible]

februar

marche

Aprill

May

Iune

Iuly

August

Septem

8

PAPER COSMOS

APIAN, *ASTRONOMICUM CAESAREUM* (1540)

Give me the Ways of wandring Stars to know:
The Depths of Heav'n above, and Earth below.
Teach me the various Labours of the Moon,
And whence proceed th' Eclipses of the Sun

VIRGIL, 29 BCE[71]

Long before they had developed the language to describe it, or the writing to record it, our prehistoric ancestors looked up at the night sky in awe. In time, they came to see patterns and rhythms both in space and across time – the celestial bodies, whatever they might be made of, and however near or far they might be, appeared to follow prescribed paths at regular intervals.

For the ancient Egyptians, Isis's tears over the death of Osiris made the Nile rivers swell. But its annual flooding, crucial to the lives of the region's populace, could be predicted to follow the dawn rising of the sky's brightest star, Sirius. Furthermore, the moon's influence on tides, the sun's heat and light, and its connection to seasons for planting and harvesting were surely proof enough that the heavens exercised significant influence over earth and its inhabitants.

ARISTOTLE'S ORBS

Expanding on the work of his predecessors Eudoxus and Callippus, Aristotle's chief cosmological treatise, *De caelo* (*On the Heavens*), written in 350 BCE, conceives the cosmos as a set of solid nested orbs or spherical shells, rather like a matryoshka doll or a series of nested snow globes. Aristotle's impenetrable, immutable and incorruptible spheres were made of an exotic fifth element or ether. Astute observers noticed that all but seven of the stars moved across the sky uniformly. The Greeks called them *planetes* (literally, wanderers). According to Aristotle, those wandering stars or planets were embedded in transparent spheres that rotated about a stationary Earth at the very centre of the cosmos. The outermost celestial sphere carried the regular or fixed stars; motion imparted to the outside

46 Miniature of the so-called Zodiac man, illustrating the intimate symbiosis of astrology and medicine. Nicholas of Lynn, early fifteenth century.

surface of that sphere – from God or angels – was transmitted to all the other successive planetary spheres.

Improvements to Aristotle's cosmological model were proposed by, among others, the father of trigonometry, and the earliest known author of comprehensive star charts, Hipparchus (*c*.190–120 BCE),[72] Aristotle's cosmology was most thoroughly realized, however, by the brilliant mathematician, astronomer and geographer Claudius Ptolemy (*c*.100–170 CE), from Alexandria (then the capital of Roman Egypt). For Aristotle and the generations of natural philosophers or scientists who came after him, it was inconceivable that the Earth should move. Ptolemy claimed, in somewhat dramatic fashion, that if the Earth were in motion it risked 'falling out of the heavens'.[73] To maintain an immobile Earth at the centre of the cosmos, and to improve astronomical predictions, required the construction of a complex geometrical system of epicycles and deferents, their ratios and positions reverse engineered from observation. Each planet is described as moving around a small circle or sphere – the epicycle. The centre of the epicycle moves around the circumference of a larger circle or sphere – the deferent.

47 Working lunar volvelle. Nicholas of Lynn, early fifteenth century.

Of course, this sophisticated and ingenious geometric model of multiple nested spheres was not at all how the cosmos worked in reality, but the predictions derived from it typically proved accurate enough. Moreover, this model also provided plausible explanations for the erratic or retrograde motion of the 'wandering stars' or planets, including variations in their apparent brightness and size. Thereafter, the Ptolemaic cosmos remained the orthodox view for almost fifteen centuries. Alfonso X of Castile (1221–84), Spanish monarch and sponsor of the famed Alfonsine Tables (Europe's most popular astronomical tables for several centuries), suggested that, had he been present at creation, he might have given some pointers. Although almost certainly apocryphal, the sentiment was perhaps shared by untold astronomers throughout history.

ASTRONOMICUM CAESAREUM

The renowned historian of astronomy Owen Gingerich described *Astronomicum Caesareum* (*Caesar's Astronomy*) as 'the most spectacular contribution of the bookmaker's art to sixteenth-century science'.[74] Published in Ingolstadt in 1540, this fabulously deluxe book was dedicated to Emperor Charles V and his brother Ferdinand. However, before we take a closer look, let us first meet its author and designer.

Peter Apian (or Petrus Apianus or Peter Bienewitz), son of a shoemaker, was born

on 16 April 1495 in Saxony. He began his studies at the University of Leipzig, later transferring to Vienna in 1519 where he pursued mathematics and astronomy. By 1527 he had been appointed professor of mathematics at Ingolstadt University, a post he held until his death despite, no doubt, receiving lucrative offers from other universities. Apian was not only a mathematician, geographer, astronomer, and designer and maker of astronomical instruments, but he also established his own private press, working as printer-publisher for himself and others. In 1524 he published his first major work, *Cosmographia*, an introduction to astronomy, geography, cartography, navigation and instrument-making that, via edited and expanded editions brought out later by the Dutch physician, mathematician and instrument-maker Gemma Frisius (1508–55), became a sixteenth-century bestseller. It was Apian's *Cosmographia* that caught the eye of Emperor Charles V. He was impressed, publicly praising it and awarding Apian printing privileges or monopolies. This episode marked the beginning of a generous and lifelong royal patronage.

NO ASSEMBLY REQUIRED

Apian's *Astronomicum* is primarily an astrological toolbox for the potentially maths-phobic but assuredly enthusiastic beginner. Writing in the introduction, Apian is clear about his intended audience: 'We see how hated is mathematics, on account of its apparent difficulty. We have tried to simplify it and have worked out new ways in which we may help those who are perplexed by arithmetic.'[75]

The copy of *Astronomicum* now held at the Bodleian Library is one of the world's most complete. It is a large folio edition measuring 49.5 × 33.3 cm and contains 114 printed pages, numerous woodcut illustrations, diagrams, tables, and decorative and historiated woodcut initials populated with astronomers, geometers and putti. After a dedication and preface, the book proper commences with an alphabetical index that uses chapter references (page numbers were still not ubiquitous by 1540). At first sight the index, other than its placement at the front of the book, appears as we would expect. Under the letter A are listed all entries beginning with A. So far, so good – but the alphabetization ends there. Entries under each letter are not in alphabetical order but rather in the order in which they appear in the book. If, for example, you wished to find out about errors in determining the vernal (spring) equinox, then 'obviously' they are listed under the letter A – *Abhominabilis error quotundam de æquinoctio vernali* ('abominable errors concerning the vernal equinox').

48 Constellations of the northern and southern hemispheres combined. After Albrecht Dürer's celestial maps. From Apian's *Astronomicum Caesareum*, 1540.

Effusio Aquarii
Aquarius
Sagittarius
Ara
Scorpius
Fera
Libra
Centaurus
Corvus
Crater
Hydra
Leo
Cancer
Procyon
Orion
Lepus
Eridanus
Cetus
Pisces
Pegasus
Draco
Hercules
Bootes
Arcturus
Erichthonius
Gemini
Argonauta

The first full-page illustration is a splendid hand-coloured octagonal planisphere (star map), illustrating forty-six of the forty-eight classical constellations. Apian used the very same woodcut for a standalone print in 1536, published under the title *Imagines syderum coelestium* (*Images of the Heavenly Stars*). The constellation figures appear to be inspired by those of Albrecht Dürer's hemispherical maps of 1515. If the star map appears unusual, this is because it is drawn on the outside of a globe, from the standpoint of a viewer outside and above rather than below and inside – which is why the stars and constellations appear reversed.

Ten pages are devoted to the apparitions and observations of five comets, including the comet of 1531 which would later be named after Edmond Halley. Also included was the frequently forgotten notion that the tails of comets point away from the Sun (mentioned by, among others, Robert Grosseteste, *c.*1230); this at a time when the nature of comets and their distance from Earth were not at all understood. In fact, at least since Aristotle, comets were considered disturbances in Earth's atmosphere and thus a meteorological phenomenon.

In chapter thirty, for the first time in print, Apian recommends the use of coloured or black glass through which to safely observe solar eclipses. Chapter thirty-eight is devoted to finding the date for Easter (connected to the first full moon after the spring equinox) and other moveable feasts in the Christian liturgical calendar. Part two of *Astronomicum* begins with the meteoroscope, a device used to solve spherical triangles without any mathematics, and concludes with the *torquetum* (or *turketum*), a rather complex medieval astronomical instrument for observing and measuring the positions of celestial objects in either equatorial, ecliptic or alt-azimuth coordinate systems. It famously appears in *The Ambassadors*, painted in 1533 by Hans Holbein the Younger.

Undoubtedly, the most striking feature of *Astronomicum* is its full-page woodcut prints of equatoria – instruments adapted from the astrolabe. Twenty-two of these paper equatoria have moving parts made from printed and hand-coloured volvelles (paper discs, named after the Latin *volvere*, to turn). Some of these volvelles have silk strings threaded with tiny seed pearls functioning as sliding indicators, most of which have long since been lost. Volvelles were not Apian's invention, although he certainly had a hand in popularizing them. They worked much like a flat or two-dimensional astrolabe, mechanizing the process of computing planetary positions (in longitude

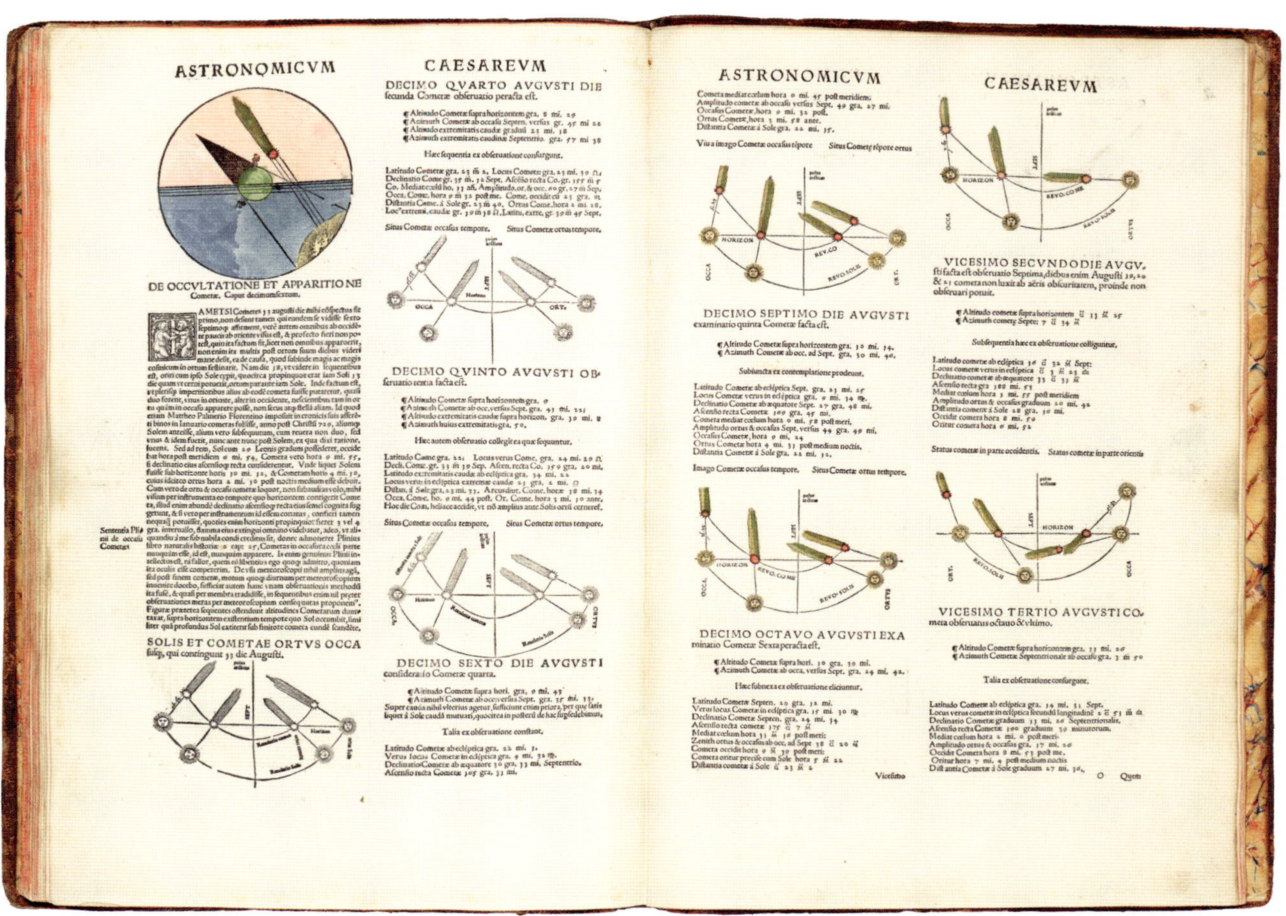

49 Two of the ten pages devoted to the apparitions and observations of five comets, including the comet of 1531, later named after Edmond Halley. From Apian's *Astronomicum Caesareum*, 1540.

and latitude), and thus doing away with the need for tricky mathematical calculations. A relatively simple lunar calendar version appeared in a printed book in 1474, published by the brilliant mathematician, instrument-maker and very first astronomer-printer, Regiomontanus (1436–76). But volvelles had appeared long before in medieval manuscript books, with the earliest surviving examples dating to the thirteenth century. The Bodleian Library has a fine example of a working lunar volvelle in an early fifteenth-century English manuscript (MS. Ashmole 370, fol. 25r).

Some of the earliest printed books to incorporate volvelles supplied the various moving parts separately, to be cut out and

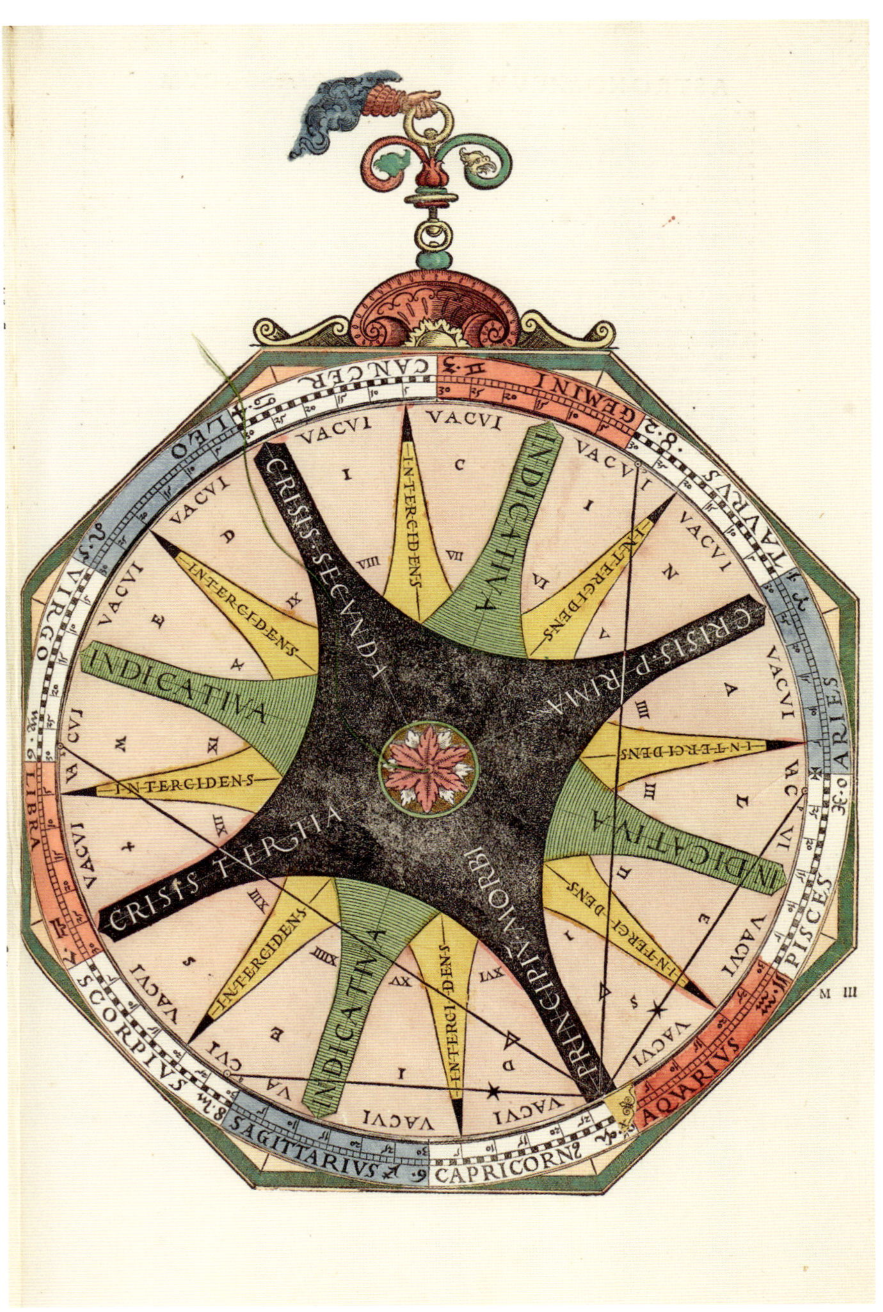

assembled at home. These were cheaper and smaller books aimed at students, whereas Apian's *Astronomicum* was well beyond the reach of most students. It was an unashamedly luxurious book with a price tag to match, and dedicated to none other than the emperor. To ensure that everything was just right, all the volvelles (some with as many as nine parts) were assembled in Apian's printshop. Usually, colouring would be left to the book buyer to arrange post-purchase but Apian, not wishing to leave anything to chance, took the unusual step of having all copies coloured in-house too.

ASTROLOGY

Throughout most of history, astronomy played a supporting role to astrology. In many respects, and for many centuries, advances in astronomy were often motivated by and important only insofar as they aided astrological practice. In addition to improving calendrical accuracy, astronomy satisfied astrology's desire for increasingly more accurate predictions for planetary positions and other celestial phenomena, like solar and lunar eclipses. This data could then be used in constructing horoscopes, in compiling almanacs and to determine the most propitious time to perform a ceremony to travel or to do business. Perhaps most crucially, right up until the eighteenth century astrology was intimately involved in many aspects of medicine, from diagnosis to determining the best time to perform surgeries or bloodletting, and for prescribing medications. Astrological decumbiture charts (from the Latin *decumbo*, to lie down), that were cast based on the time at which a patient took to their bed, were used to determine the nature, course and outcome of the illness that had put them there.

It is important to remember that even the ostensibly astronomical parts of *Astronomicum* ultimately serve important astrological functions. For example, the planetary volvelles in the first part of the book, used to compute the position and paths of the planets for any given time, were not for casual backyard astronomers hoping to catch glimpses of the planets. They were very practical and necessary tools for use in astrology. Two of the graphically most striking equatoria are the dragon volvelles – the Lunar Latitude (FIII) and Lunar Phases (GIII). They were to be used in conjunction with others to determine the date, duration and size of eclipses. Why? Because such information was crucial in medical prognostications where eclipses signified particularly inauspicious times for treating patients. The final volvelle (MIII; fig. 50), in the fortieth and final chapter of Part One, serves as an aid to physicians to 'find the critical days for doctors for effecting cures', as Apian explains in his introduction to the chapter.

ASTRONOMICAL FOLLY?

In 1543, less than three years after the publication of *Astronomicum*, a certain Polish mathematician and astronomer, Nicolaus Copernicus, published in print his literally Earth-moving *On the Revolutions of the Heavenly Spheres* – better known by its abbreviated Latin title, *De revolutionibus*.[76] He proposed a heliocentric universe, one in which all the planets, including Earth, orbit the Sun.

You might think this revolutionary book would have rendered Apian's didactic and artistic masterpiece, his astronomical and astrological magnum opus, immediately obsolete. But that was not to be. The world was not quite ready for Copernicus's newly rearranged cosmos. Not only would it meet theological, philosophical and even scientific opposition, but the Ptolemaic system had become deeply ingrained; it had served astrology and its allied disciplines well, like medicine, for many centuries. Furthermore, although overall the computed planetary positions derived from Copernicus (in the Prutenic tables) were more accurate, that was

50 Volvelle and decumbiture chart for medical astrology. From Apian's *Astronomicum Caesareum*, 1540.

not the case for all the planets. For the inferior planets, namely Mercury and Venus, and for lunar eclipses, Ptolemy's predictions, via the Alfonsine tables, proved a little more precise than the Copernican ones.

As for astrology, it continued to flourish until its eventual fall from scientific grace in the eighteenth century. It began to lose its intellectual footing when, across Europe, astrology as a subject of study began to disappear from university curricula. But its decline was protracted. Even Brahe, Kepler and Galileo practised astrology. And Francis Bacon, one of the fathers of empiricism, who one might assume would have been vehemently opposed to astrology, proposed not its abandonment but instead its scientific reform. In some respects, *Astronomicum* was the last encore of Aristotle's and Ptolemy's cosmos before the wrecking ball of new science and Copernicanism demolished the crystalline spheres and deposed Earth – and us – from the centre of the universe. More than a century would pass before Copernicus's revolutionary ideas were more generally accepted – helped along and clarified by Kepler and his laws of planetary motion that described the planets moving not in circular but in elliptical orbits, and moving faster in those orbits the closer they are to the Sun.

While the emperor loved Apian's book – knighting him, feting him and making him a very wealthy man – not everyone was as magnanimous. In a scathing review, Kepler decried Apianus's *Astronomicum* as a waste of his time and talents. However, Apian's work was intended not for professional mathematical astronomers like Kepler, but for keen non-specialists, most especially those without a mathematics background. In that regard he succeeded. Apian's *Astronomicum* is both art and science, geometry and mathematics, astronomy and astrology, vision and folly – realized magnificently in what is surely one of the most beautiful astronomy books ever produced.

51 Detail of Hans Holbein the Younger's *The Ambassadors*, 1533. Note the astronomical instruments, including the torquetum.

following pages

52 Lunar phases dragon volvelle and volvelle for eclipse times. From Apian's *Astronomicum Caesareum*, 1540.

IVLIVS
AVGVSTVS
SEPTEMBER
OCTOBER
NOVEMBER
DECEMBER
IANVARIVS
FEBRVARIVS
MARTIVS
ANNI CVRRENTES
IVNIVS
UMBRA

¶ Cautela obseruanda in dispositione rotarum.

Operandi modus huius secundi instrumenti verus qdem & certus est, quoties annus currens siue propositus in arcu limbi inferioris rotæ ab indice X Y procedendo secundum dieꝝ ordinem, usqꝫ ad 29 diem Ianuarii, horam 12, Mi. 44 siue stellam lunæ sic depictam ✳☽ reperitur. Annus ille cum filo (vt prius dictū est) signatur, eidemqꝫ denuo index XY adducitur, qui inuariatus ad operationis finem sic perdurabit. Si uero post primam siue radicalem indicis locationem annus ꝓpositus à stella prædicta (supputatione secundum dierum ordinem facta) usqꝫ ad indicem X Y occurrat, iam dictæ stellæ centrum inspice, ꝑ huncqꝫ filū tende, cui subducis indicem T. Mox deinceps filum ducatur per ꝓpositum siue currentem annum, ubi intersectio fili cum circulo T diem tantū, aut diem horamqꝫ dabit. Dies ille tandem in limbo Ianuarii requisitus, cum filo signatur, eidemqꝫ denuo ostensor X Y subiungitur, ita autem rota illa ultimum sui locum sortita est. Atqui nunc mihi uideor satis superqꝫ positionem rotæ X Y declarasse, admonens interim, ut similia de rota Z V intelligantur, qualia de rota X Y prodita sunt, interesse tamen hoc vnum quod hic considerandus erit index Z V, & centrum stellæ iuxta 27 Ian: diem signatæ cū charactere draconis sic ✳☊

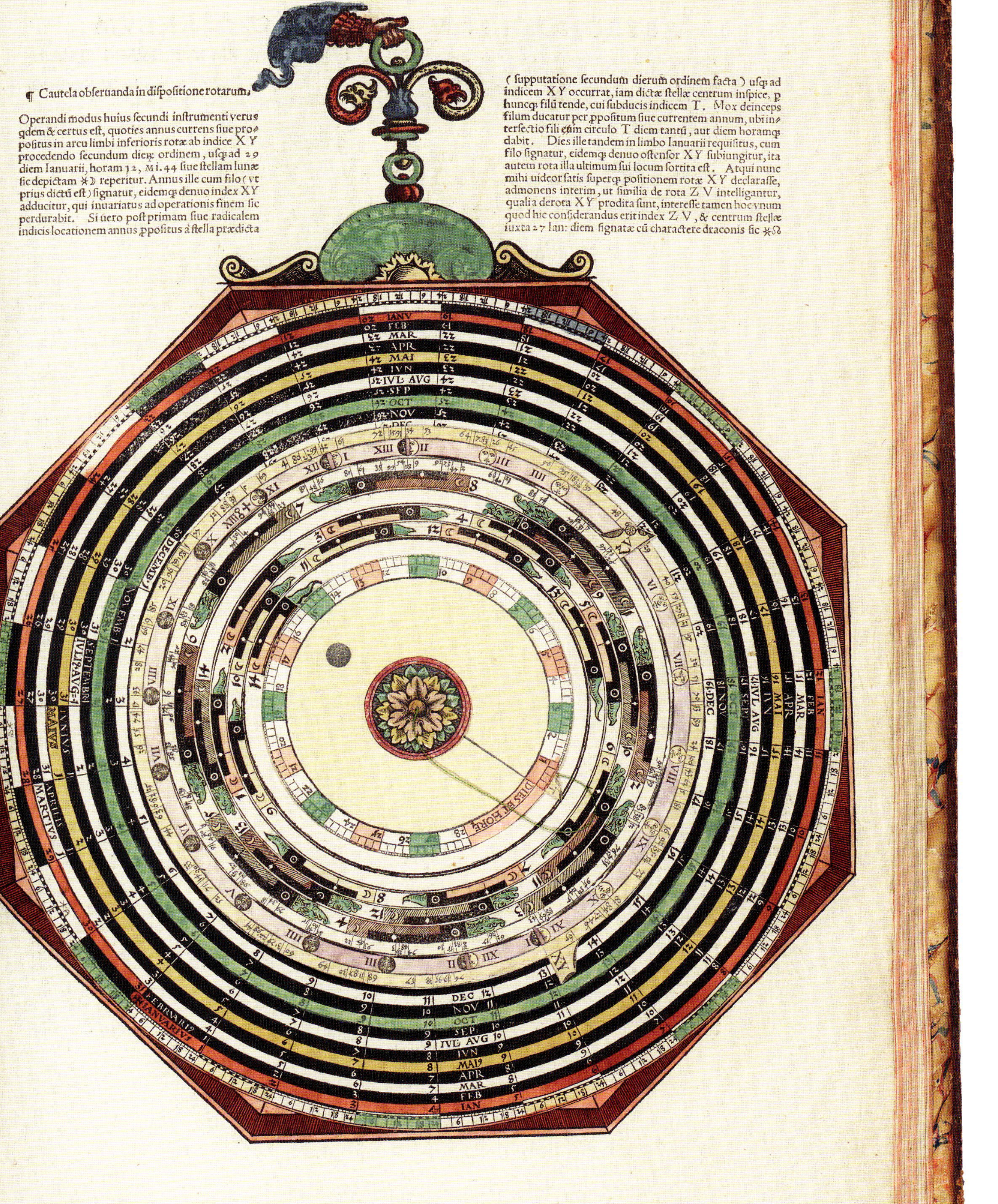

ANDREAE VESALII
BRVXELLENSIS, SCHOLAE
medicorum Patauinæ professoris, de
Humani corporis fabrica
Libri septem.
CVM CAESAREAE
Maiest. Galliarum Regis, ac Senatus Veneti gra-
tia & priuilegio, ut in diplomatis eorundem continetur.

9

THE WALKING DEAD

VESALIUS, *DE HUMANI CORPORIS FABRICA* (1543)

It is better to dissect nature, than to reduce her to abstraction.

FRANCIS BACON, 1620[77]

We can be thankful that we do not live at a time when haemorrhoids were cauterized with hot irons. Mercifully, there are now gentler alternatives. The same goes for headaches: had you lived in Europe during the Middle Ages, your doctor might have suggested tying a mole to your head.[78] If that did not work, then removing a sizeable piece of your skull with a hand-operated drill – without anaesthesia – might do the trick. Practised since the Neolithic period, this technique, known as trepanation, was also recommended for, among other ailments, epilepsy and melancholy. Mercury, now understood to be lethal even in small doses, was once commonly prescribed to treat everything from constipation and influenza to syphilis. It was sold, along with countless other potions and salves by *quacksalvers*, from which the term 'quack' is derived. Mercury was even included as an ingredient in medications for teething babies well into the twentieth century! Many common ailments and injuries that in the past would have led to our premature demise are now easily remedied. The Black Death, a fourteenth-century pandemic that killed a third of Earth's population in the space of about five years, can now be cured with a prescription of antibiotics – widely available since the 1940s. Before the advent of modern medicine, many medical treatments and pharmacological concoctions were rather hit and miss, their success often predicated more on them not killing you than on their curing you.

The fact is that until relatively recently, we understood very little about human physiology. But perhaps the most obvious way to learn how something works is to take it apart. And, in the third century BCE, that's exactly what

53 Frontispiece to Andreas Vesalius's *De humani corporis fabrica* (*On the Fabric of the Human Body*), 1543.

Herophilus and Erasistratus did. They founded a school of anatomy in Alexandria and 'were the first to engage in systematic dissection of the human body'.[79] Four centuries later, Galen (129–216 CE), the most famous ancient anatomist, considered dissection crucial to understanding human physiology. Although limited to animal dissections, Galen assumed or hoped that human anatomy was not all that different from that of other animals – an assumption which led to many long-standing misconceptions. For most of the Middle Ages cadaveric dissection was not practised, but not because the church prohibited it, as is often claimed.[80] By the early 1300s anatomical dissections and autopsy had been revived, most notably at the more progressive medical faculties of Bologna, Padua and Paris.

THE BELGIAN BODY SNATCHER

Built in Paris in the late thirteenth century, the Gibbet of Montfaucon was an enormous three-sided colonnade for public hangings, with room enough for forty-five executees, their corpses left on display *pour encourager les autres*. As the corpses decayed and were fed on by birds and rats, they would naturally disintegrate, with various bits and pieces falling to the ground. In the 1530s a young student frequented the site in the hope of picking up a leg, an arm or even an entire torso. He and his fellow students would also drop by the Holy Innocents' Cemetery, behind where the Louvre Museum now stands, to recover bones from the charnel houses. These arched buildings, constructed along the perimeter of the cemetery, were designed to cope with overcrowding; bones were disinterred and moved to the charnel houses to make room for new burials. In the autumn of 1536, back in Belgium, the same student recounts how he, along with his friend, the Dutch polymath Gemma Frisius, would go for long walks on country roads in search of hanged criminals. Later, and with evident enthusiasm, he reports how on successive trips he brought home legs, arms, and, on another night, a thorax, which proved a particularly challenging haul owing to its being secured to the gallows with a chain.

But it is high time we introduced our curious grave-robbing protagonist. Andreas Vesalius was born in Brussels in 1514 to a family of physicians. He grew up surrounded by books and soon developed an interest in the ancient authors, all of whom were available to him in the family's well-stocked library. He began his medical studies at the University of Paris in 1533, but in 1536 he was forced to leave when war broke out between King Francis I of France and Charles V, Holy Roman Emperor and king of Spain. Vesalius returned to Leuven

54 The *lector*, *sector* and *ostensor* at work during a public dissection. *Fasciculo di medicina*, 1494.

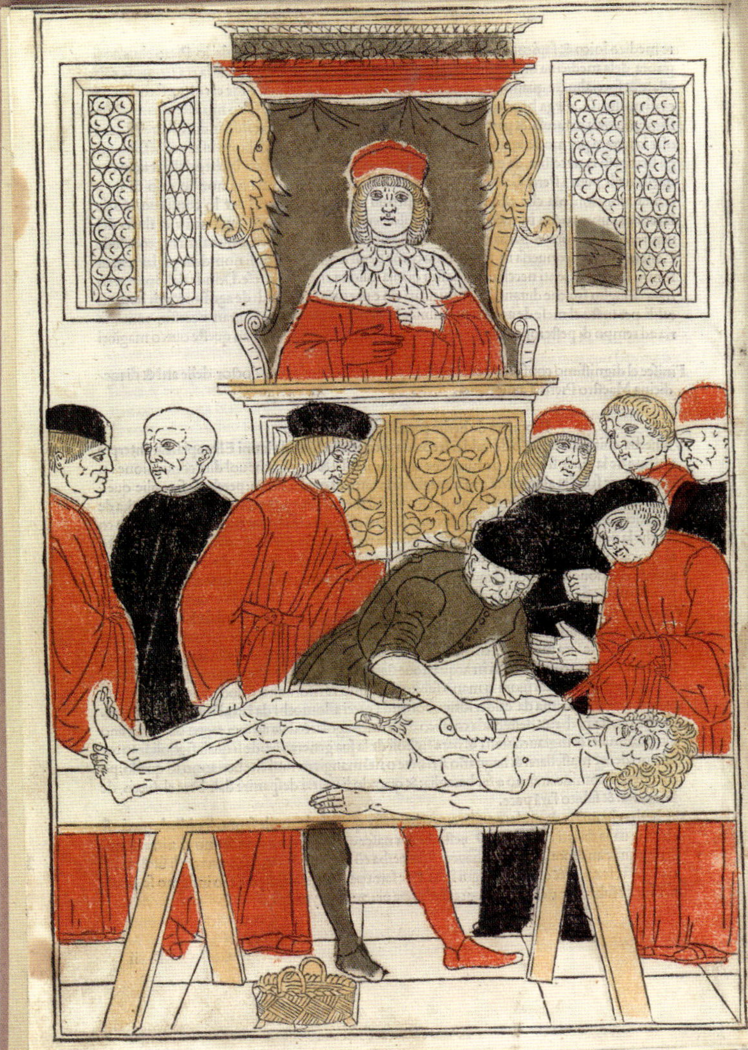

Commincia la Anathomia ouero diſſectione del corpo humano :cõpoſta e compilata per el fa
moſiſſimo & eximio doctore del arte & de medicina maeſtro Mundino .

P

Er che diſſe Galieno nel ſeptimo della terapentica che la doctrina per aucto
rita di Platone aiuto in alcuna ſciẽtia ouero arte per tre caſoni ſi contribuiſce
La prima e per ſatiſfare agli amici. La ſecõda acio che ſi exerciti per ultimo ex
ercitio el q̃l e per lo intellecto. La terza cio che ſi rimedii alla obliuiõe: la qual
procede dala uecchieza. Et de qua uiene che mi ſon moſſo per queſte tre raſo
ni ad componere una certe opera in medicina alli miei ſcolari. &perche la co
gnitione delle parti del ſubiecto nela medicina e el corpo humano el qual ſi chiama li luoghi
dele diſpoſitiõi e una delle parti della ſcientia dela medicina: ſi come dice Auerroi nel primo
del ſuo colliget nel capitulo dela diffinition dela medicina. & de qua naſce che fra tucte laltre
coſe douemo hauer cognitione del corpo humano & delle parti de eſſo: la qual cognitione ĩ
ſurge & procede dalla anathomia. La quale ho prepoſto de dimoſtrare: non obſeruando ſtile
alto: ma ſecondo la manuale operatione uene daro notitia .

Poſto adonq; deſteſo ala ſupina el corpo ouero homo morto per decollatiõe ouero ſuſpendio
Primamẽte deuemo hauer notitia del tucto. Secõdariamente delle parte. Impoche cõcioſiaco
ſa che ogni noſtra notitia comenzi dale coſe piu note ad noi: & q̃lle coſe che ſono cõfuſe ſono
piu manifeſte: &el tucto ſia piu cõfuſo che le parti douemo cõminciar dala cognitiõe del tucto
Ma circa al tucto el quale prima douemo cognoſcere e ĩ che lhõ e differẽte da glaltri aĩali. Impo
che in tre coſe ha tal differentia: cio e nela figura ouer ſito dele parti: & ĩ neli coſtumi ouero ar
ti: & ĩ alcũe parti . Et certamente nela figura lhõ e di ſtatura dritta & ha hauta q̃ſta per q̃tro ra
ſoni . Impoche el corpo humano ha fra glaltri aĩali la materia leuiſſima ſpumoſa & aerea: &po
eleuabile ale coſe ſupiore. Secõdariamente tra glaltri aĩali di medeſima q̃tita ha piu calor natu
rale al q̃l ſi appertiene ſemp̃ eleuare ĩ alto. La terza raſone e perche lhõ ha la forma pfectiſſima
la q̃l comunica cõ gli anzoli & cõ le ĩtelligẽtie le q̃le regono tucto lo uniuerſo: & po coſi deue
eſſere eleuata la forma delhõ ſcd'o q̃lla del uniuerſo. La quarta e p reſpecto del ſuo fine . Impo
che eſſo hõ e finalmẽte ordinato ad ĩtendere: al q̃le ſeruono li ſentimenti & ſpecialmẽte el ſen
timẽto del uiſo ſi cõe e manifeſto nel ꝓhemio dela metaphiſica. & po in eſſo hõ douea colocar
ſe la uiſta: &el ceruello: &cõſequẽtemẽte la teſta ĩ tal logo del corpo che poſſeſſi ĩprẽdere tucte
le coſe ſenſibile. Et perche q̃n e poſto ĩ alto ſe extẽde ad piu coſe uiſibili: el che appariſce pche
li guardiani dele citta acio che poſſino ben ueder de lõga põgono li ſoi ſpectaculi in logo alto
cõe nele torri & altri loghi ſimili cõe dice Galieno nel nono deli iuuamenti deli mẽbri . & p q̃
ſto lui dice li & ancho Aui. nel prĩcipio del terzo canone: che nõ fo neceſſario p el ceruello col
locare la teſta in alto ne per le orecchie ne per la bocca ne per el naſo ma ſolamente per gli oc
chi per le raſoni dicti di ſopra. Et coſi appariſce dalla parte dele quatro raſoni che lhõ fo di ſta
tura drietta formato: per el che ſi chiama piãta reuerſa & mũdo minore pche ha di ſopra & di
ſotto cõe mũdo & lo uniuerſo &q̃ſta e la prima differentia. La ſecõda e dali coſtumi ouero dal
arte . Impoche tra tucti glaltri aĩali lhõ ha li coſtumi piu mãſueti perche e aĩal politico & ciuile.
Ma naturalmente nõ ha arte alcuna: cõe el ragno e lapa & ſimili ad queſti acio che poſſa ĩpren
dere ogni arte. Impoche ſe naturalmẽte haueſſe arte alcũo : nõ potrebe alcunaltra piglare cõe
dice Gal. nel quarto degli iuuamẽti. Differiſce anchora daglaltri nele parti. Impoche ñ ha mol
te parte ĩtrinſeche le quale hãno glaltri aĩali. Imperoche nõ ha le parti le quale ſono date dalla
natura: cõe arme ad defẽdere cõe ſon corne unge lõghe &q̃ſti nõ gli ha lhõ. Impoche ha lo or
gano degli organi el quale e le mano cõ le qual ſi puo apparechiare ogni generation de arme
ad ſua defenſione: cõe ancora dice Gal. nel primo degli iuuamenti . & pero la natura non gli
ha date le ſopradicte arme acio poſſa eligere quelle che piu gli piaciono . Nõ gli ha date ancho
ra le parti le quale ſon piloſe pẽnoſe & ſquamoſe per la medeſima raſone & ancho perche nõ
ha ĩ ſe mã terrena molto ſouerchia la q̃l materia e di quele pti . Nõ gli ha data anchora la coda

for a year, then went to the University of Padua where he was awarded his doctorate on 5 December 1537. The very next day, he was appointed to the chair of surgery and anatomy.

When it came to performing dissections, Vesalius soon became something of a celebrity, impressing his students and peers alike. Typically, public dissections were hosted by a team of three: a *lector* (lecturer) who read from a textbook, perhaps Mundinus's *Anatomia* (1316), a *sector* (barber-surgeon) who wielded the knife, and an *ostensor* (demonstrator) who pointed out the various features described in the text. Vesalius derided this method, describing the lector, 'perched on a pulpit like a crow, haughtily repeating ideas that he did not learn directly from the cadaver, but that he read in other's books'.[81] What made Vesalius's public dissections so remarkable – and remarkably popular – was not only his profound knowledge of anatomy, but that he did not mind getting his hands dirty. In fact, he performed all three roles, declaiming, dissecting and describing to a packed amphitheatre, even passing around bloodied organs to an inquisitive and sometimes boisterous audience (see fig. 53).

For his anatomy students, Vesalius prepared large anatomical drawings. These proved so popular that he decided to publish them in print. They were printed in Venice in April 1538 as *Tabulae anatomicae sex* (*Six Anatomical Tables*), a summary anatomical atlas comprising six large broadsheet posters. Three of the drawings were Vesalius's own, and three were supplied by Jan Stephan van Calcar, talented pupil of the great Venetian master Titian. The drawings were designed to be used in the classroom or as reference during dissections. Towards the end of the introduction to these plates Vesalius suggested that, if they were well received, he would consider producing something more substantial.

FABRICA

Published in 1543, when Vesalius was just twenty-eight years old, *De humani corporis fabrica libri septem* (*On the Fabric of the Human Body in Seven Books*) was the more substantial work Vesalius had hinted at five years earlier in *Tabulae sex*. Known colloquially as *Fabrica*, it is organized into seven main sections or books, each concerned with a different system or part of the body: from bones to ligaments, muscles, veins and arteries, the organs and, lastly, the brain.

Fabrica is a large and formidable work, comprising 700 pages of Latin accompanied by more than 250 woodcut illustrations. In medieval books, useful anatomical figures had been rare. The recently translated texts of Galen likewise were not accompanied by drawings. Even during Vesalius's time, some were opposed to illustrations on principle, arguing that they did not reflect the classical tradition. But Vesalius forged ahead and set new standards with his remarkably precise and detailed drawings of articulated skeletons; musculature; the organs; vena cava; and the alimentary, arterial and nervous systems. The illustrations are usually attributed to Stephan van Calcar, who, as we have already learned, contributed to Vesalius's *Tabulae sex.* Among the best known and frequently reproduced *Fabrica* drawings are the iconic myological figures of Book Two, a series of fourteen Muscle-Men arranged with their skin, fascia and muscle progressively peeled back – what one art historian likens to 'a choreographed muscular ballet'.[82]

In addition to the anatomical illustrations and drawings of surgical instruments, *Fabrica* is filled with dozens of charming, comical and macabre historiated (story-telling) initials. Some depict scenes of putti preparing for dissections, robbing graves or being otherwise mischievous. In such a large book these initials are not merely decorative, but are part of a typographical hierarchy designed to help readers navigate the long and complex text.

Who was *Fabrica* intended for? It was dedicated to Charles V, and aimed to elicit a job offer. Vesalius presented him with a beautiful hand-coloured copy, and the emperor was so impressed that he appointed Vesalius as one of his imperial physicians, calling *Fabrica* 'without question the greatest of all books which have been written about anatomy'.[83] *Fabrica* was not at all aimed at students. It was far too expensive. Instead, it was pitched to an audience of predominantly affluent doctors and scholars. For the student market, and published simultaneously with *Fabrica*, Vesalius issued an *Epitome*, a slim 'student edition' of just twenty-three pages printed on larger but cheaper paper. It is also the first printed anatomical pop-up book, being supplied with loose sheets which students were encouraged to cut out and glue to certain figures in the book. These are sometimes called anatomical fugitive sheets.

DESIGN AND TYPOGRAPHY

When it came to the design and printing of *Fabrica* (and the *Epitome*), Vesalius was exceptionally hands-on. Once the woodblocks for the illustrations were completed in Venice, Vesalius had them carefully packed up and sent on a three- or four-week journey across the Alps, to Johannes Oporinus, his printer-publisher in Basel. When they arrived in the middle of September 1542, Oporinus found not only the many engraved pear-wood blocks but printed proofs and captions too,

55 A selection of historiated initials: the large initial I (opposite) shows grave-robbing putti; the smaller initial D depicts putti sawing off the top of a skull in preparation for dissection of the brain.

accompanied by a letter from Vesalius outlining details about the books' design, including page layout, typography and even font sizes. He also repeated how crucial it was that the woodblocks be printed well, ensuring that even their finest details were reproduced, right down, specifically, to the very fine crosshatching in the shadows. And later, when it came to proofing, Vesalius was even more exacting, noting every misprint and typo – even remarking on a broken comma!

WOODCUT WANDERLUST

The story of the woodblocks used to print the anatomical illustrations in *Fabrica* is a fascinating one. Seldom do the original blocks of such early books survive. Most have long since been lost, many used to destruction, or reused and recycled; some no doubt ended their lives rather ignominiously as kindling. But the *Fabrica* woodblocks tell a Homeric tale of miraculous survival. Carved in Venice and then crossing the Alps to Oporinus's printshop in Basel, they were used for the first edition of *Fabrica* in 1543 and the second in 1555. Upon the death of Oporinus in 1568, the woodblocks passed to Erasmus's favourite printer, Ambrose Froben. In 1706 they made a brief appearance in Augsburg, then went on to Landshut via Ingolstadt, and then, at some time in the early

ANDREAE VESA

BRVXELLENSIS, DE HVMANI C

RIS FABRICA LIBER SECVNDVS, LIGAMENTIS

& Musculis, uoluntarij atque è nostro arbitratu pendentis motus in
dedicatus, ac propemodum figuras omnes ipsi proprias, ante Ca
contextum, uti nunc subijcitur, spectandas offerens.

N PRAESENTIS
ponenda sedecim tabularum series,
cundi libri Capitibus communis erit
bri calce, quàm hîc modò in fronte
Primæ enim quatuordecim, integro
nes, ac harum ordine prima, anter
delineatam continet, secunda latus
quarta, quinta, sexta, septima, octau
ciem quoq; proponunt, in hoc illud ue
lorum, qui indicantur, natura & situ
Sex uerò octauam consequentes, po
ris faciem referunt, omnes propemoc
ut quod in priori conspicuum est, in subsequenti resectum, ab insertione pendea
tabulæ ita inuicem congruunt, ut uni quæ anteriorem faciem exprimit, alia suc
steriorem exhibens. Integrum namq; erat tertiæ subiungi nonam, mox quartan
insuper quintam, illi uerò undecimam, postmodum sextam, ab hac duodeciman
mam, quã sequeretur decimatertia, cui rursus succederet octaua, & huic deci
etiam non inopportunè feceris, si utraq; serie has musculorum tabulas intueari
læ potißimùm exprimant, ex ipsarum earundemq; characterum indicibus illis

nineteenth century, to Munich University Library. Here, those splendid monuments of early scientific printing sat unlabelled and forgotten in an out-of-the-way cupboard before, in 1893, someone happened to open that cupboard and record their existence. They were again mislaid, but reappeared in the early 1930s in a wooden chest in the Munich University Library attic. In 1934 the woodblocks, now almost 400 years old, were dusted off and used to print a commemorative edition of *Fabrica*, published jointly by the New York Academy of Medicine and the University of Munich. A decade later, on the evening of 16 July 1944, 200 Allied planes bombed Munich, destroying the Munich University Library and the woodblocks.

A NEW PRINCE OF ANATOMY

Vesalius emphasised repeatedly the importance of direct observation over bookishness and claims to authority. He also practised what he preached in the way he taught anatomy – not with readings from ancient authorities and not with his head buried in a book, but with sleeves rolled up and up to his elbows in blood and viscera, describing what he saw and felt, not what he had read and memorized. Not only did he dare to challenge Galen, but he proved through dissections that Galen was fallible. Vesalius claims to have corrected more than 200 of Galen's anatomical errors, but he was also quick to admit his debt to his ancient forebear, referring to him as 'the prince of anatomists'.[84] *Fabrica* established Vesalius as the founder of modern anatomy, and his work remains one of the most important books in the history of medicine, setting the standard for anatomical illustration and paving the way for future breakthroughs in the fields of anatomy, physiology, neuroscience and neurosurgery.

The sixteenth century marked both the revival and decline of Galenism. The classics, including the Galenic corpus, had been resurrected by the Italian Renaissance – rescued from the stranglehold of scholasticism, scrubbed clean of corruption by the greatest philologists, and was expected, in this pristine form, to signal a neo-golden age of medicine. Petrarch had characterized the period from the collapse of the Roman Empire until his own day as 'a sleep of forgetfulness', an unremarkable and unenlightened *medium tempus*, a purgatorial Middle Ages.[85] But no sooner had Galen been resurrected than Vesalius entered with a wrecking ball that not only hastened the demise of Galenism, but bolstered a growing consensus that even the most hallowed ancient authors could be flat-out wrong. This newfound scepticism towards ancient authorities such as Galen had been a long time coming, but when the dam broke it ushered in a new science of the human body and laid the foundations for modern medicine.

As we began with the grisly, it feels only fitting that we go full circle and conclude there too. If you have never heard of anthropodermic bibliopegy, you can be forgiven. Binding books in human skin (there were clues in 'anthro', 'dermic' and 'biblio'), although thoroughly grisly, was extremely rare. So why mention it? Well, the Bodleian copy of the 1543 *Fabrica*, reproduced in this chapter, was rebound in the eighteenth or early nineteenth century in brown sheepskin over the original wood board. It is one of 300 surviving copies. Without a doubt, the most unusual of these must be the copy held at the John Hay Library at Brown University in Rhode Island, which was confirmed in 2015 to be bound in human skin.

following pages

left 56 Articulated skeleton from Andreas Vesalius's *De humani corporis fabrica*, 1543.

right 57 One of fourteen Muscle-Men figures, from Andreas Vesalius's *De humani corporis fabrica*, 1543.

HVMANI CORPORIS OSSIVM CAETERIS QVAS SVSTINENT PARTIBVS LIBERORVM, SVÁQVE SEDE POSITORVM EX latere delineatio.

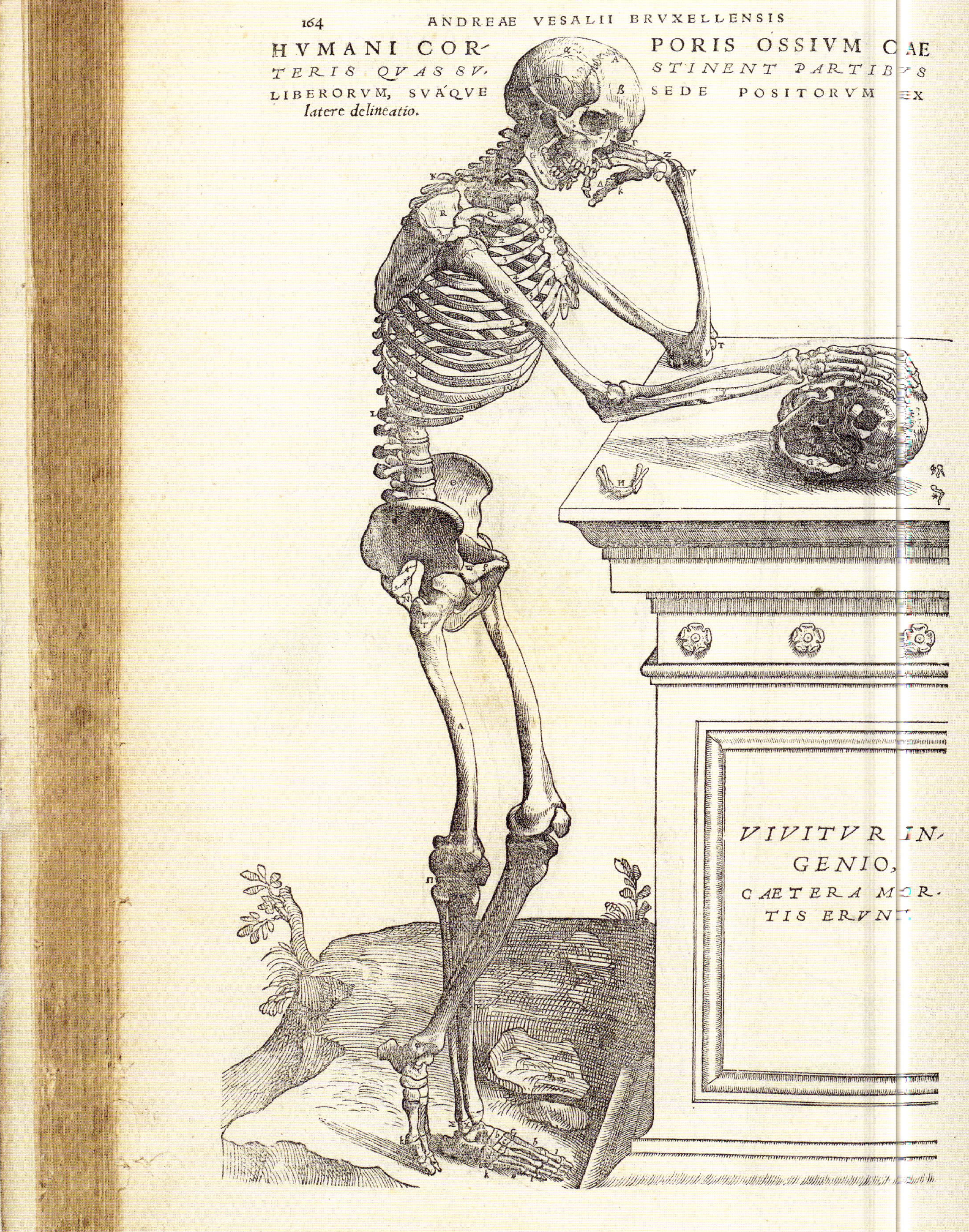
VIVITVR INGENIO, CAETERA MORTIS ERVNT.

PRIMA
MVSCVLO-
RVM TA-
BVLA.

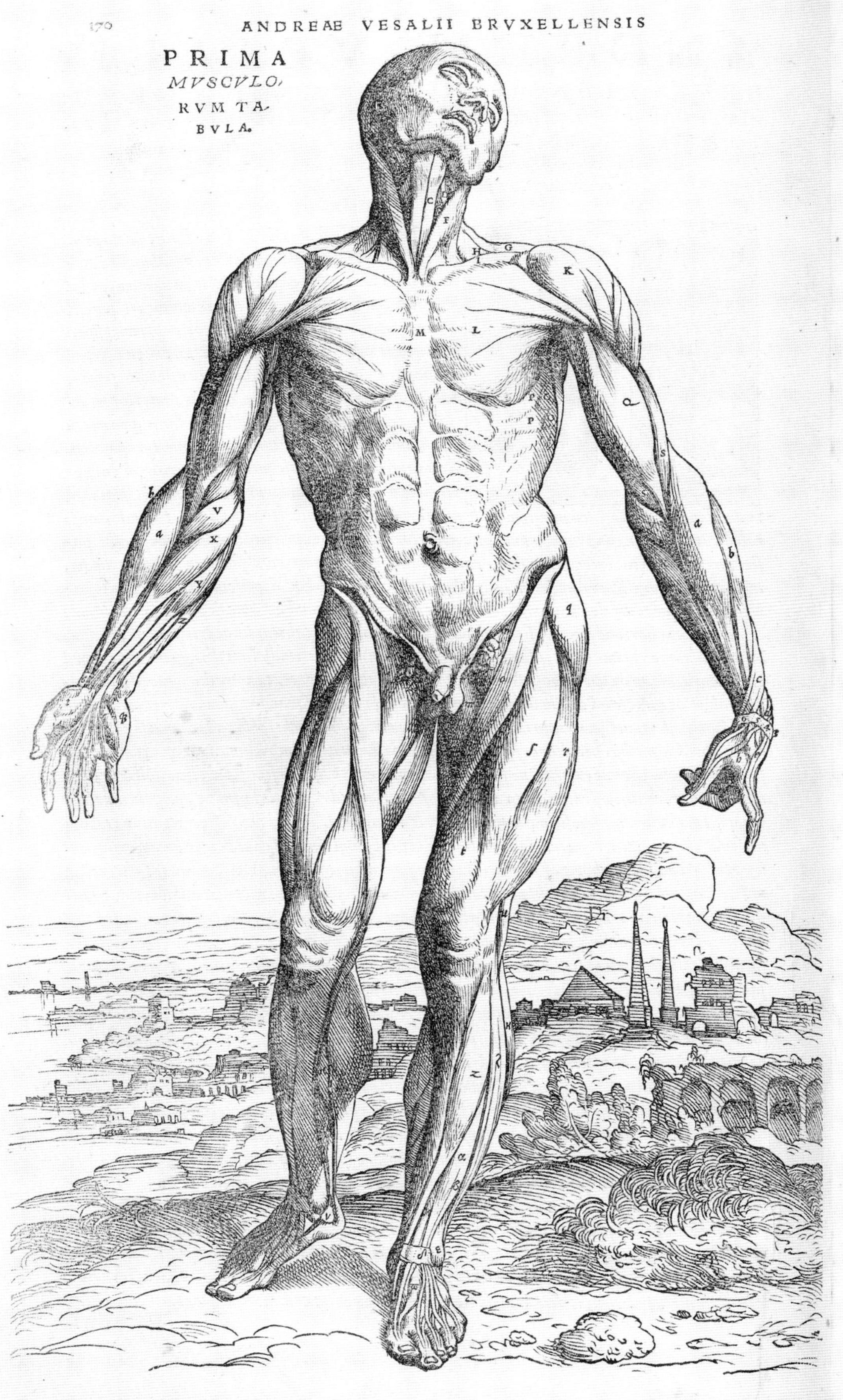

PRIMA

PRAESE
pus exprimit, à quo cut
neruis, uenis & arteri
beram relinquere prop
tia ferè prima eſt, quam
oculis ſubijcit, quod no
ſculptoresq́; indies etia
bulæ facie & ceruice u
& plaſtem (quorum ſt
ſit, muſculos in ſuperfic
tionem, ſumma diligent
muſculū aliquē aut bre
debeāt, hoc axioma per
uentrem retrahit, bre
quum autem è conuerſo
tur, muſculi uentrem (
minimumq́; protuberar
perſtringam, characte
uatim expreſſurus ſum,
hic obiter ſpectare lice
illi tenues exactè & m
modò occurrant.

A Glandulæ quàm plurim
dem repoſitæ, cauitate
quas in pueris humorū
ſubinde infeſtantur. H
præſciſſæ hic auris for
B Siniſtri lateris muſcul
C Muſculus à pectoris o
D Muſculus gracillimus
rum figura, V & V,
ra uiſitur, cauaq́; eſt, ne
bus, & arterijs ſopora
F Muſculus à pectoris
tione implantatus.
G Portio eſt muſculi, ſc
tati ſunt. Præſentis mu
meri ſedem claniculæ c
Δ inſignitus.
H Sedes hæc iugulares u
nem, in uiuis duntaxat
ademptis, ille occurrit
anteriorem tranſuerſo
ſculorum tabula notat
I Clauiculæ anterior ſe
K Muſculus brachium a
naſcitur, atq; hic ipſius
L Muſculus brachium p
M Pectoris os excarne a

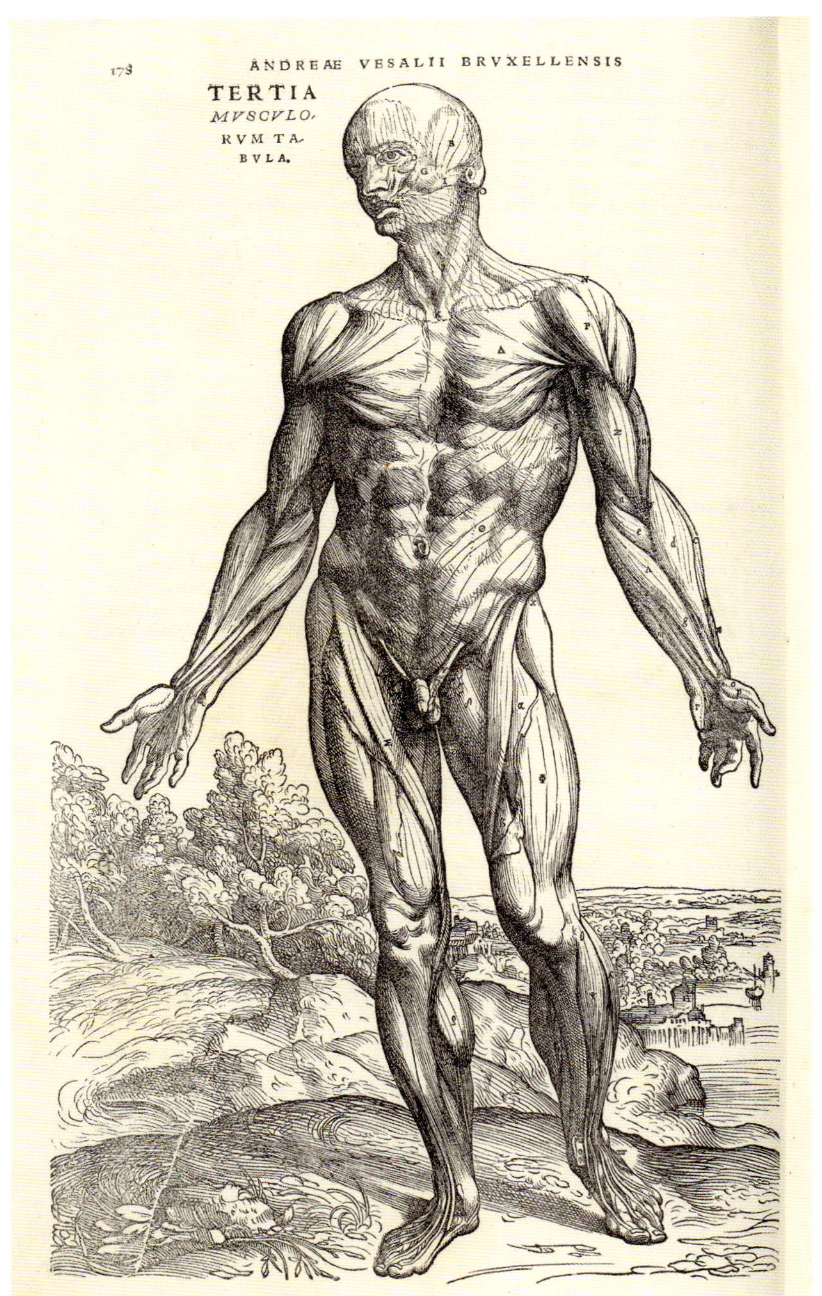
178 ANDREAE VESALII BRVXELLENSIS
TERTIA
MVSCVLO-
RVM TA-
BVLA.

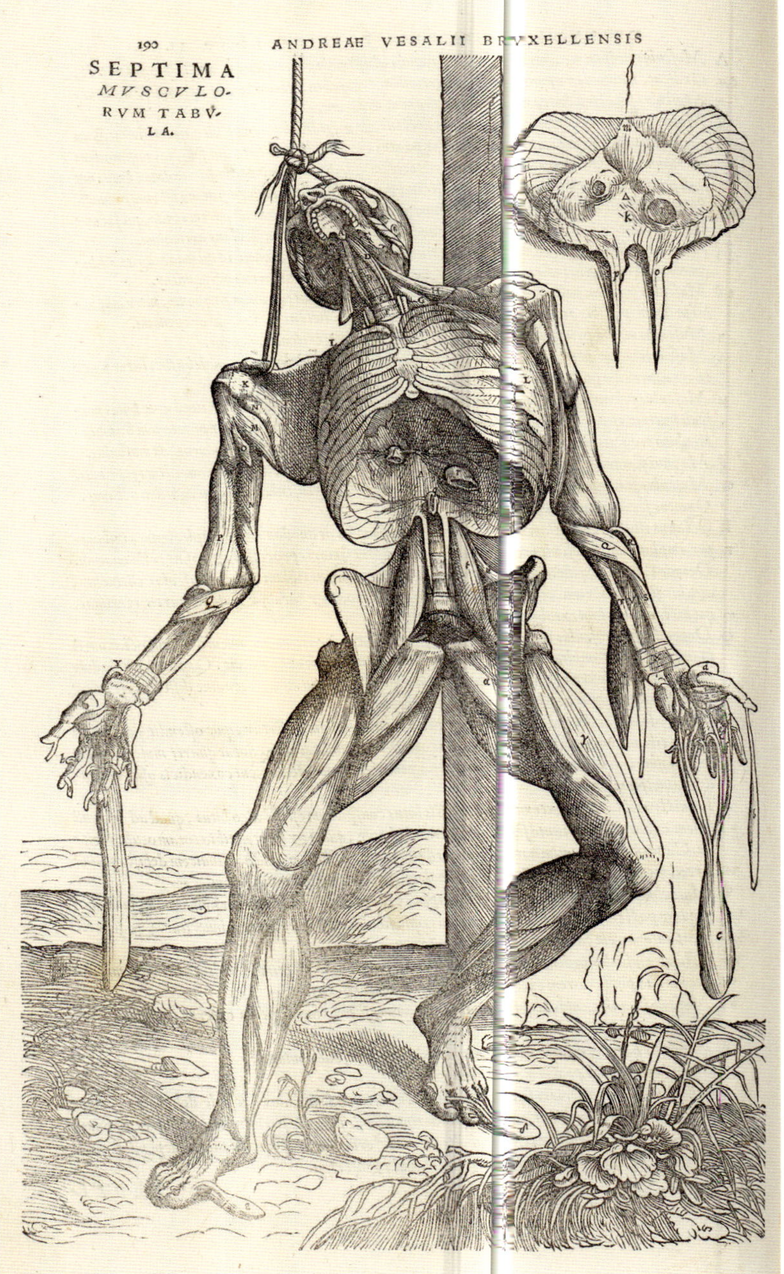
190 ANDREAE VESALII BRVXELLENSIS
SEPTIMA
MVSCVLO-
RVM TABV-
LA.

opposite 58 Two Muscle-Men figures from Andreas Vesalius's *De humani corporis fabrica*, 1543.

above 59 Nineteenth-century engraving by Theodor Josef Hubert Hoffbauer of the Saints Innocents cemetery in Paris, as it was *c*.1550. Note the arched charnel houses on the left (for the storage of disinterred bones).

appellatur; Quod ipsas linces sentire hoc documento probatur; Nam egestum liquorem arenis in quantum potuerint contegunt. inuidia quadam naturae ne tal. egestio in usum transeat humanum; licet dicat plinius exceptum unum non admittere fetum; DE GRIFE.

A grype. or a gryffon.

Grifes uocatur. quod sit animal pennatum et quadrupes. hoc genus ferarum in hiperboreis nascitur locis uel montibus. omni parte corporis leoni. alis et facie aquilis simile. equis uehementer infestum. nam et homines uiuos discerpit; DE ELEF.

A olyfaunte. or a olyphaunte

Est animal quod dicitur elephans in quo non est concupiscencia coitus; Elephantem greci a magnitudine corporis uocatum putant. quod formam montis preferat. Greci enim mons

10

UNICORNS AND THE SAUSAGE SUPPER AFFAIR

GESSNER, *HISTORIA ANIMALIUM* (1551–58)

We should venture on the study of every kind of animal without distaste; for each and all will reveal to us something natural and something beautiful.

ARISTOTLE, fourth century BCE[86]

According to the biblical story of creation, God created animals on the fourth day. He then tasked Adam (Eve was not yet on the scene) with naming all the animals.[87] No doubt this took Adam quite some time. It is estimated that there are now about 8.7 million animal species living on Earth. We have names for about 1.2 million of them, meaning that we have yet to discover, catalogue and name another 7.5 million. And this is likely to be a gross underestimate.

The ancient Greek philosopher Aristotle (384–322 BCE) was among the first to attempt seriously to describe the natural world in purely natural rather than supernatural terms. According to legend, Alexander the Great commissioned him to compile an encyclopaedic history and description of the entire known animal world. The result was Aristotle's *Historia animalium* (*History of Animals*), describing 500 species across nine books. Although Alexander's part in this tale is almost certainly apocryphal, Aristotle's work counts as the earliest substantial work of zoology – one that was destined to dominate the field for the next 2,000 years.

MEDIEVAL BESTIARIES

In the first century, when Pliny needed information about animals for his own encyclopaedia, he often turned to Aristotle. In the same way, a century or so after Pliny, when Aelian needed material for his seventeen-book encyclopaedia of animal behaviour, *On the Nature of Animals*, he borrowed from both Aristotle and Pliny. In the third century, an anonymous author in Roman-occupied Egypt wrote the remarkably popular *Physiologus*, a

60 A mythical Griffin and a real-world elephant ridden into battle from the Ashmole Bestiary, early thirteenth century.

didactic compendium of moralising animal tales that again borrowed from earlier authors such as Aristotle and Pliny, but supplemented them with many excerpts from the Bible. These Christian allegories later served as models for a new genre of book, the medieval bestiary (literally a 'books of beasts'), which similarly commandeered animals and animal stories to teach moral lessons.

While medieval bestiaries were often illustrated, books of natural history seldom were. It might appear strange to us that books about animals should not contain any pictures of, well, animals. But, as Pliny had pointed out, their usefulness depended on the talents of the copyist. Moreover, there was no guarantee that future copies would remain faithful to the original, and that over time even the best copies were susceptible to alteration and corruption. A rather late solution to this latter problem was woodblock printing. Popularized in the latter half of the fifteenth century, it enabled the mass production of ostensibly identical images. Now it is time for us to meet one of the most exceptional early champions of woodcuts for scientific illustration.

THE FATHER OF BIBLIOGRAPHY

Conrad Gessner was born in 1516 in Zurich. His parents were so poor that they could not afford to keep all their children at home. Gessner was sent to live with his great-uncle Johannes Frick, whom he credits with instilling in him a love of botany. By the age of fifteen, Gessner was already fluent in Latin and Greek. His father died in October 1531, and the next year Gessner was sent to Strasbourg, where he learned Hebrew. In 1533 he was dispatched to Bourges in France, on a scholarship, by way of Basel and Paris – a journey that took six weeks on foot! He was now almost seventeen years old. After a year in Bourges, where he had little time to devote to his studies because he was so busy teaching rich kids Latin and Greek, Gessner moved to Paris. By 1536 he was married to Barbara Singerin and living back in his hometown of Zurich. Despite his incredible learning and talents, he was only able to get a poorly paid teaching job at a local school. To supplement his meagre income, he worked on a 1,000-page revised edition of a Greek and Latin lexicon. After a short stint in Montpellier he completed his studies in Basel, and in February 1541 graduated as a Doctor of Medicine.

Nowadays, Conrad Gessner is known as the father of bibliography. In 1545 he published his *Bibliotheca universalis* (*Universal Bibliography*), an incredibly ambitious 1,300-page bibliography of everything ever written in Latin, Greek and Hebrew. He completed this Herculean task, the first of its kind, in just three years. Besides bibliography, linguistics and philology, Gessner's other interests included botany, medicine, pharmacology and zoology.

HISTORY OF ANIMALS

It is for zoology that Gessner is best known. Just as he had done for literature in his *Universal Bibliography*, so he would do for every animal in the world. The result was *Historia animalium* (*History of Animals*), a long-overdue overhaul of Aristotle's work of the same name. Gessner's illustrated encyclopaedia of animals was published by Christoph Froschauer in Zurich, in four volumes, between 1551 and 1558. In his *Ad lectorem* (letter to the reader), Gessner suggests that the book should not be read from cover to cover but used as a reference book, like an encyclopaedia or dictionary; his books are organized to facilitate this kind of use.

The four volumes follow Aristotle's classifications: Volume 1 for viviparous quadrupeds (four-legged animals bearing living offspring), Volume 2 for oviparous quadrupeds (four-legged, egg-laying animals), Volume 3 for birds and the fourth volume for fish and aquatic animals. Unlike Aristotle's history, Gessner's animals are also organized alphabetically, with each entry subdivided into eight sections labelled A–H. In addition to recording the names of animals in various languages, he considers their habitats, characteristics, physiologies and, finally, matters related to philology. This latter entry is the richest and most extensive, and is further subdivided into eight sections, incorporating details on etymology and thousands of references to animals in history and in literature.

Gessner's four-volume *History of Animals* ran to almost 3,500 pages, and featured 1,100 woodcuts. At almost 7 florins it was already pretty expensive but, as Gessner explains in his preface, 'for customers who are not deterred by the higher price',[88] a hand-coloured edition was available for 19 florins. At almost three times the price of the plain, uncoloured edition, it would have taken weeks if not months to prepare.[89] In 1553 Gessner also brought out a much more affordable picture-book edition – *Icones animalium* (*Animal Pictures*) – using the woodcuts from the first two volumes. This proved popular enough to be reprinted in 1560. Gessner's illustrations were widely copied. Some, including his iconic cat, even turned up in embroidery pattern books, and famously appeared in the embroidery of Mary Queen of Scots during her eighteen-year exile at the hands of her cousin, Elizabeth I. Four hundred years later, and from high-born to high fashion, Gessner's cat was still making the news –

this time on the catwalk, appliquéd onto a Gucci sweater.[90]

Of the 1,100 woodcuts in Gessner's magnificent *History of Animals*, one of the most familiar is the rhinoceros that appears in volume one (p. 953). It is a fairly faithful copy of Albrecht Dürer's stylized rhinoceros poster print of 1515, perhaps the most famous of all sixteenth-century animal portraits. It should be noted that neither Gessner nor Dürer ever saw a rhinoceros in the flesh. Dürer probably based his drawing on a written description and sketch in a Portuguese newsletter, dispatched when a rhino, gifted to King Manuel I, arrived in Lisbon. Many other drawings in *History of Animals* were either contributed by Gessner's correspondents or borrowed from other books. For example, the giraffe woodcut was drawn by Erhard Reuwich and appeared in Bernhard von Breydenbach's *Peregrinatio in terram sanctam* (1486), a kind of tourist guide for pilgrims visiting the Holy Land.

61 Cat woodcut from Conrad Gessner's multi-volume *History of Animals*, 1551–58.

following pages

62 Rhinoceros woodcut after Dürer, from Conrad Gessner's multi-volume *History of Animals*, 1551–58.

Gessner's *History of Animals* was an incredibly ambitious undertaking. His work on the monumental *Universal Bibliography* had certainly prepared him for the task, but his new zoological work was much more than an illustrated bibliography of existing works on zoology. He aimed to bring up to date the field that had been dominated by Aristotle for 2,000 years. Gessner's book would serve as more than a contemporary snapshot of the animal kingdom; it would be a new historiography of it. In addition to drawing from ancient and medieval sources, Gessner corresponded with a vast network of scholars, doctors, artists, printers, professors and students. They sent him not only letters, but also plant and animal specimens, drawings and books. Gessner could rely on a vast network of at least 240 people throughout Europe, from Poland to France, Germany, Italy, England, and of course his native Switzerland. Thus, in addition to what could be gleaned from his own large library (and others he had access to), he was able to incorporate countless contemporary accounts and observations from his network of learned and trusted contacts. He incentivized his correspondents by promising to include their names in his books – a promise that he kept.

HERE BE UNICORNS

In addition to hundreds of familiar species, Gessner's *History of Animals* also includes a few fabled or mythological creatures and monsters. The more freakish and implausible they are, the further away from civilization these creatures tend to live – something the second-century Greek philosopher and essayist

ponit: uocatur & uulgò hodie apud Græcos κάτης. Italicè gatta, gatto. Hispanicè gato, gata. Gallicè chat. Germanicè katz. Anglicè cat. Illyricè koczka. Furioz apud Albertum Magnũ pro cato legitur, quod nomen ab Auicenna sumptum puto, & Arabicum uel Persicum esse: Albertus significationem eius ignorauit, & alicubi pro capro montano uel ibice, ut supra dixi, ineptissimè exponit: sed catũ esse constat, quoniam & in eo loco ubi Aristoteles de æluro, & eadem scribit. Eiusdem forsan originis est etiam uocabulum furo, quod uiuerram significat, utpote cõgenerem feli. Aegyptij felem bubastum uocant, Stephanus: Hinc forte nomen Bubasto ciuitati in Aegypto: quã Herodotus Bubastin appellat: sacras enim feles Aegyptij habebant, ut infra dicam. ¶ Apud Columellam (lib. 8. cap. 3.) & Varronem (lib. 3. cap. 12.) feles accipi uidetur pro fouino: sic enim uulgus appellat bestiolã gallinis maximè infestam noxiãq;, & sæpe gallinaria tota contrucidantẽ, Philippus Beroaldus. Feles Varronis & Columellæ fouinus uel marturellus uidetur, Aug. Niphus. Idẽ alibi, felis est, inquit, quę uulgo dicitur fouina: ictis, marturus uel marturellus: mustela uerò, donula. Sed de his omnibus in Mustela dicam. Meles auibus animal inimicum, puto esse id quod uulgus fouinum & marturellum appellat, Ge. Alexandrinus in litera M. in Enarrationibus priscarum uocum: citat aũt Varronis locum de re rust. lib. 3. cap. 12. ubi sic legimus, Quis enim ignorat septa è maceriis ita esse oportere in leporario, ut tectorio tecta sint, & sint alta. Alterum ne feles, aut meles, aliáue quæ bestia intrare possit: alterum, ne lepus transilire. Ego Ge. Alexandrinum felem interpretari uoluisse, lapsum autem memoria melem (quem suo loco taxum uulgò dictum esse docebo) posuisse puto. Felẽ certe pro cato siue domestico siue syluestri apud ueteres authores semper acceperim. Errant qui felem putauerunt martem dici, Perottus. ¶ γαλῆ Græcis mustelam significat, diuersum à fele animal, ut copiose probat Perottus in Cornucop. Recentiores tamen quidam Græci, ut Galeomyomachiæ author, & ab iis decepti quidam Latini, γαλῶ pro cato accipiunt. Sunt sanè quędam horum animalium, mustelæ & cati, naturis communia, ut corporis ferè figura, & ingenium: calliditas, uictus, musculorum uenatus: utrunq; fœtus suos ore de loco in locum transfert, ut & canes interdum: & Græci mustelam non solum γαλῶ simpliciter, sed sæpe γαλῶ κατοικίδιον, id est domesticam, & in domibus nobiscum uersantem uocitant: sunt autem ubiq; cati domestici, mustelæ nimirum nõ item: Quæ omnia errandi occasio fuisse illis uidentur, qui galen pro cato interpretantur. Miror autẽ non dixisse illos, si gale catus est apud ueteres Græcos, quo nomine mustelam iidem appellarint. Michael Ephesius etiam in Græcis scholiis in lib. 3. de gener. animal. cap. 29. γαλῶ exponit catam, ut refert Aug. Niphus: Et Gaza γαλῶ non semper mustelam transfert, sed aliquando catum: ut galen agrian, catum syluestrem. Marcellum Vergilium quoq; mustelam domesticam, felem existimasse, apparet ex commentariis eius in Dioscoridis caput de mustela domestica, & in caput de lychnide. Feles genitale osseum non habet: mustela, ictis, lupus & uulpes habent, Sipontinus. Mustelæ hyeme cubant, æstate expergiscuntur, Aristot. Hoc mustelis accidere (inquit Sipontinus) compertum est: quod ipsi quoq; coemptis in hunc usum utriusq; generis (paruis & magnis, siue domesticis & rusticis) mustelis aliquando

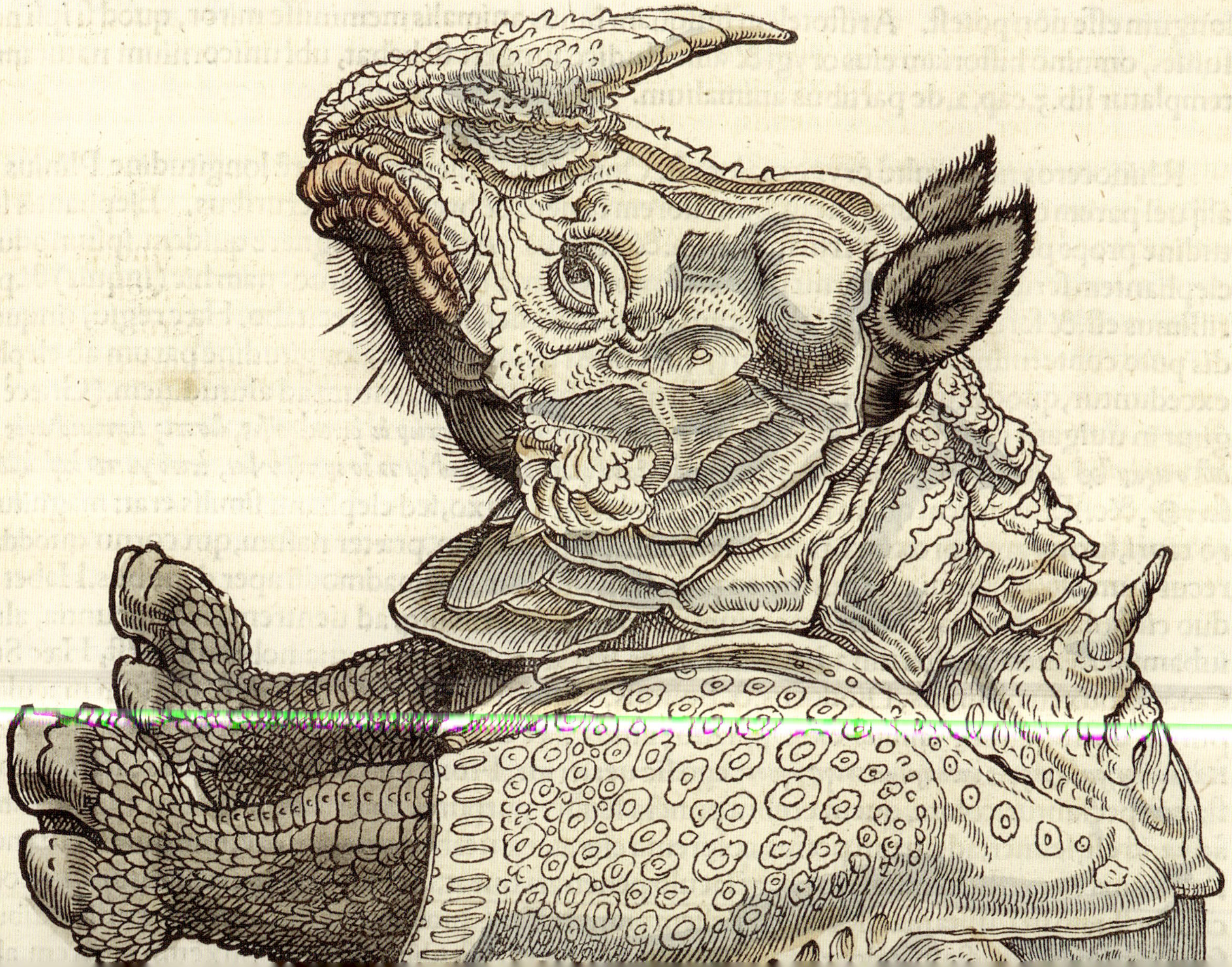

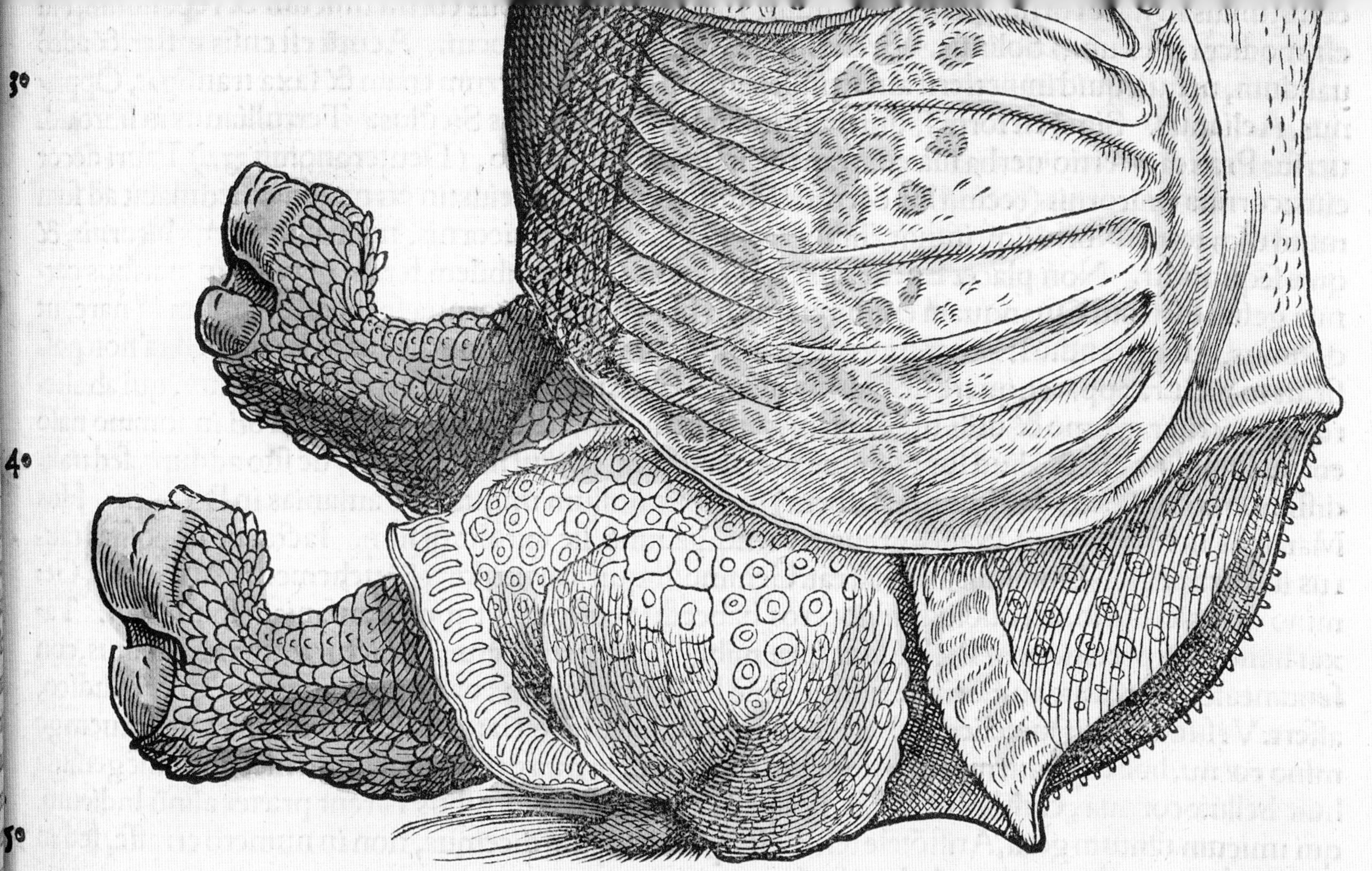

decem, ut ipse mensuraui, longitudine excedit: & diameter eius in radice sesquipalmum, (sesquidodrantem intelligo,) superabat, Hæc ille. Ineptè autem facit, primum quòd asinum Indicum ex Aristotele scribens solipedem esse, mox rhinocerotem animal bisulcum interpretatur: deinde, quòd rhinocerotem & unicornem confundit: tertio, quòd archa uel archos Arabicum nomen faciens libro secundo, (corruptum forte à uoce karas,) duodecimo principem interpretatur ac si Græca esset. Sed et proceritas ista cornu, decem pedes excedens, rhinoceroti puto non conuenit, sed monoceroti cartazono, nam Oppianus rhinocerotis cornu paruum (hoc est breue. Gillius quoque paruum transfert) esse scribit: ὀλίγον δ᾽ ὑπὲρ ἄκρεα ῥινὸς Ἀντέλλει κέρας αἰνὸν, ἀκαχμένον, ἄγριον ἄορ. Quod si quis uerbum ὀλίγον non ad cornu quantitatem, sed ad loci distantiam referat, hoc sensu: paulò supra extremum nasum crudele & acutissimum cornu oritur: nos tamen ex ipsa picturæ quam ad uiuum dedimus, proportione, cornu breue esse conuincemus: nam cum supra nares incipiat, & multò infra aures desinat, poterit. μηλὶς etiam in Lexico Græcolatino arbor malus exponitur, ſed ſine authore. Μελία fraxinus eſt, cuius lignum haſtis conficiendis idoneum habetur: quare eodem nomine haſtam quoq; nominant Græci. Mali certe arboris lignum haſtis ineptum eſt. ¶ Leucrocutæ feræ caput eſt melium, Plin. camelinum, Solin. ¶ A taxo Ferrariæ nobiliſſima Taxonorum familia nomen ſortita eſt, Braſauolus. ¶ Fiente, id eſt fimus Gallica lingua, non de quibuſuis feris, ſed propriè fœtentibus dicitur, ut uulpe, mele.

DE MONOCEROTE.

Figura hæc talis eſt, qualis à pictoribus ferè hodie pingitur, de qua certi nihil habeo.

A.

MONOCEROS, hoc eſt unicornis fera, ab alijs aliter deſcribitur: ſiue quoniam diuerſæ ſunt unicornes animantes, ut conſtat: ſiue quòd aliqui notas diuerſarum tanquam unius confuderunt. Minus autem mirum de fera tam peregrina & toto à nobis orbe diuiſa, nec unquam in Europam adducta, diuerſa ab Europæis ſcriptoribus auritis ferè omnibus non oculatis, memoriæ prodita eſſe. Hoc magis mirum, recentiores etiam, ut Ludouicum Romanum & Paulum Venetum, qui regiones illas in quibus reperiuntur luſtrarunt, diuerſas tamen monocerotes deſcribere. Ego ſingulorum uerba adnumerabo, ut doctioribus diligentioribusq; olim certius aliquid his de feris ſtatuendi occaſionem præbeam. ¶ Orſei Indi uenantur aſperrimam feram monocerotem, reliquo corpore equo ſimilem, capite ceruo, pedibus elephanto, cauda apro, mugitu graui, uno cornu nigro media fronte cubitorum duum eminente. hanc feram uiuam negant capi, Plinius. Phyſiologus quidam author obſcurus, & alij eum ſecuti, monocerotem animal paruum eſſe ſcribunt, hœdo ſimile, acerrimum, uno in capite cornu. Sed illi ex Plinio acerrimum pro aſperrimum legerunt: & hœdo pro equo, unde neceſſarius ferè alter error ſecutus eſt ut animal paruum eſſe putarent. ¶ Montes (inquit Aelianus) eſſe dicuntur in intimis regionibus Indiæ, ad quos difficulter eatur, ubi præter alias beſtias feras reperiatur monoceros, quem (Indi) uocant cartazonon: eumq; magnitudine ad confirmatæ ætatis equum accedere dicunt, iubaq; & pilis fuluum eſſe: pedū bonitate & totius corporis celeritate excellere: atq; ſimiliter ut elephantos pedum digitis indiuiſis eſſe: apri caudam habere, inter ſupercilia cornu uno, eodemq; nigro, non læui quidem, ſed uerſuras quaſdam naturales habente, atq; in acutiſſimum mucronem deſinente ornatum exiſtere, Hęc Aelianus. Mihi omnino Plinius & Aelianus unam eandemq; beſtiam deſcripſiſſe uidentur: ſed nec aliam Philes ſimia Aeliani, cuius uerba ſingulatim in ſequentibus per partes recitabo. Quinetiam aſinum ſiue onagrum Indicum, ſi non idem, inter unicornia tamen animalia iam deſcripto omnium proximum eſſe dixerim. Conueniunt ſanè pręter cornu utriq; unicum è media fronte, locus natalis India, equi magnitudo, ungulæ ſolidæ, celeritas, uita ſolitaria, robur inexpugnabile, & quòd confirmata ætate nulli capiuntur. Colore tantum differre uidentur: cum aſinus Indicus albus ſit reliquo corpore, ſed capite purpureo: monoceros fuluus, qui color etiam rhinoceroti à quibuſdam tribuitur: ſic & cornu color non idem: monoceroti enim ſimpliciter nigrum Plinius tribuit: aſino Indico Aelianus medium tantum nigrum, inferius album, ſuperius puniceum: ſed forſitan omnes iſti colores in corpore potius quàm in cornibus ſpectantur, caput purpureum, media pars corporis nigra, poſtrema alba, Philes quidem cornu totum nigrum eſſe ſcribit, excepto mucrone. Sed de aſino Indico unicorne

LAENA ERECTA GRANDEM NAVEM SVBMERGENS.

r & alia quædam cete ex eodem Balænis adnumeranda, quæ ipse simpliciter cet[e] præter magnitudinem balænis præcipuè conuenientem, nullam in se corporis [...] it monstrosam habeant. Eiusmodi sunt:

VS INGENS, QVEM INCOLAE FARAE INSVLAE ICH-thyophagi tempestatibus appulsum, unco comprehensum ferreo, securibus dissecant & partiuntur inter se.

TAE IN DORSA CETORVM, QVAE INSVLAS PVTANT, anchoras figentes sæpe periclitantur. Hos cetos Trolual sua lingua appellant, Germanicè Teüffelwal.

SIMILIS EST ET ILLORVM ICON APVD EVNDEM, CAPITE, ROstro, dentibus, fistulis, quos montium instar grandes esse scribit, & naues euertere, nisi sono tubarum aut missis in mare rotundis & uacuis uasis absterreantur: quod & in Balthico mari circa balænam Brunfisch dictam fieri diximus.

B Maximum animal in Indico mari pristis & balæna est, Plinius. Et rursus, Plurima & maxima in Indico mari animalia, è quibus balænæ quaternûm iugerum, pristes ducenûm cubitorum. Indica maria balænas habent ultra spacia quatuor iugerum, Solinus. Quatuor iugera Massarius interpretatur nongentorum sexaginta pedum longitudinem. Ad litora Noruegiæ appelluntur aliquando immensæ magnitudinis pisces balænæ, quarum nonnullæ ad ulnas centum longitudinis accedunt. Hæ per æstatem circa Noruegiam inter Fosam insulam & arcem Vardehusam pariunt: magnis eò agminibus adnantes, adeò ut naues quæ fortè inciderint, in maximo uersentur discrimine, etiam cum in profundo sub aqua balænæ fuerint, Incertus. Cum balænæ ui tempestatū aut ab alijs cetaceis animalibus in Septentrionalibus oris ad litus expelluntur, multa plaustra plena de uno pisce ab incolis auehūtur, Olaus. Balænæ & in nostra maria penetrant. in Gaditano Oceano non ante brumam conspici eas tradunt, Plinius. Sunt & prægrandes in mari Britannico. Quantum delphinis balæna Britannica maior, Iuuenalis Sat. 10. De balænarū magnitudine plura leges infra in Cetis in genere B.

Balæna quemadmodum Delphinus, lac habet, colore quanquam nigro non est, maxime tamen cyaneo, qui medium inter nigrum & uiridem locum tenet, conspicitur: non branchijs, sed fistula (sic enim huius respirandi uiam appellant) spiritum ducit, Aelianus. Branchiæ non sunt balænis, nec delphinis. hæc duo genera fistulis spirant: quæ ad pulmonē pertinent, balænis à fronte, delphinis à dorso, Plinius. Et rursus, Ora balænæ habēt in frontibus: ideoq; summa aqua natantes in sublime nimbos efflant. Per ora (inquit Massarius) Plinius intelligit fistulas, quas balenę, uti retulimus, habent à fronte, quod & sequentia indicant: non autem ora quibus deuorant, ea nanq; non à fronte, sed subter habent, ex Aristotele 8. de historia. Cæteris, inquit, piscibus captura minorum à fronte agitur ore, ut solent meare. At cartilaginei, & delphini, & omnes cetacei generis resupinati corripiunt: habent enim os subter, unde fit ut periculum minores facilius possint euadere. Balæna mammas & lac habet, Aristot. Balæna, delphinus & quęcunq; fistulam gerunt, tum aërem recipiunt ut terrestria, tum aquam ut aquatilia, Idem. Balænas & pristes Plinius inter pilo intecta & animal gignentia numerat. Ceti quidam sunt hirsuti, ijq; maximi: quidam uerò minores & planæ pellis, qui in nostro mari capiuntur duorum generum, alij dentati: alij sine dentibus, qui ore sugunt, sicut muræna (lampreda,) aliquanto minores dentatis, & multò melioris carnis, Albertus. Et alibi, Balænæ genus quoddam sugit ore & extrahit alimentum, sicuti sturio & muræna, (sic uocat lampredam.) Puncta ueru balena nuper in oris Germaniæ emisit per oculum undecim amphoras magnas saginis, Idem. Apparet autem ipsum quoque balænæ nomine communiùs quàm ueteres scriptores usum. ¶ Balæna copiosum sanguinem habet, & respirat in aëre miro modo, Galenus sexto de usu partium. Cutis eius summè dura, & propemodum insensibilis est, Ibidem libro 3. A castro Vuardhus litus totum uerno tempore procul infestum est balænis uastæ magnitudinis, adeò quòd ad centum perueniunt cubitos. Spiracula duo habent in summa fronte patentia ad cubiti proceritatem, (*negat hoc Rondeletius.*) hæc tecta sunt folliculo. Respirantes efflant undas in modum densi nimbi. Spina dorsi reperitur continēs amplexu ulnas tres, internodia singula unam, Iac. Zieglerus in descriptione Schondię. ¶ Oculi cancris, balænis, (*in Græco etiam φαλαίναις legitur, sed perperam ut uidetur*) carabis & omnibus animalibus capitis expertibus, ceruicibus prælongis insunt. Habent enim hęc omnia testaceam ac duram cutim: unde facile erat oculos altis ceruicibus tutò imponere, &c. Galenus de usu partiū 8.5.

Plutarch (46–120 CE) was all too aware of when he described this tendency of historians and geographers to 'squeeze what they don't know into the outer fringes of the maps'[91] – or of map-makers' fabled 'here be dragons'.[92]

Among the more dubious animals, but one with an antique pedigree, was the child-eating Lamia which, according to Aristophanes, possessed unwashed and foul-smelling testicles. By the time this creature appears in Gessner, it resembles a desiccated shark. Another was that staple of medieval Christianized folklore, the Monocerote or Unicorn. In Gessner's day 'unicorn horns', sometimes ground into a powder, were sold by apothecaries. It was believed that they possessed healing powers. In most cases the unicorn horns were the spiral tusk or teeth of the narwhal. Gessner writes that he had hoped to buy one to test claims about its medicinal properties, but says they were prohibitively expensive, concluding, 'I leave this way of experimenting to the rich'.[93]

Perhaps there was a commercial motive too in including these fabulous and fantastic monsters; and frankly their omission would have been even odder at a time when interest in such monsters was at a new high. What is more, the inclusion of even patently mythical creatures was still justified by Gessner's philological aims. These creatures had existed, if only in the popular imagination, since antiquity. Whether real or not, they possessed historical and cultural value.

THE SAUSAGE AFFAIR

In 1559 Gessner's *History of Animals* was placed on the Catholic Church's index of prohibited books, simply because of Gessner's Protestantism. It probably did not help that Gessner's printer, Christoph Froschauer, a fellow Protestant, had printed a huge number of pamphlets and books for the Swiss reformer Huldrych Zwingli. But it went from bad to worse. On Friday, 9 March 1522, Froschauer and his wife Elise invited some of their printshop workers and friends over to dinner – Pastor Zwingli was among the guests. Word soon got out that sausages had been served, and there was pandemonium. Now, the church had nothing against sausages per se, but it was the season of Lent, a period of forty days during which Christians were supposed to abstain from meat. Arrests were made and Zwingli, who was present but reportedly had not partaken of the sacrilegious sausages, came to Froschauer's defence. This unholy, dare we say unsavoury, gastronomical gaffe, now known as the Affair of the Sausages, was one of the sparks that ignited the Protestant Reformation in Switzerland.

previous pages

left 63 Monocerote (Unicorn) woodcut, from Conrad Gessner's multi-volume *History of Animals*, 1551–58.

right 64 Monstrous whales attack a sailing ship, from Conrad Gessner's multi-volume *History of Animals*, 1551–58.

ALWAYS ON THE CLOCK

Gessner always worked incredibly hard. Not only was he the town physician, seeing patients and providing support for local hospitals, but he taught classes every day at the local high school too – all for a very meagre salary. And he devoted his nights not to sleep but to study and writing. Gessner was, we might say, always on the clock. Even while visiting the Alpine hot springs in Bormio in the hope of finding some relief for his debilitating arthritis and sciatica, he was sampling the water for its mineral content and collecting plants for his next great work, a botanical encyclopaedia. In addition to the epithet 'father of bibliography', he was also one of the founders of modern botany and modern descriptive zoology. Gessner was a man of principles with deeply held religious convictions. Despite working all hours, to the detriment of his health, he was never able to achieve the kind of financial independence that would have afforded him the leisure his mind and ailing body so sorely needed. He was offered lucrative positions – even Emperor Ferdinand I offered Gessner a job as imperial court physician and scholar-in-residence. Not only was he unwilling to abandon Protestantism to serve the Catholic emperor, but a full-time position would have meant that he could not complete the many books he had planned.

A particularly deadly outbreak of the plague in Switzerland took the life of Froschauer in 1564. The following year, the overworked and somewhat emaciated forty-nine-year-old Conrad Gessner succumbed to the plague and died.

A genuine polymath, Gessner was profoundly well read, and skilled in gathering, collating and indexing. He organized vast amounts of information on myriad slips of paper, indexed and catalogued – leading one scholar to describe him as 'a one-man search engine'.[94] His interests spanned an almost impossibly broad range of subjects, from bibliography, classical philology, linguistics, theology, geology, medicine and pharmacology to biology, botany and, of course, zoology. But Gessner was much more than a scholar. He possessed a profound reverence for nature and enjoyed the outdoors. In a letter to his friend Jakob Vogel, he resolved to climb at least one mountain a year and, in typical Gessner fashion, such expeditions were working holidays.

Gessner's legacy is remarkable. He was editor and author of more than sixty books, and left material enough for the posthumous publication of a dozen more. One only wonders what else he might have accomplished had the Fates been kinder.

11

RENAISSANCE INVENTION

STRADANUS, *NOVA REPERTA* (*c.*1588)

It is hardly too much to say that since the invention of writing there has been no more important invention than that of the exactly repeatable pictorial statement.

William Ivins Jr, 1969[95]

In the early 1500s the brilliant German artist and leading light of the Northern Renaissance, Albrecht Dürer, had an epiphany. He describes it in a letter to a client dated 29 August 1509. In it he writes that, rather than laboriously producing countless unique works of art, he could make considerably more money – and with a great deal less effort – by selling not the originals, but prints of his work. His only regret, he says, is not having thought of it sooner. Dürer was among the first Western artists to fully exploit 'art publishing' or printmaking. He sold copies of his art as loose prints, such as *Knight, Death and the Devil* (1513), and also as sets of prints, as in, for example, his acclaimed *Apocalypse* woodcut series, published in 1498. He attained considerable fame during his lifetime, and today is best known for his woodcuts and engravings. He was commissioned by some of Europe's leading figures, including the Holy Roman Emperor Maximilian I, for whom he created one of the largest woodcut prints ever produced.

PRINTMAKING

Standalone prints were not entirely new. In fifteenth-century Europe, woodcut prints of biblical scenes and characters were popular, and were used for private religious devotion – in this respect, prints can be seen as affordable alternatives to expensive devotional paintings.

From the beginning of the sixteenth century, woodcut was steadily replaced by intaglio methods like engraving, drypoint and etching. Intaglio is, ostensibly, the opposite of relief. In relief printing, it is the raised surface of the woodcut and metal type that comes

65 *La Vanité, la Modération (ou la Modestie) et la Mort*, painting by Johannes Stradanus, oil on canvas, 1569.

into contact with the paper and is printed. In intaglio (from the Italian *intagliare*, to cut), the surface of the metal plate is cleaned, and it is the ink that remains – in the incised or engraved lines and grooves of the plate – that is printed. For the paper to be pressed into these engraved lines demands considerable pressure. Although time-consuming, it is possible to print intaglio plates by rubbing the back of the paper. To speed up the process and improve the consistency of intaglio prints, the rolling-press was developed (fig. 66). Its broad adoption coincides with a boom in intaglio printing, and with it the emergence of the reproductive print as a popular and independent art form.

Printmaking was not immediately and widely embraced by Renaissance artists. Although some of Michelangelo's paintings were reproduced as engravings, he was not as interested in printmaking as, say, Raphael, who collaborated with the engraver Marcantonio Raimondi (*c.*1480–1534) to produce some of the most famous prints of the Renaissance, including *The Massacre of the Innocents*, published around 1512. Marcantonio later got into hot water when he collaborated with Giulio Romano on a series of erotic engravings, for which he was briefly imprisoned by the Pope.

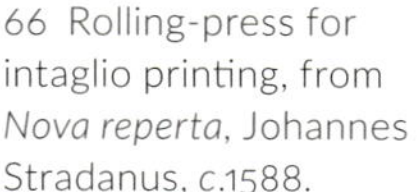

66 Rolling-press for intaglio printing, from *Nova reperta*, Johannes Stradanus, c.1588.

The sixteenth century saw the expansion and consolidation of printmaking, away

Phls Galle excud.

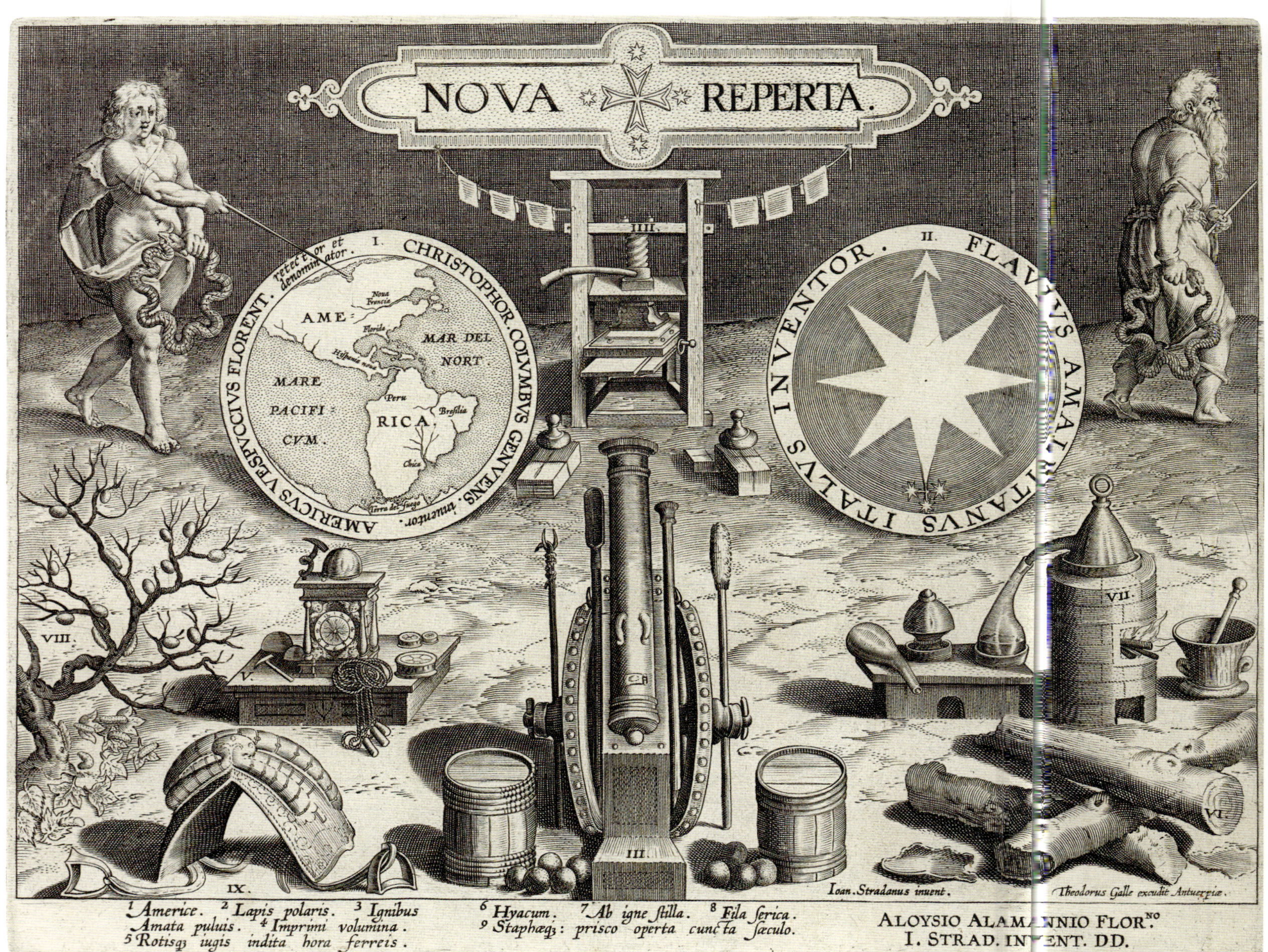
NOVA REPERTA.
I. CHRISTOPHOR. COLUMBUS GENUENS. inventor.
AMERICUS VESPUCCIUS FLORENT. retector et denominator.
AME RICA
MAR DEL NORT
MARE PACIFI CUM
II. FLAVIUS AMALPHITANUS ITALUS INVENTOR.
IIII.
III.
V.
VI.
VII.
VIII.
IX.
Ioan. Stradanus inuent.
Theodorus Galle excudit Antuerpiæ.
1 Americe. 2 Lapis polaris. 3 Ignibus
Amata puluis. 4 Imprimi volumina.
5 Rotisq; iugis indita hora ferreis.
6 Hyacum. 7 Ab igne stilla. 8 Fila serica.
9 Staphæq;: prisco operta cuncta sæculo.
ALOYSIO ALAMANNIO FLOR.NO
I. STRAD. INVENT. DD.

from individual artists and painter-engravers trying their hand at printmaking towards the emergence of dedicated print publishers, who commissioned designs and orchestrated production and distribution.[96] Husband and wife team Hieronymus Cock (1517/18–70) and Volcxken Diericx (*c.*1522–1600) were a good example of this collaborative endeavour typical of the burgeoning sixteenth-century art trade. Between 1548 and 1600, the internationally acclaimed duo issued more than 2,000 prints from their famed home-cum-workshop, Aux Quatre Vents, in Antwerp, one of the world's largest trading centres, and the printmaking capital of the world. They collaborated with scores of artists at home and abroad, commissioning both original works and ones after leading Renaissance artists, including Raphael, Bronzino and Vasari.

STRADANUS

Among the many artists with whom Hieronymus Cock and Volcxken Diericx collaborated was Jan van der Straet, better known by his Latinized name, Johannes Stradanus. Born in Bruges in 1523, Stradanus wound up in Florence via Antwerp, Lyon and Venice. Many young northern artists made their way to Italy to complete their intellectual and artistic education, and in the hope of finding patrons. In about 1550 Stradanus moved to Florence and began designing tapestries for Grand Duke Cosimo I de' Medici. He worked under Giorgio Vasari on the decoration of the Palazzo Vecchio, where some of his tapestries still hang. It was during his time at the Medici court that Stradanus made a name for himself. However, from the early 1570s he was ready to move on from Vasari and the Florentine court, and so he began to work independently, increasingly directing his energies towards designs for engravings.

NOVA REPERTA

Stradanus was prolific, producing designs across every conceivable genre of religious and secular subjects, including single prints such as *The Practitioners of the Visual Arts*, and popular series such as *The Life of Christ* and *The Twelve Emperors*. But he is best known for a print series published in around 1590, when he was back in Florence. *Nova reperta* (*New Discoveries*) is a set of twenty engravings depicting significant 'modern' or postclassical inventions and discoveries. When it came to engraving and publishing the series, Stradanus sent his drawings to Antwerp, to his favoured printmaker and publisher Philips Galle, who oversaw their transformation into engraved copper plates and fine prints. The series was

67 Title page for *Nova reperta*, Johannes Stradanus, *c.*1588.

Ioan. Stradanus inuent.
Theodor. Galle sculp.

dedicated to Stradanus's patron, the Florentine noble and scholar Luigi Alamanni (1558–1603), whose name appears prominently on the title page to the series (fig. 67). Alamanni was much more than a patron – Stradanus refers to him as his *auctor intellectualis* (intellectual advisor).[97] They had worked closely together before, and surviving records such as Alamanni's notes in Stradanus's sketchbooks and on his preparatory drawings, including directions for the engravers in Antwerp, reveal an intimate intellectual and artistic collaboration.

PRINTS AND PROPAGANDA

A recent biographer describes Amerigo Vespucci (1454–1512) as a self-confident raconteur, amateur sorcerer, former pimp, small-time jewel trader and salesman who 'rebranded himself as an expert in navigation and cosmography'.[98] It was this particular reinvention that led Vespucci, in 1499, to the northern shores of South America. He wished to learn more about the landmass that Columbus had encountered seven years before, and was also hoping to find a westerly route to Asia. Vespucci's first contact with the Americas is portrayed in the first 'invention' of Stradanus's *Nova reperta* series. It might sound rather odd to call the discovery of the Americas an invention, but in Latin *inventio*

68 Allegory of America from *Nova Reperta*, Johannes Stradanus, c.1588.

also has the sense of 'discovery'. Holding a mariner's astrolabe (a navigational aid), dressed in armour and wearing a sword, Vespucci is both explorer and saviour, his God-given authority manifest in his banner and crucifix. The half-naked figure of an Indigenous woman seated on a hammock personifies America awakened from slumber, with a scene of cannibalism depicted in the background. Vespucci's sensational accounts of cannibalism in the Americas appear to have been concocted essentially for self-promotion (some sixty editions of Vespucci's pamphlets appeared before 1530). But an even more sinister motive is at play too, with such tropes intended to highlight the dissimilitude between the 'civilized' world and the 'wild west', and thus the need for intervention from Christian liberators who would save their mortal bodies from savagery – cannibalism and nudity – and their immortal souls from hell.

RENAISSANCE WONDER DRUG

When European colonizers first landed in the Americas, they brought with them invisible stowaways – deadly pathogens responsible for smallpox, measles, whooping cough, chicken pox, bubonic plague and typhus – which decimated local populations who had no immunity to them.[99] However, by 1495 Europe itself was also in the throes of an epidemic that would go on to kill millions. It was long believed that Columbus had brought syphilis to Europe from the Americas, but recent DNA analysis suggests that it had existed in Europe long before Columbus's time. Usually curable nowadays with antibiotics, syphilis was during the Renaissance, considerably more virulent and often fatal.

In Stradanus's day, the only treatments for syphilis were mercury and guaiacum. Guaiacum was a medicine made from the bark or sap of the guaiacum tree, also known as holy wood and native to the Caribbean and South America. Its use in Europe appears to have begun in Spain around 1500. The earliest written source for its medicinal use appears in a Spanish recipe obtained in 1516. In 1519 Ulrich von Hutten (1488–1523), German Imperial Knight and scholar, and enthusiastic advocate for guaiacum as a cure for syphilis, claimed in his book *Morbus gallicus* that guaiacum had cured him of the disease. He died four years later – from syphilis. Guaiacum was even recommended as a treatment for syphilis and epilepsy by the famed sixteenth-century anatomist Andreas Vesalius. This expensive new Renaissance wonder drug, entirely ineffective in the treatment of syphilis, is the subject of plate 6 of *Nova reperta*. The scenes of a bedridden syphilitic and the preparation of the drug are separated by a painting of promiscuity, an allusion to how the disease was typically contracted.

EASTERN INVENTION, WESTERN APPROPRIATION

Several decades after *Nova reperta*, Francis Bacon singled out three inventions that he believed were the most consequential and that had also come to distinguish the so-called civilized world from the 'barbarous': printing, gunpowder, and the compass.[100] All three appear as plates in *Nova reperta* and are three of the nine inventions highlighted on the series' title page. However, none of Bacon's triad were European inventions. Printing from moveable type, although 'reinvented' by Gutenberg in Germany around 1450, had been invented by Bi Sheng in China between 1041 and 1048. Gunpowder, described in Stradanus's caption as *videtur infernis ab invidis* (a gift from a jealous hell), had been invented by Chinese alchemists in the ninth century. The mariner's compass, wrongly attributed to Flavio of Amalfi (Flavio Gioja) in plate 2, was yet another Chinese innovation. Its use in China for maritime navigation dates to the end of the eleventh century CE – a century before its appearance in Europe.

In fact, only a handful of Stradanus's inventions were of Western origin. We do not know who invented oil paints (plate 14), but their use is described by a German monk writing under the pseudonym Theophilus in about 1125 CE. Stradanus, like Vasari several decades before him, wrongly ascribed the invention of oil paints to the brilliant Flemish painter Jan van Eyck (*c.*1395–1441), one of the early masters of the medium. Spectacles or eyeglasses (plate 15) were invented in Italy by an anonymous glassmaker in about 1285. Armour polishing, illustrated in plate 17, was a European development of the fifteenth century, and metal engraving for the purpose of printing (plate 19) was developed in Germany in the 1430s.

For the other inventions we must head east. The vertical-axle windmill (plate 11), nowadays typically associated with the Netherlands, was used in Persia (modern-day Iran and Afghanistan) from about 1180, long before its use in Europe. Plate 8, *Ser, sive sericus vermis* (*Silk, or the silkworm*), illustrates an event recorded by the Byzantine historian Procopius of Caesarea. For centuries Chinese silk production had been a closely guarded secret, and although silk had been traded routinely with the West since the second century BCE, sericulture was not introduced into the West until about 550 CE. Stradanus's plate depicts Emperor Justinian in Constantinople, capital of the Eastern Roman Empire, receiving two monks who have just returned from Serinda (China or India) with a tube of silkworm eggs. In the background a painting resembling a large window depicts the various stages of silk production, from the cultivation of mulberry trees whose leaves are a favourite of the silkworm (the caterpillar of the silk moth) to, on the right, cocoons being spun into silk thread (fig. 69). A single cocoon can produce a thread more than a kilometre in length, with a half dozen or so spun together to produce silk yarn.

It goes without saying that silk production, like almost all inventions, did not appear suddenly and fully formed. Invariably, inventions are collaborative undertakings that emerge from an iterative process of successes and failures, modifications and refinements. Plate 18, *Astrolabium*, is a case in point. The astrolabe dates to ancient Greece, and during the Middle Ages it was the most widely used astronomical instrument. From the eighth century CE onwards, it was substantively improved by Islamic scientists. In the fifteenth century the mariner's astrolabe appeared. Its simplified design made it easy to use as an instrument to determine the latitude of ships at sea; during the day it would be pointed at the Sun, and at night aligned with Polaris

69 Plate 8, *Ser, sive sericus vermis* (*Silk, or the Silkworm*) illustrates an event recorded by the Byzantine historian Procopius of Caesarea. *Nova reperta*, Johannes Stradanus, c.1588.

Phls Galle excud.

or the Southern Cross, depending on which hemisphere one was in. However, it is evident that Stradanus was neither a navigator nor an astronomer. The astrolabe in his drawing, held aloft by Vespucci, is not an astrolabe but an armillary sphere, a complex multi purpose scientific instrument which simulated the movements of the celestial bodies. It was a costly device that required considerable expertise to operate (fig. 70). By Stradanus's time it had been largely retired as an observing instrument, and was used mostly as a teaching aid or displayed as an expensive ornament, reflecting its owner's evident refined taste, wealth and intellectual curiosity.

THE NOT SO DARK AGES

By the end of the Renaissance, people had already begun to see that classical antiquity was not the cultural terminus that many humanist scholars had made it out to be. *Nova reperta* invites us to a retrospective and celebration of postclassical civilization and its considerable innovations. In this respect, it is a resounding repudiation of Petrarch's conception of a middle or dark age during which little happened besides the bastardization of Cicero's Latin and the eclipse of antique genius. The so-called early modern period that followed the Renaissance was distinguished by a coming of age, of Europe emerging from the long shadow of antiquity and its latter-day renaissance, no longer content to refashion the antique but determined to forge its own golden age.

Nowadays, Renaissance-era and early modern prints are sold at auction or displayed behind glass in museums. But during Stradanus's day, when such prints were very affordable, they were affixed to walls, collected and bound into books, or sometimes even cut up and pasted into manuscripts and printed books. It is difficult for us, surrounded as we now are by billions of images, to fully appreciate the revolutionary nature of the printed image. But just as moveable type and the printing press brought books to the masses, so did the rolling-press, and intaglio techniques such as engraving and etching, bring affordable fine art into the homes of ordinary folk.

70 Detail from plate 18, *Astrolabium*. From *Nova reperta*, Johannes Stradanus, *c.*1588.

CAVRVS·CHORVS·VEL·IAPIX·SIVE·ARGESTES·
AQVILO·VEL·BOREAS·
FAVONIVS·ZEPHIRVS
SVBSOLANVS
EVROPA
ASIA
LIBIA INTERIOR
AFFRICA
ETHIOPIA INTERIOR
MARE·INDICVM
MARE·INDICVM
PRASODVM
MARE
AFRICVS·VEL·LIBS·
LIBONOTVS·EVROAVSTER
EVRNOTVS
VLTVRNVS·EVRVS

12

YOU ARE HERE

MERCATOR, *ATLAS SIVE COSMOGRAPHICAE* (1595)

A map is the greatest of all epic poems. Its lines and colours show the realization of great dreams.

GILBERT H. GROSVENOR, early 20th century[101]

We humans have always sought to understand our place in the world. Not only in a figurative or existential sense, but in relation to where we stand in physical space too. That quest has involved mapping our surroundings – to locate ourselves within them and to give us a sense of where *here* is in relation to everywhere else. We do not know when humans first began drawing maps. Some archaeologists see evidence of primitive maps in cave paintings that date back to the late Palaeolithic, some 30,000 years ago. Older candidates might qualify as maps, but without additional context it is impossible to know whether they were intended as an image of a place, a map of a location or something else entirely. It is perhaps more likely that prehistoric maps, if we can even call them maps, 'served broadly pictorial, religious, ritual, symbolic, or magical functions'.[102]

For more unambiguous evidence of mapmaking, we can fast-forward to the seventh or sixth century BCE. At that time, in Sippar, on the outskirts of what is today Baghdad, someone took a small piece of soft clay, measuring 12 × 8 cm, and proceeded to draw a map of the world. The circles, triangles and rectangles impressed in the clay could easily be mistaken for neo-Babylonian abstract art. Fortunately, we are not left guessing their true purpose. The graphical elements are accompanied by texts written on both sides, in Akkadian cuneiform, making it the earliest surviving map of the world, a bird's-eye – or perhaps god's-eye – view of the disc-shaped Babylonian world.

Many centuries later, the geographer Strabo, born in Amaseia (now Amasya, in present-day Turkey), who worked at the library of Alexandria in the late first century CE, decided that a globe

71 A world map from Ptolemy's second-century *Geography*, published in 1486.

82
7-14
509
92687

at least 10 feet (3 metres) in diameter would be ideal for depicting Earth. It would provide space enough for all major place names; if a globe was not practical, then a seven-foot-long map would suffice.[103] By the second century, the astronomer and geographer Claudius Ptolemy, from Alexandria in then Roman-occupied Egypt, was among the first to use mathematics systematically as an aid to mapmaking, when in about 150 CE he published his *Geography*, the earliest known atlas and manual of cartography.

The *oikoumene* (inhabited world) that Ptolemy described was considerably smaller than ours.[104] It spanned just 180 degrees of longitude from the Iberian Peninsula at its western limit to the Indus and Ganges in India and to China at its far eastern edge. Its southern limit was little more than 16 degrees south of the equator, reaching as far as Agisymba, an unidentified place in the southern region of Ethiopia; its northern limit was the island of Thule, at a latitude of 63 degrees. Beyond those far-flung fringes were the *terra incognita* (unknown lands). Ptolemy understood that hand-drawn maps would be especially susceptible to corruption through continual copying and recopying, so he added longitude and latitude coordinates for almost 8,000 locations. If Ptolemy produced maps to accompany his *Geography*, and I think he probably did, none have survived. But his coordinates proved to be more valuable than maps could ever be. Later they were used to reconstruct the maps he described. For centuries, knowledge of Ptolemy's work was all but lost in the West, until it resurfaced during the Renaissance via earlier Arab scholars in the ninth and tenth centuries and then Byzantine scholars in Constantinople at the end of the thirteenth.

GERARD MERCATOR

On 5 March 1512, Emerentia and Hubert Kremer had their seventh child, a son they named Gerard. At the time they were living in poverty in rural Rupelmonde, modern-day Belgium. Hubert Kremer, a shoemaker and farmer, died suddenly in 1526 when Gerard was only about fourteen. Hubert's brother Gisbert, a Catholic priest who had graduated from the University of Louvain, took Gerard under his wing, using his influence to enrol him in the Brethren of the Common Life in 's-Hertogenbosch, a school that boasted Erasmus as an alumnus. Gerard would have grown up hearing incredible tales of recent adventures and the discovery of a 'New World'. In August 1530 he enrolled in the University of Louvain. His name appears in the register as the Latinized Gerardus Mercator, the form he was to use for the rest of his life. It was

72 Map of the world from Sippar, Iraq. Seventh or sixth century BCE. British Museum.

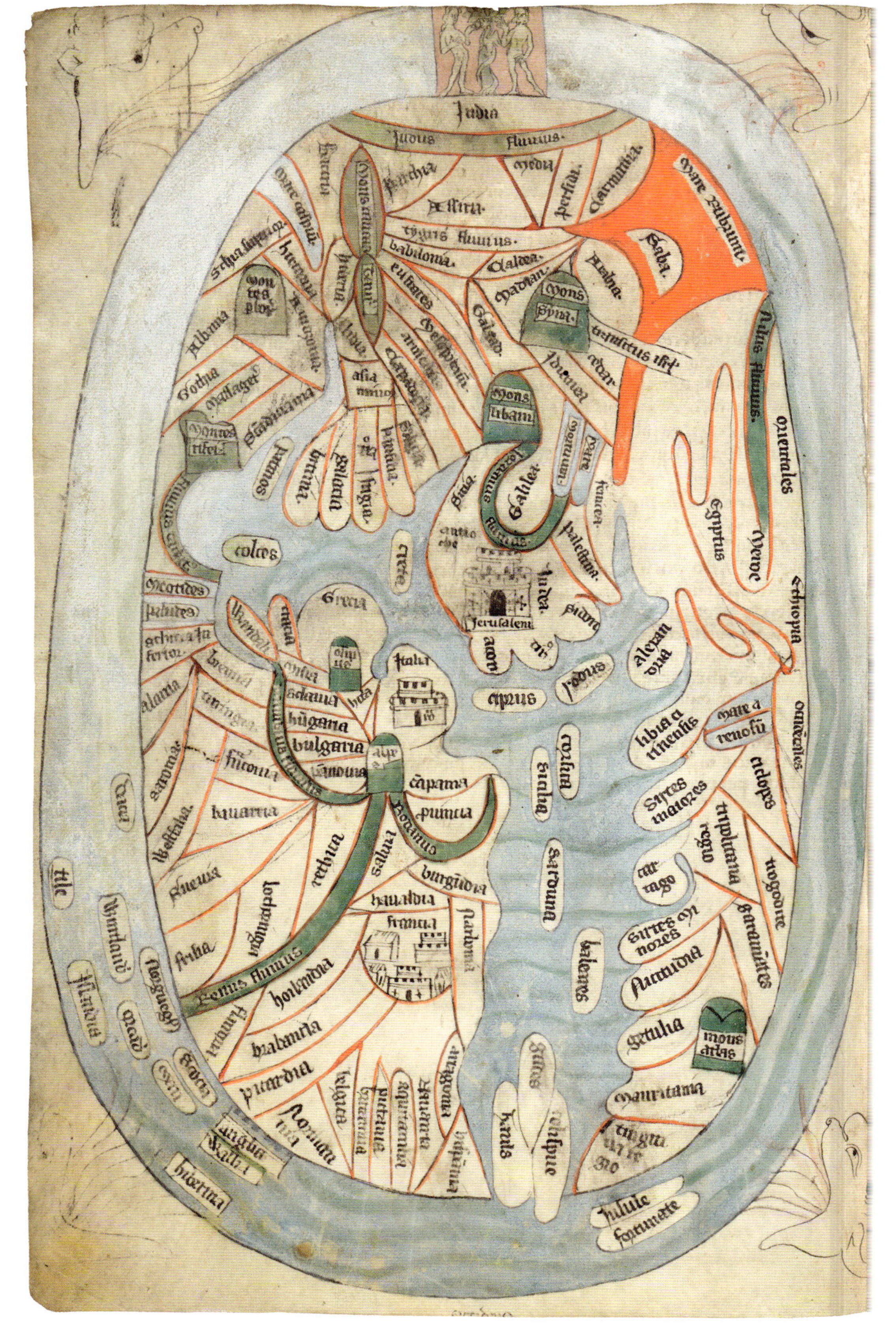

India
Indus fluuius
Assiria
tygris fluuius
babilonia
mons synai
mons libani
Jerusalem
Grecia
Italia
cyprus
bulgaria
capania
burgundia
francia
Renus fluuius
brabantia
picardia
getulia
mons atlas
mauritania
insule fortunate

in Louvain that Mercator met the polymath Gemma Frisius. Not only did Frisius, a brilliant mathematician, tutor Mercator in mathematics, but he also became a mentor and friend to him. In the 1530s Gemma and Gerard collaborated on the production of celestial and terrestrial globes. Already by his mid-twenties, Mercator was an accomplished engraver, calligrapher and globemaker, and was well on his way to establishing his reputation as one of Europe's foremost mapmakers and geographers.

While Mercator was forging his formidable reputation, the Protestant Reformation was sweeping through Europe. In October 1529 Charles V decreed that reading banned books and unauthorized Bible translations would now be treated as crimes, and that of those found guilty, 'men were to be beheaded, women buried alive, and the relapsed burnt'.[105] The infamously cruel procurer-general Pierre Dufief, who had been instrumental in the arrest and execution of the English Reformer and Bible translator William Tyndale came knocking at the door of Mercator's Louvain home in 1544. Mercator's intellectual pursuits concerning philosophy and the creation of the world, his extensive travelling and the company he kept were enough to raise suspicions of heresy. He was not at home when Dufief came knocking – his absence might have been construed as evidence of his guilt. Had the fugitive been forewarned of Dufief's visit? Mercator was apprehended and arrested in Rupelmonde. At least five of those arrested along with him were executed: two were burned at the stake, two buried alive and one beheaded. After nearly eight months in prison, Mercator was finally released. The Inquisition was not obliged to explain itself.

Today, Mercator is best known for his eponymous map projection. In the simplest terms, it is the spherical Earth projected onto a cylinder and then unrolled. It was first introduced in Mercator's world map of 1569. Designed especially for use by mariners, it was in fact the very first sailing chart for the entire world. The printed map comprised eighteen printed sheets, assembled to produce a map measuring an enormous 202 × 124 cm. Lines of latitude and longitude were drawn as a graticule (grid of straight lines) intersecting at right angles. This is important because a map drawn in this way 'preserves angles', which in practical terms means that navigators can plot a straight-line course on the map, then measure the angle of that rhumb line (a line crossing all meridians of longitude at the same angle) to acquire a compass bearing.

Even ancient cartographers understood that every map projection is a compromise. A sphere cannot be transferred to a flat plane

73 Late fourteenth-century map centred on Jerusalem, *Polychronicon*, Ranulf Higden.

without deformation. The main drawback of the Mercator projection is that land masses at higher latitudes, or regions closer to the poles, become significantly distorted and larger; for example, the continent of Africa appears to be about the same size as Greenland, when in fact Africa is more than fourteen times the size of Greenland. When it comes to map projections, one cannot have one's cartographic cake and eat it. The moment one attempts to correct for land mass distortion, then its ease of use for, say, navigation is compromised.

ATLAS

In addition to his interest in cartography and mapmaking, Mercator was one of the foremost cosmographers of his age. The now archaic science of cosmography was concerned with describing the general features of the cosmos, including its substance, creation and chronology – a kind of physics, history and geography all rolled into one. As part of his interest in cosmography, in 1569 Mercator published *Chronologia*, a history of the world from the Creation until 1568. In its preface he outlines his plan for subsequent volumes. It was a project that would consume the rest of his life. First conceived of as two volumes, one each for heaven and earth, it would become a mammoth five-part universal description of the entire cosmos, of which *Chronologia* was the first part.

Included in Mercator's grand scheme for a universal cosmography was a modern compendium of maps of the world, and he published the first two instalments in 1585 and 1589. He named his collection of maps *Atlas*, not after the Titan who was part of a failed rebellion against the Olympian gods and who was condemned by Zeus to carry the heavens on his shoulders for eternity, but rather, according to Mercator's preface and a rather unusual and convoluted family tree, a late descendent – Atlas the king of Mauretania, a learned philosopher and astronomer credited with inventing the celestial globe. A year after publishing the second instalment, Mercator suffered a stroke that paralysed his left side and affected his speech. Most frustrating for him was not the illness itself, but the time it cost him – he still had so much more to do, including completion of the maps for his *Atlas*.

When Mercator died in December 1594, aged eighty-two, his *Atlas* was still unfinished. But his youngest son Rumold immediately took up the baton, and within the space of a few months had published a completed collection. In addition to republishing the parts previously issued in 1585 and 1589, Rumold completed Mercator's *Atlas* by reusing a world map from 1587, and maps of the continents based on

74 Title page from Gerard Mercator's *Atlas sive cosmographicae* of 1595.

ATLAS
SIVE
COSMOGRAPHICÆ
MEDITATIONES
DE
FABRICA MVNDI ET
FABRICATI FIGVRA.
Gerardo Mercatore Rupelmundano,
Jllustrißimi Ducis Juliæ Cliviæ & Mõ-
tis &c. Cosmographo Autore.
Cum Privilegio.
DVISBVRGI CLIVORVM.

Mercator's world map of 1569, in addition to maps for Iceland, the British Isles, Scandinavia and parts of southern and south-eastern Europe. The book Rumold published was not quite the one his father had, for so many decades, envisaged. Missing are detailed maps of regions beyond Europe, and – considering the market for this atlas was Europe – the most conspicuous omissions are detailed maps for Spain and Portugal.

The presentation of maps in *Atlas* roughly follows that proposed by Ptolemy, from the whole to its parts, and so it opens with a full-spread world map. However, rather than use the Mercator projection, the Earth is presented as two hemispheres, one showing Europe, Asia and Africa, the other the Americas. Next follow large double-spread maps for each of the continents: Europa, Africa, Asia, America and *Polus Arcticus* (the Arctic). This detailed map of the Arctic is almost entirely fictional – the North Pole was not explored until the twentieth century. At the geographic centre of Mercator's Arctic map sits *Rupes nigra* (Black Rock), which Mercator had decades earlier described as a giant magnetic island mountain measuring 33 French miles (approximately 66 km) in circumference. Then follow country maps beginning in the north with *Islandia* (Iceland), followed by Britain and detailed individual maps for its constituent parts, beginning with *Scotia*.

75 A detailed and yet entirely fictional map of *Polus Arcticus* (the Arctic). From Mercator's *Atlas sive cosmographicae* of 1595.

following pages

76 Map of Britain from Mercator's *Atlas sive cosmographicae* of 1595.

COLOUR MAPS

By the sixteenth century copperplate engraving had almost entirely replaced woodcuts for printed maps. There was also a shift in the method and style of hand-colouring, from opaquer colours to light translucent washes that did not obscure the printing underneath. Also, by this time map colouring had become an independent trade, with colourists, often women, working from a style guide or set of exemplars.

When Mercator's *Atlas* was published posthumously in 1595, Abraham Ortelius's bestselling atlas, *Theatre of the World*, first published in 1570, had already appeared in twelve Latin editions. Unsurprisingly, Mercator's *Atlas* was not a great financial success. However, it was given a new lease of life, and undoubtedly better marketing by the Dutch cartographer Jodocus Hondius who purchased the engraved plates from Mercator's heirs in 1604. He and his sons used them as the basis for a revised and expanded edition that quickly superseded Ortelius's *Theatre of the World* atlas, and that was reissued a further thirty times between 1609 and 1641.

SEP: TENTRIO: NALIUM Terrarum de: scriptio.
Per Gerardum Mercatorem Cum Privilegio
Frisland insula
Farre in: sule
Scetland insulæ
AMERICAE PARS
ASIAE PARS
California regio sola fama Hispanis nota
Anian regnum
Bergi regio
El streto de Anian
Circulus Arcticus
Polus magnetis
Polus magnetis respectu Corui insule
POLUS ARCTICUS
Hic mare est dulcium aquarum, cuius terminum ignorari Canadenses ex relatu Saguena ensium aiunt
Vng quæ a nostris Gog dicitur
Desertum de Belgian arenosum
Bargu campestria quorum incole vocantur Merciti
Ciorza
Cauona PARS
OCEANUS SCYTHICUS qui et Mare Tabin
NOVA ZEMLA
PETZORKE MARE
MVRMANSKOI MARE
RUS SIA
GROENLAND
Grocland
Mare glaciale
OCEANUS SEPTENTRIONALIS
ISLAND
SCOTIA
Gradus latitudinis
Lago de Conibaz
Fretum

ANGLIA, SCOTIA et HIBER: NIA.
OCEANVS DEVCALI
DONIVS
OCCIDEN:
TALIS
OCEANVS
Hiberniæ aliquot nomina
2 Glanarme ab. 9 C. Beale
3 Torane 10 Englishe. cast.
4 Belfast 11 New cast.
5 C. Letrum 12 C. Eiland.
6 Moschenes ca. 13 Dereshame
7 Drommemer 14 Clancauras
8 Tripperain 15 Kylmyuoge
Miliaria Anglica parua
10 20 30 40 50 60 70
VERGIVIVS OCEANVS
Per Gerardum Mercatorem Cum Priuilegio

OCEANUS
NORVEGIAE PARS
DANIAE PARS
Nomina aliquot quę ſuis orbiculis aſscri bere loci anguſtia prohibuit
Scotiæ
2 Leyn
3 Lonet
4 Rangue
5 Narden
6 Tornway
7 Rothes
8 Inuerury
9 Inuermegy
10 S.t Johans tou
11 Luccurs
12 Masad
13 Bergomum
14 Duglyn
15 Neyum
16 Monoch
17 Dunblain
18 Falkirk
19 Quenes ferry
20 Cornwall
21 Dunbriton
22 Craufurdihou
Hebridum Inſul:
1 Dunweg
2 Kirk morich
3 Reuenſa
4 Roſay
5 Arrois
6 Bailmoir
7 Colanzay
8 Sodore
Angliæ
2 Kirſopfoot
3 Wulſty
4 Wigen
5 Rothedale
6 Stopford
7 Garthpibo
8 Chalmondelay
9 Whitchurch
10 Bramcroſt
11 Barkway
12 Biſshops tartford
13 Waltham ab.
14 Eltham
15 Leneham
16 Minching hampton
GERMANICUS
ANGLIA
Seelant
Flandria
Artois
Picar: die
OCEANUS BRITANNICUS

MAPS AS MORE THAN MAPS

Nowadays, we tend to think of maps primarily as wayfinding aids. But maps have not always been considered this way. Most medieval *mappaemundi* (maps of the world) were not at all concerned with precisely rendered topographies and geographical coordinates. Instead, their purpose was didactic. They were often historiated or schematic maps depicting the world as God's creation and dominion, or illustrating biblical narratives and moralizing tales presented in a geographical framework for readers' spiritual edification.

In Europe, since at least the thirteenth century, mariners had used portolan charts. At a time when sailors seldom strayed far from shore, these charts, mapping coastal features, were invaluable. But as sailors ventured beyond sight of land and out into open waters, new maps and new methods of navigation were developed, including Mercator's projection, which to this day is still used for most navigational charts. The Web Mercator, a modern variant of the Mercator projection, has become the standard for online mapping applications.

There is no such thing as a definitive map or even a best projection. Maps are not synonymous with the environments they seek to represent, but then neither are they completely divorced from them.[106] All maps (and there are more than 400 kinds of map projection) are compromises, scaled down, stretched, distorted and crammed into only two of three dimensions. Moreover, our built and natural environments are continually changing. Topographies evolve, national borders shift in the face of wars of aggression or attrition, rivers carve new courses or run dry and, as polar ice caps melt and sea levels rise, low plains are flooded and coastlines are redrawn. Maps are always in flux. Precisely what a map is or what constitutes a map is still debated. From primordial efforts painted on cave walls or carved on bones, and ancient depictions impressed in clay, to modern-day celestial charts mapping long-dead galaxies at the edge of the observable universe, all maps tell stories across time and space of past, present and future worlds.

On 14 February 1990, Voyager 1, traveling at a speed of 64,000 kph, snapped a photograph of Earth from a distance of 6 billion km. There were no discernible or mappable features. Earth was now just a single point, a coordinate on a larger cosmic map, appearing, as Carl Sagan famously narrated, as nothing more than a 'pale blue dot'[107] – indelibly and invisibly inscribed with the words, 'you are here'.

77 Portolan chart of the Western Mediterranean, including parts of Spain and the coasts of Algeria and Morocco. Illustrated by Maestro della Parousia, early fifteenth century.

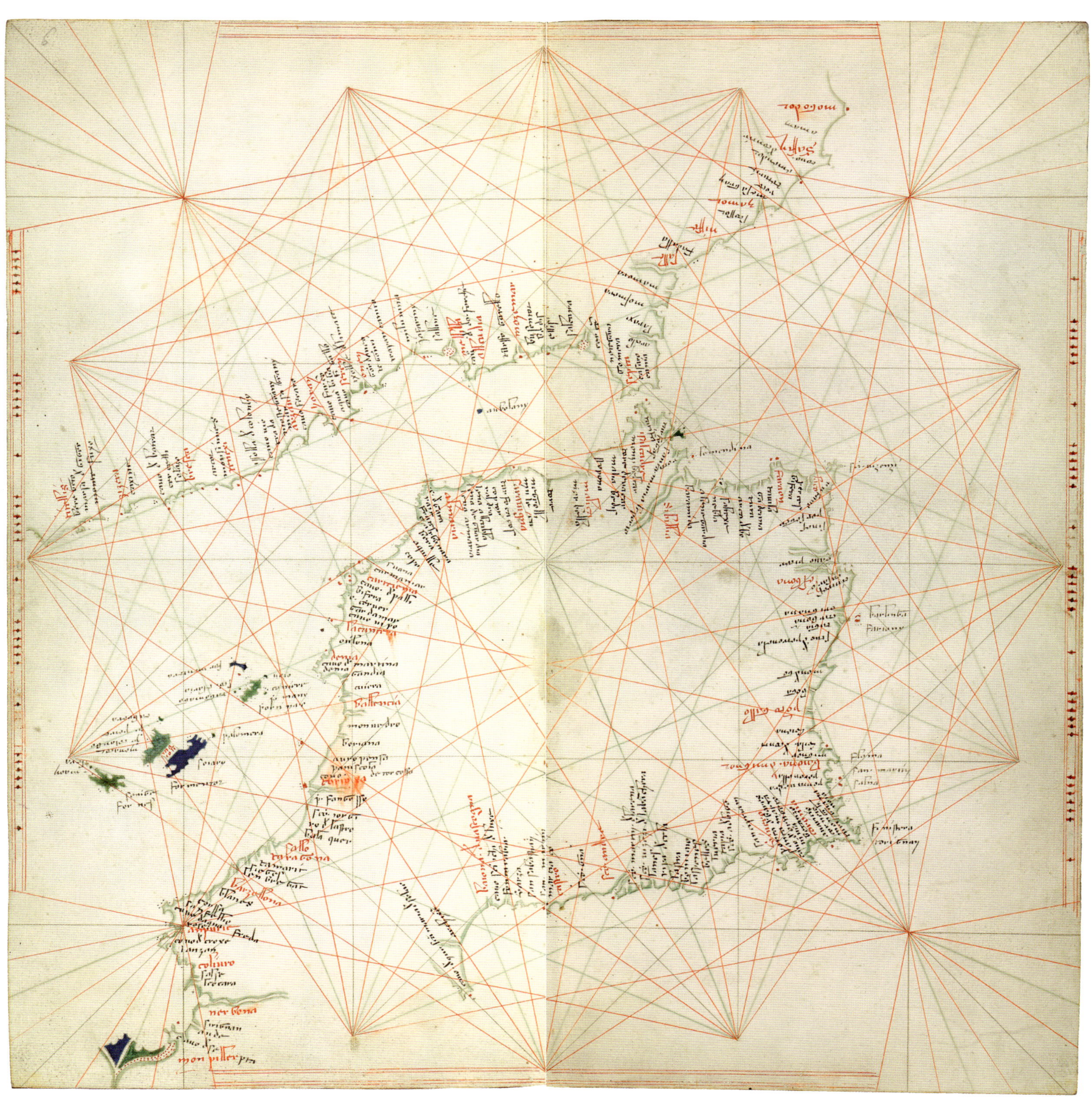

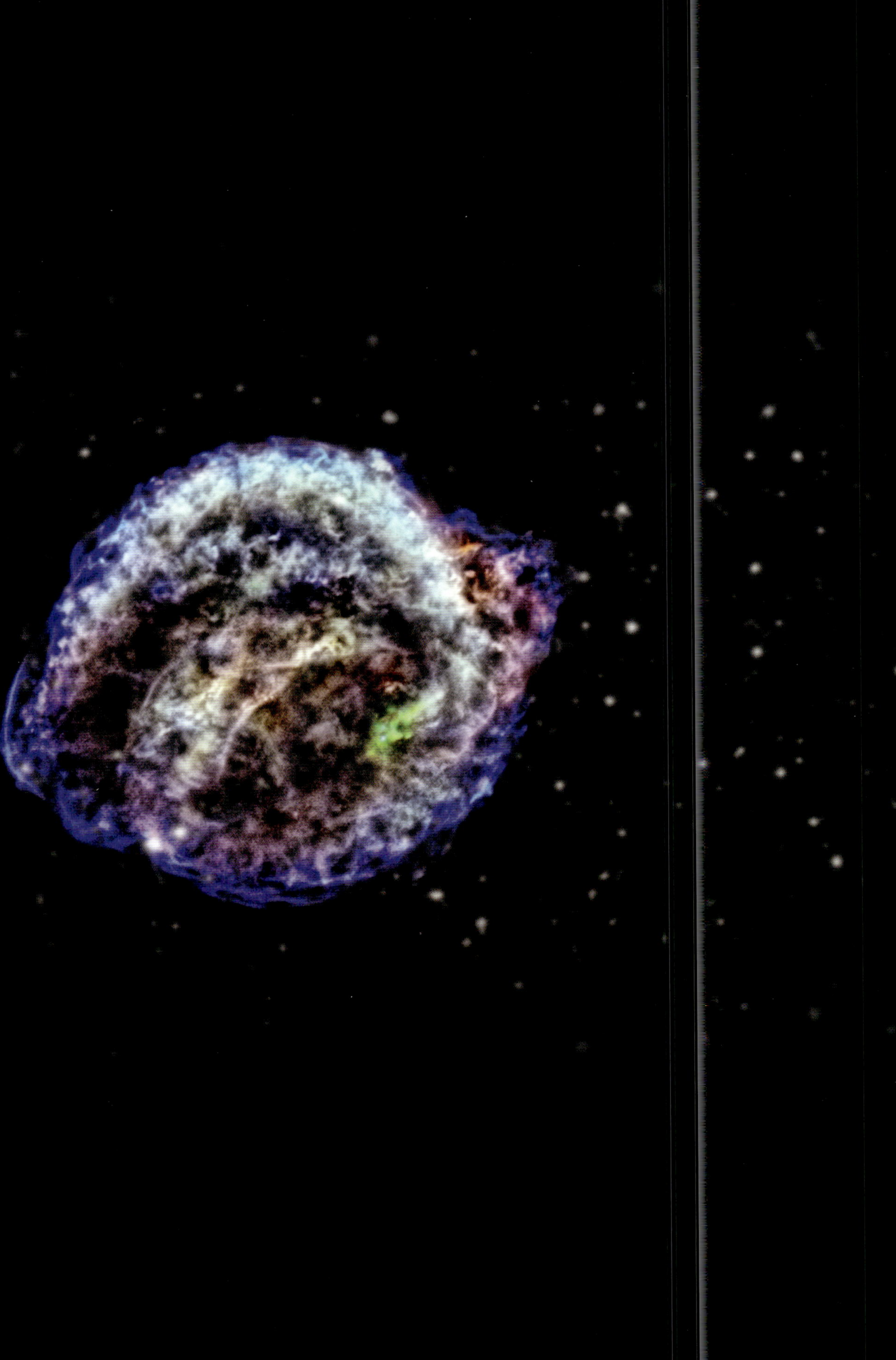

13

A STAR IS BORN

KEPLER, *DE STELLA NOVA* (1606)

The cosmos is within us. We are made of star-stuff.
We are a way for the universe to know itself.

Carl Sagan, 1980–81[108]

On 4 July 1054 Chinese astronomers recorded a bright new star in the sky. They, and contemporary Japanese sources, described it as a 'guest star'. Located in the constellation of Taurus, initially it shone so brightly that it was clearly visible even during the daytime. It remained visible in the night sky for another two years before vanishing without a trace on 6 April 1056. Five-hundred and fifty years later, in 1604, a similar guest star appeared in the constellation Ophiuchus (also known as the Serpent Bearer), outshining all the stars and planets in the sky. This time it was also documented by astronomers in Europe. Those two guest stars were, unbeknown to their observers, stellar explosions or supernovae. The remnants of the supernova of 1054, now spanning more than ten light years, is today known as the Crab Nebula, while the star of 1604, designated SN 1604, is now known colloquially as Kepler's Nova. In 1606 this latter star was the subject of a book by a quite brilliant German astronomer who would refashion our conception of the cosmos.

Johannes Kepler was born on 27 December 1571 in Weil der Stadt, a small town west of Stuttgart in south-western Germany. In his twenties, Kepler described his father as 'immoral, rough and quarrelsome'.[109] He was raised by his mother Katharina Guldenmann. They lived in his grandfather's inn, where as a young boy Kepler helped to serve the inn's patrons. Despite a difficult childhood, including a bout of smallpox that almost killed him, Kepler recalled two standout events from his youth. The first was in 1577, when his mother took the six-year-old Johannes to see a comet; the second in 1580, when he and his father

78 Remnant of Kepler's supernova (SN 1604), discovered by Johannes Kepler in 1604. Composite X-ray and optical image.

PLANISPHÆRIVM
Sive
MVNDI TOTIVS,
TYCHONIS
PLANO
Prostant Amstelædami apud
GERARDUM VALK. et
PETRUM SCHENK.
CAPRI
CORNVS
AQVA
RIVS
PIS
CES
ARI
ES
TAV
RVS
GE
MINI
IVPITER
CIRCVLVS MARTIS
MARS
MARS
IVPITER
SATVRNVS

BRAHEVM,
Structura
EX HYPOTHESI
BRAHEI IN
DELINEATA.
SAGIT TARIVS
SCOR PIVS
LI BRA
VIR GO
LE O
CAN CER
CIRCVLVS SATVRNI

witnessed a total lunar eclipse. Soon after, his father, a mercenary soldier, went off to fight and never returned. A precocious, remarkably pious, conscientious and hard-working boy, Kepler was awarded a scholarship to study at Tübinger Stift, the seminary at the University of Tübingen. When it came to renewing the scholarship, the board was fulsome in its praise of the young student, commending Kepler's 'superior and magnificent mind'.[110] It was in Tübingen that Kepler first met Michael Maestlin, a professor of mathematics and astronomy, through whom Kepler was exposed to the cosmology of Nicolaus Copernicus.

Kepler soon became an ardent disciple of Copernicus's heliocentrism, and sought to confirm this revolutionary conception of the cosmos through mathematics and observational astronomy. He was a devout Lutheran and a practising astrologer. He later came to believe rather fervently that astrology was long overdue for substantial reform. For example, he rejected the twelve signs of the zodiac as arbitrary and fantastical human inventions, and was more comfortable ascribing his own success not to the stars but to brilliant mentors and teachers, writing, 'my stars were not Mercury as the morning star in the angle of the seventh house, in quartile with mars, but they were Copernicus, they were Tycho Brahe'.[111] Kepler is most well known for his three laws of planetary motion: that planetary orbits are elliptical rather than circular, that their velocity varies in relation to their distance from the Sun and that a planet's orbital period is related to the radius or semi-major axis of its orbit.

THE NEW STAR

In 1600 Kepler took a job in Prague as Tycho Brahe's assistant, and was promptly assigned to the Mars problem – that is, to determining with greater precision the orbit of Mars. Following Brahe's sudden death in October 1601, and Kepler's promotion to *Mathematicus Imperialis* (mathematician to the emperor), Kepler continued with his work on the orbit of Mars. And then the new star appeared in the constellation Ophiuchus – although, owing to cloudy skies, it was not visible to Kepler in Prague until 17 October 1604. In November of that year he dashed off a seven-page pamphlet in German that was promptly printed in Prague and Strasbourg, following it up in 1606 with the publication of a more substantial scholarly Latin treatise titled *De stella nova in pede serpentarii* (*On the New Star in the Foot of the Serpent Handler*).

In *De stella nova*, Kepler attempted to answer a number of questions raised about the new star, including why and how it appeared,

previous pages

79 Tycho Brahe's geoheliocentric model in which the Sun and Moon orbit Earth, while the other five planets revolve around the Sun. *Harmonica macrocosmica*, 1708.

its significance or purpose, what it was made of, how big it was and how far away it was. The new star appeared during an already astrologically significant conjunction of Saturn and Jupiter in Sagittarius that began in 1603. Saturn and Jupiter are in conjunction once every twenty years or so, but this particular conjunction in this part of the sky was calculated to occur only once every 800 years! By the autumn of 1604 Jupiter and Saturn were joined by Mars in a triangular configuration. A similar conjunction had already been associated with momentous historical events, such as the birth of Jesus and the appearance of the Star of Bethlehem. In fact, Kepler devoted a substantial appendix in the book to this very topic.

Some of the topics discussed and the arguments presented in *De stella nova* might appear rather peculiar to modern readers. But they begin to make sense when we pause to think about what physics, cosmology and astronomy looked like at the turn of the seventeenth century. For context, it is crucial to recall that the new star appeared before the era of telescopic astronomy, and four years before publication of Galileo's world- and cosmos-changing telescopic observations reported in *Sidereus nuncius* (*Starry Messenger*) in 1610. And although some sixty years had passed since the publication of Copernicus's seminal work of heliocentrism, *De revolutionibus orbium coelestium* (*On the Revolutions of the Heavenly Spheres*), many still could not conceive of a universe in which the Earth was not at its centre – for both theological *and* scientific reasons. Although Kepler was an ardent heliocentrist, Tycho Brahe, his former boss, categorically and enthusiastically rejected Copernicus's Sun-centred cosmos in favour of his own geoheliocentric or Tychonic system, a hybrid Ptolemaic and Copernican model in which the Sun and Moon orbit Earth while the other five planets revolve around the Sun. The final crucial piece of the early seventeenth-century scientific landscape was the brilliant but ancient Aristotle, whose enduring legacy still loomed large. Aristotle believed that the terrestrial and celestial spheres were made of different stuff – the former from combinations of the four elements (earth, water, air and fire) whose natural motion was rectilinear, while the heavens were composed of an enigmatic *quintessence*, an immutable fifth element whose natural motion was circular, hence the circular motion of the heavenly spheres.

Let us not forget, too, that when this new star suddenly appeared very little was understood about stars. Frankly, no one had a clue what they were made of, why they shone or how distant they really were. Most astronomers, including

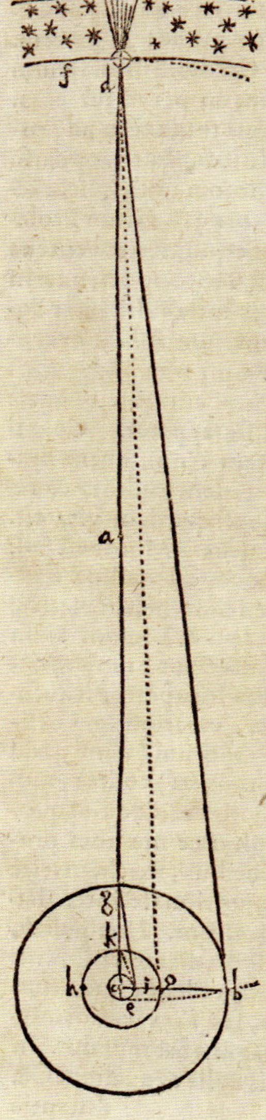

distantia Solis & terræ est 1432. Sit Sphæra Saturni altior GB. Jam Saturnus decuplo distat ejus, quo Sol distat, nimirum CG est decupla ipsius CK. Minus quidem aliquid est, sed tamen & hic impleatur numerus. Distabit igitur Saturnus 14320 terræ semidiametris, & hæc est longitudo ipsius CG. Jam itaque sit, ut semidiameter corporis solaris CO, sex semidiametrorum terræ, ad semidiametrum orbis Saturni CG vel CB, 14320 semidiametrorum terræ; sic hæc CB ad CD semidiametrum fixarum: quod fit continuatâ CG, & super hac lineâ constituto semicirculo EBD, per signa E,B traducto, cujus centrum A: prodibit nobis pro fixis, summa semidiametrorum terræ, trecenties quadragies centena septuaginta septem millia, hoc est $34077066\frac{2}{3}$, quæ summa nondum est pars quarta de illa priore, quam ad exemplum multiplicatæ in veteri sententia celeritatis assumpseramus.

Quid igitur satagunt Philosophi, eximere ex oculo Copernici festucam hanc immensitatis fixarum, cùm interim dissimulent in suo oculo, trabem ingentem, amplius quàm quater majorem, insanæ celeritatis fixarum; tantò absurdiores, quàm Copernicus; quantò difficilius est, accidens præter modulum subjecti intendere, quàm subjectum augere sine accidente. Tycho Braheus aliquid hic adjuvit sententiam veterum, retentâ de Saturni altitudine parte solummodo tertia, paulò plus; quia ponit illam semidiametrorum terræ septem millium: fixis verò largitur duplum hujus: illud quidem necessaria demonstratione, ex supposita propria Mundi forma: hoc verò ex probabili conjectura. At sive duæ tertiæ, sive una; utrinque adhuc pars quarta vel quinta exceditur. Et quid unica Saturni stella ad immanem fixarum multitudinem? quæ omnes apud receptas hypotheses illo perniciſſimo

Brahe (the greatest observational astronomer of his day), believed that the stars were situated just beyond the orbit of Saturn. We must also remember that *De stella nova* was written eighty years before Isaac Newton's law of universal gravitation – and another two centuries before Einstein's general relativity, an account of gravity's effects on the fabric of space-time.

The new star's appearance ignited frenzied prophetic speculation. For some it portended a blessed new era of rejuvenation; for others it was a harbinger of impending catastrophe and the end of the world. Kepler believed that the star's appearance could not be a coincidence, even admitting that it could well be associated with the Second Coming. But he avoided making or endorsing any concrete prophetic interpretations, explaining in his defence that he had been appointed as a mathematician rather than a prophet. In *De stella nova*'s thirtieth and final chapter, Kepler summarizes his opinions on the significance of the star by concluding that, although he considered the cause of the new star to be natural rather than miraculous, divine providence was involved in staging its appearance.

OF MITES AND MEN[112]

Hold a pencil at arm's length, then look at it through first one eye and then the other. The pencil's apparent position against, say, the backdrop of your living-room wall shifts because your left and right eyes are seeing the pencil from different angles. Promote the pencil to a star and the living room wall to even more distant stars, and you will see (stellar) parallax in action. This same principle had been used by astronomers since antiquity. Kepler, in chapter sixteen of *De stella nova*, used parallax to determine the relative distance of the *stella nova* (new star). In the absence of any discernible parallax, the new star must be at a distance comparable to the other so-called fixed stars. If it were closer, then one would expect it, like the planets or wandering stars (as the ancients used to call them) to move relative to the backdrop of the even more distant fixed stars.

In the second century, Claudius Ptolemy of Alexandria used parallax to calculate the distance to the Moon. To the sphere of fixed stars, he suggested a distance equal to 20,000 Earth radii (e.r.) or almost 105 million km.[113] Ptolemy's guesstimates were accepted with only minor adjustments for the next 1,400 years. When Copernicus introduced the world to his revolutionary Sun-centred cosmos, a major sticking point for Tycho Brahe was that for Copernicus's model to make any sense, the stars would have to be ridiculously far away.

80 A diagram illustrating stellar parallax. *De stella nova*, Johannes Kepler, 1606.

81 The new star, or nova (N), appearing at the foot of the Serpent Bearer constellation. *De stella nova*, Johannes Kepler, 1606.

Ad fol: 76.
ſignum * * *

To account for no discernible stellar parallax, Brahe estimated that the stars in Copernicus's cosmos were required to be almost 8 million e.r. from Earth.[114] Not only was such a vast distance incomprehensibly large, but it would also leave a gargantuan void between the sphere of Saturn and the sphere of the stars (the ancients had claimed the spheres were contiguous) – and why would God waste space! For Brahe, these facts were evidence of a fundamental flaw in the Copernican hypothesis. Kepler proposed a distance of a little over 60 million e.r. to the stars. He was quick to admit that this figure seemed implausibly large, but explained that it was no more ridiculous than the stars orbiting a stationary Earth at 2,257,500 mph (3,633,094 kph), as demanded by the geocentric model.

Copernicus had transformed not only the configuration of our universe but its scale too. The universe, and the stars in it, became unimaginably larger. To get some idea of how large the universe had grown, consider that from Ptolemy in the first century until Copernicus in the sixteenth, the entire observable universe was thought to be about 209 million km in diameter – and thus would fit inside the present-day orbit of Mars! By the turn of the seventeenth century, it had grown, by Kepler's estimate, to a diameter of some 764 billion km.

THE LIVES OF STARS

We now understand that Kepler's star had always been there, but like trillions of others it was too distant and too faint to be seen with the naked eye. Only when the star exploded did it become visible to observers on Earth. Stars are born when their core densities increase to the point where they can sustain nuclear fusion – this is when the star turns on, so to speak. From then on, it is an astrophysical balancing act between the outward pressure generated in the star's core and the star's own gravity exerting pressure in the opposite direction. All stars are destined to die, but the precise nature of their demise, whether they go out with a whimper, a pop or a bang, largely depends on their mass. Very massive stars quickly exhaust the hydrogen fuel in their cores, leading to eventual core collapse and a supernova explosion.[115] Medium-sized stars like our Sun, a yellow dwarf, are not massive enough to end their days as supernovae. But like all stars, they too eventually run out of fuel, and shed their outer layers, exposing a hot dense stellar core known as a white dwarf. But without any mechanism to accrete more mass, white dwarfs are destined to survive for trillions of years until, in theory, they turn into cool, dim and inert black dwarfs – this is theoretical because their life expectancy exceeds the present age of the universe.

Stellar post-mortems point to most Type Ia supernovae, like Kepler's, originating in binary star systems that include a white dwarf. As just mentioned, white dwarfs are not massive enough to go supernova, but when they exist in a binary system they have a companion star to eat – their strong gravitational force slowly strips away material from its unfortunate donor star until enough mass is accreted to take it beyond the Chandrasekhar limit of 1.4 solar masses. Once the star crosses this threshold, it is destined to go out with a very big bang, as a supernova, leaving behind exotic stellar remnants like black holes and neutron stars.

Of course, the explosion that destroyed Kepler's star did not actually occur in 1604 – it just so happens that the light from its explosion first reached Earth in 1604. The actual explosion occurred in our prehistory, perhaps about 13,000 years ago.[116] Today, the shockwave from Kepler's Nova is still expanding through space at about 24 million kph.[117] Since Kepler's Nova, there have been no naked-eye observations of supernovae in our galaxy (at least not by humans). Kepler's Nova prompted widespread debate about astrology, astronomy and cosmology, and ultimately ushered in a new era of observational and mathematical astronomy.

It is estimated that throughout the entire observable universe several hundred million stars are born and die every day. A relatively small number of those terminal stars end their lives in cataclysmic thermonuclear explosions, as supernovae. And yet without their sacrifice we would not exist. Those stellar explosions, among the most powerful and destructive events in the cosmos, are at the same time engines of creation and progenitors of life. Most of the atoms in your body and in the very fingers that hold this book were forged in the hearts of stars and seeded into space during their annihilation. Their ensuing shockwaves tear through space at millions of kilometres per hour, on their way heating older stellar flotsam and, with gravity's help, coalescing it into new galaxies and solar systems where those star-forged elements might, with a lot of luck, evolve over the course of billions of years into complex intelligent life – like you!

14

FORGING HEAVEN

GALILEO, *SIDEREUS NUNCIUS* (1610)

... the broad white road in heaven,
Pathway of the ghosts, the shadows,
Running straight across the heavens,
Crowded with the ghosts, the shadows.

LONGFELLOW, 1855[118]

In a small spectacle shop in Middelburg in what is now the Netherlands, about half-way down Kapoenstraat, next to the church, 'on the left side coming from the vegetable market' was the home and workshop of the German immigrant Hans Lipperhey and his many children. In 1608 Hans applied for a patent and was subsequently invited to demonstrate his newfangled invention. The letter of introduction reads: 'The bearer of this letter declares to have [found] a certain art with which one can see all things very far away as if they were nearby, by means of sights of glasses, which he pretends to be a new invention.'[119]

Hans was not granted a patent because his instrument was considered too easily copied. However, he did receive the handsome sum of 1,200 guilders, more than enough to buy his neighbour's house. By the spring of 1609 spyglasses (the word 'telescope' was not coined until 1611) were on sale in Paris, and by the winter they were sold throughout Europe.

It was in May 1609 that news of the spyglass reached a certain professor of mathematics at the University of Padua – one Galileo Galilei (1564–1642). He was convinced he could improve this novelty spyglass, which at the time was considered little more than a toy. His first effort, a telescope with three-times magnification, was no more powerful than those already available. He understood that a more powerful instrument was still next to useless if it produced distorted or blurred images. Unable to find lenses of a high enough quality for telescopic observation, he learned how to grind and polish his own.

In Padua, on a chill November evening in 1609, Galileo pointed his new twenty-times magnification telescope at the sky. At first,

82 In Greek mythology the breast milk of Hera spilled across the sky, creating the Milky Way. *The Origin of the Milky Way*, painting by Jacopo Tintoretto, oil on canvas, c.1575.

he could hardly believe what he saw. It was staggering, and he knew immediately that this was going to change everything. He also understood that he had to publish his findings – and do so quickly. From Galileo's many surviving notes we know that on 15 January 1610, while observing Jupiter, he was already beginning to imagine how his book might look, even thinking about how he could produce the illustrations: 'They will be cut in wood, all on one block, the stars white and the rest black, and then the blocks will be sawn [into strips].'[120]

STARRY MESSENGER

Just six weeks elapsed between Galileo's first recorded telescopic observations and the publication of his book, *Sidereus nuncius* (*Starry Messenger*). Why had Galileo been in such a hurry? In a letter dated 19 March 1610, addressed to Cosimo de' Medici's personal secretary, Galileo explains: 'I did not want to prolong the publication lest I run the risk that perhaps someone else might have discovered the same and preceded me.'[121]

Galileo was right to be anxious. In the weeks leading up to publication, word was already out that he had made some extraordinary discoveries with his new spyglass, including the discovery of four new planets. Working like a man possessed, he ran back and forth between his home in Padua and the printshop in Venice, some 40 km away. He continued writing and editing in earnest while completed pages were already being typeset and printed. With no time to waste looking for a new printer, Galileo went with a team he had already used and one he could trust with his sensitive manuscript. Although often cited as the printer of *Sidereus nuncius* – and his name is on the title page – Tommaso Baglioni is better described as a publisher. The actual printing was most likely done on Niccolò Polo's press, and the whole operation was directed by Roberto Meietti. Another critical reason to get the book printed quickly was that the Frankfurt Book Fair would begin on 28 March. Frankfurt is 920 km from Venice, a journey that would have taken about two weeks at that time. With Galileo still recording his astronomical observations until 2 March, he and his printers were cutting it close. However, within two weeks of printing in Venice, *Sidereus nuncius* was announced in the Frankfurt Fair spring catalogue. There was risk involved in choosing to work with Meitti. He had a history of run-ins with the Inquisition for printing and smuggling banned books, but his invaluable network of connections in the international book trade meant that he was probably the only one who could have pulled it off in time.

MAKING THE MOON

Sidereus nuncius is a slim quarto format book of just sixty pages. It measures about 22 × 17 cm, about the size of a typical modern hardback. The book opens with a dedication to Cosimo de' Medici, whom Galileo was courting as a patron. It is overwrought, grandiloquent and fawning, but that was customary in the seventeenth century. Then, after a short general introduction, Galileo launches into his observations of the Moon, the first of three main sections. Anaxagoras (500–428 BCE) had claimed the Moon to be Earth-like. According to Plutarch, it was covered in valleys and mountains. He even speculated that it was inhabited. But again, at least in the West, it was Aristotle's view of a perfectly spherical and flawlessly smooth moon that prevailed. When, in 1609, Galileo first observed the lunar surface through his telescope, the theorizing and speculation was over. For with his own eyes Galileo saw the Moon 'to be uneven, rough, and crowded with depressions and bulges. And it is like the face of the Earth itself, which is marked here and there with chains of mountains and depths of valleys.'[122]

When it came to illustrating those features, Galileo began by painting a series of watercolours of the Moon, which evidently served as models for those printed in the book. The five Moon etchings (from four plates; one is repeated) feel as though they were rushed, which is unsurprising considering the tremendously tight schedule Galileo was working to. It also appears that the printer was unfamiliar with intaglio printing, evidenced by inky fingerprints, smudges and mis-registration of the plates. It is worth noting that Galileo's etchings were not intended as cartographic

83 Galileo presents his telescope to Doge Leonardo Donato. Fresco by Giuseppe Bertini, Villa Ponti Varese, 1858.

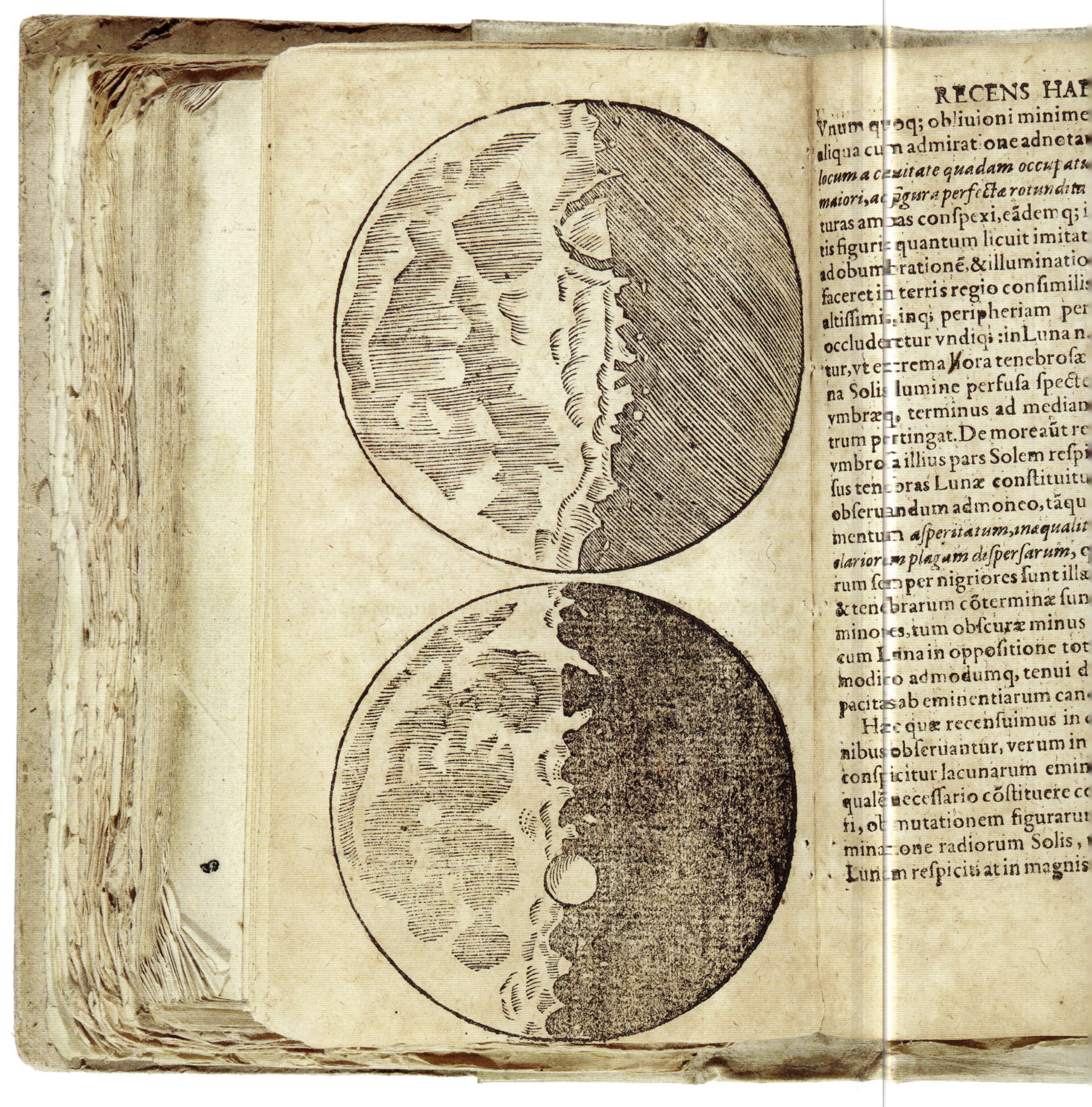

RECENS HAB

Vnum quoq; obliuioni minime
aliqua cum admiratione adnota
locum a cauitate quadam occupatu
maiori, ac figura perfecta rotundita
turas ambas conspexi, eãdemq; i
tis figuris quantum licuit imitat
adobumbrationẽ, & illuminatio
faceret in terris regio consimilis
altissimis, inq; peripheriam per
occluderetur vndiq; : in Luna n
tur, vt extrema ora tenebrosæ
na Solis lumine perfusa specte
vmbræq, terminus ad median
trum pertingat. De moreaũt re
vmbrosa illius pars Solem respi
sus tenebras Lunæ constituitu
obseruandum admoneo, tãqu
mentum *asperitatum, inæqualit*
clariorum plagam dispersarum, q
rum semper nigriores sunt illa
& tenebrarum cõterminæ sun
minores, tum obscuræ minus
cum Luna in oppositione tot
modico admodumq, tenui d
pacitas ab eminentiarum can
Hæc quæ recensuimus in
nibus obseruantur, verum in
conspicitur lacunarum emin
qualẽ necessario cõstituere co
ti, ob mutationem figurarum
minatione radiorum Solis,
Lunam respicitis at in magnis

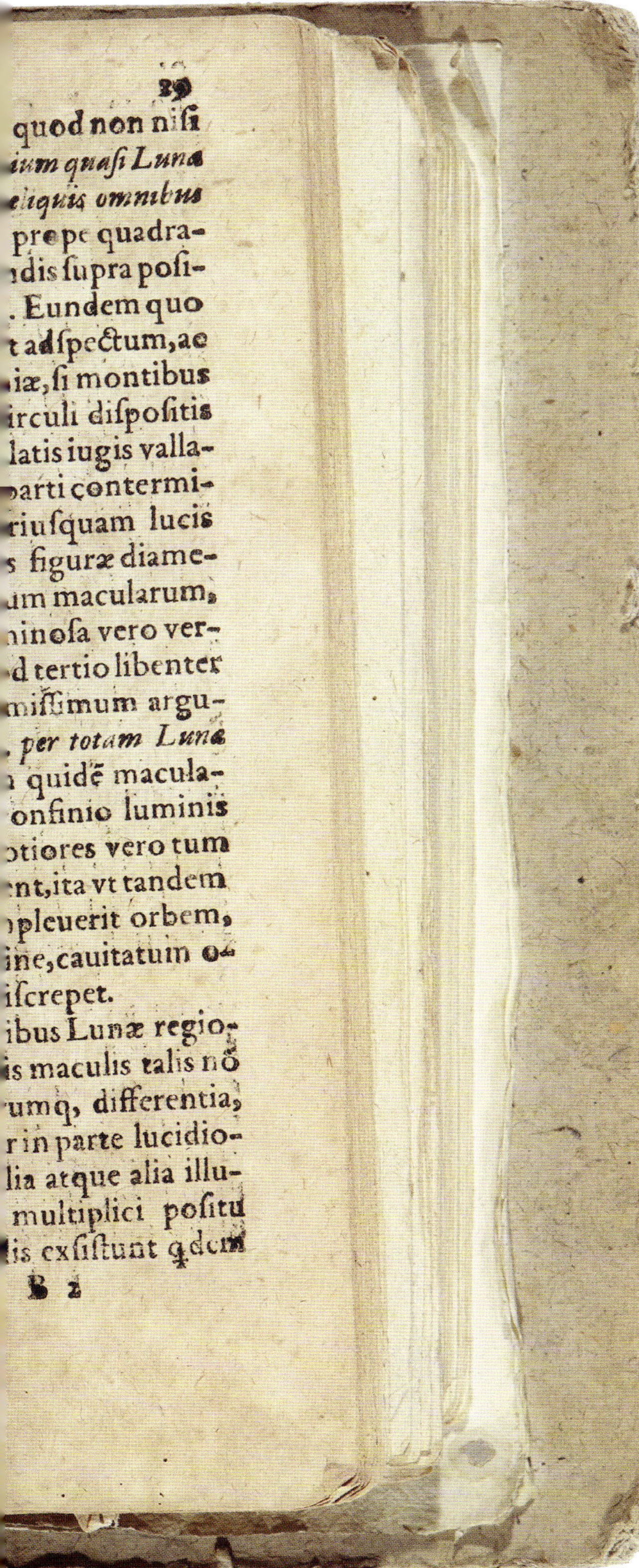
29
quod non niſi
ium quaſi Luna
eliquis omnibus
prope quadra-
idis ſupra poſi-
. Eundem quo
t adſpectum, ac
iæ, ſi montibus
irculi diſpoſitis
latis iugis valla-
parti contermi-
riuſquam lucis
s figuræ diame-
um macularum,
ninoſa vero ver-
d tertio libenter
miſſimum argu-
. *per totam Lunæ*
quidē macula-
onfinio luminis
otiores vero tum
nt, ita vt tandem
pleuerit orbem,
ine, cauitatum o-
iſcrepet.
ibus Lunæ regio-
is maculis talis nō
umq; differentia,
r in parte lucidio-
lia atque alia illu-
multiplici poſitu
is exſiſtunt q̃dem
B 2

84 Moon etchings from Galileo's *Sidereus nuncius*, 1610.

moon maps, but designed instead to highlight specific topographical features and to illustrate how light and shadow played out over the rugged Earth-like surface. A detailed map was not necessary – the big headline was the fact that the Moon was not perfectly smooth. I suspect the choice of etching over engraving or woodcut came down to a combination of two factors: detail and speed. Woodcut was the cheapest of the three methods, but the detail and tones that Galileo was trying to achieve were not possible. The finest details could be reproduced in engraving, but tones had to be built up through hatching and crosshatching. On the other hand, etching produced a warm, almost nebulous tonal quality and was the fastest of the three methods – and Galileo was in a hurry!

HERA AND HERCULES

To the Egyptians it was a reflection of the Nile; for the Babylonians it was a giant serpent or length of rope. In Greek mythology it was the breast milk of Hera spilled across the sky. The Romans, borrowing from the Greeks, called it *via lactea* (milky road) and in English we know it as the Milky Way. Aristotle wrote that Anaxagoras and Democritus (*c.*460–*c.*370 BCE) supposed the Milky Way was made up of many stars. Aristotle disagreed, believing instead that the Milky Way was a meteorological or atmospheric phenomenon, 'a dry and smoky exhalation' produced high in the Earth's atmosphere where the celestial and terrestrial spheres meet – the exact same process that was thought to be responsible for the creation of comets and shooting stars. Ancient Chinese astronomers called it Tianhe (celestial river). A popular belief among some cultures, including the Algonquian peoples, was that the Milky Way served as a pathway to the afterworld. In the West, it was Aristotle's view that prevailed.

However, confirmation of the ancient speculations of Anaxagoras and Democritus came with Galileo, who writes in *Sidereus nuncius* that 'the Galaxy is nothing else than a congeries [collection] of innumerable stars distributed in clusters'.[123] Through his telescope, Galileo saw for the first time the cloud-like Milky Way resolved into countless individual stars. But there were other milky or cloudy patches in the night sky. Ptolemy, writing in Greek in the second century, had called them *nepheloeides*, from *nephele* (cloud) or, in Latin, *nebula* (meaning mist or cloud). Galileo concludes: 'And since the milky lustre, like whitish clouds, is seen not only in the Milky Way … many similarly coloured patches shine weakly; if you direct a glass [telescope] to any of them, you will meet with a dense crowd of stars.'[124]

Galileo had discovered, without fully realising it, galactic nebulae. In *Sidereus nuncius* he also considers the so-called fixed stars, explaining that his telescope reveals more than ten times more stars than can been seen with the naked eye. He beautifully and simply illustrates this across a two-page spread, with diagrams of two very familiar constellations: on the left page, part of the Orion constellation, and on the right, the Pleiades, colloquially known in English as the Seven Sisters. Galileo writes that he had intended to include the entire Orion constellation, but, 'overwhelmed by the enormous multitude of stars and lack of time, I put off this assault until another occasion'.[125] Galileo illustrates dimmer stars with six-spoke asterisks, whereas the brightest are drawn in outline with a dot at the centre – as in the three belt stars at the top of Galileo's detail of the Orion Constellation (fig. 85).

BY JOVE!

Galileo saved his third and most unexpected – and indeed mind-blowing – finding for last: his discovery of four moons orbiting Jupiter, which Galileo named the Medicean stars in honour of the short-lived Cosimo II de' Medici, Grand Duke of Tuscany (1590–1621).

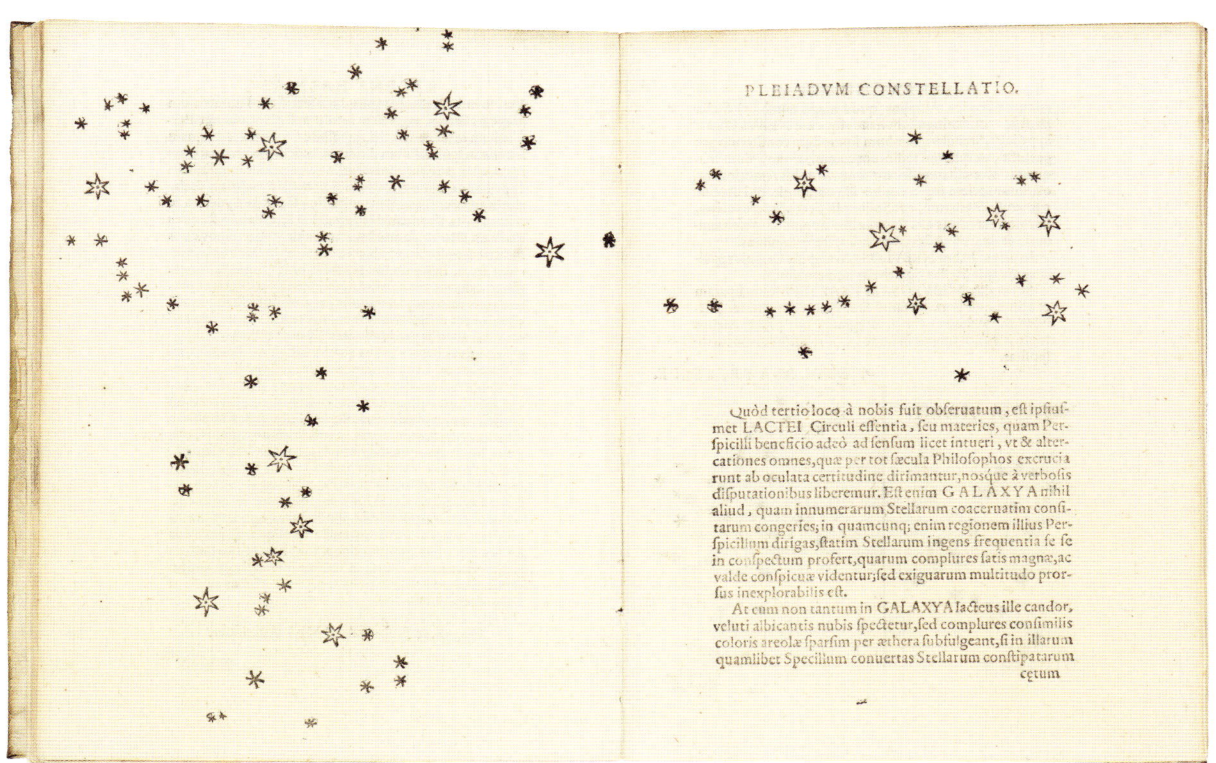

PLEIADVM CONSTELLATIO.

Quòd tertio loco à nobis fuit obſeruatum, eſt ipſiuſmet LACTEI Circuli eſſentia, ſeu materies, quam Perſpicilli beneficio adeò ad ſenſum licet intueri, vt & altercationes omnes, quæ per tot ſæcula Philoſophos excruciarunt ab oculata certitudine dirimantur, nosq́ue à verboſis diſputationibus liberemur. Eſt enim GALAXYA nihil aliud, quam innumerarum Stellarum coacervatim conſitarum congeries; in quamcunq; enim regionem illius Perſpicillum dirigas, ſtatim Stellarum ingens frequentia ſe ſe in conſpectum profert, quarum complures ſatis magnæ, ac valde conſpicuæ videntur; ſed exiguarum multitudo prorſus inexplorabilis eſt.

At cum non tantum in GALAXYA lacteus ille candor, veluti albicantis nubis ſpectetur, ſed complures conſimilis coloris areolæ ſparſim per æthera ſubfulgeant, ſi in illarum quamlibet Specillum conuertas Stellarum conſtipatarum

cętum

85 Above left: Asterism of the belt and sword of Orion. Right: Pleiades star cluster. From Galileo's *Sidereus nuncius*, 1610.

Galileo's observations of Jupiter's four moons (later named Callisto, Ganymede, Io and Europa) were yet more evidence in favour of the Copernican system, because they proved unequivocally that not all celestial bodies must revolve about Earth.

Galileo's star diagrams were printed from woodblocks, and he had initially intended to use woodblocks for his sixty-five Jupiter and moons diagrams too. But he chose instead a rather ingenious typographic solution. For Jupiter Galileo borrowed a capital O from one of the large titling fonts he had used on the title page, and simply turned it on its side. For Jupiter's moons, he illustrated those with several sizes of asterisk – appropriately enough, because in Greek *asteriskos* means 'little star'.

Sidereus nuncius really is the product of Galileo's many talents: his knowledge of physics, astronomy and mathematics; his doggedness and curiosity; and his skill in *disegno* (graphic design), a term coined only in the twentieth century but which retrospectively describes perfectly yet another of his talents.

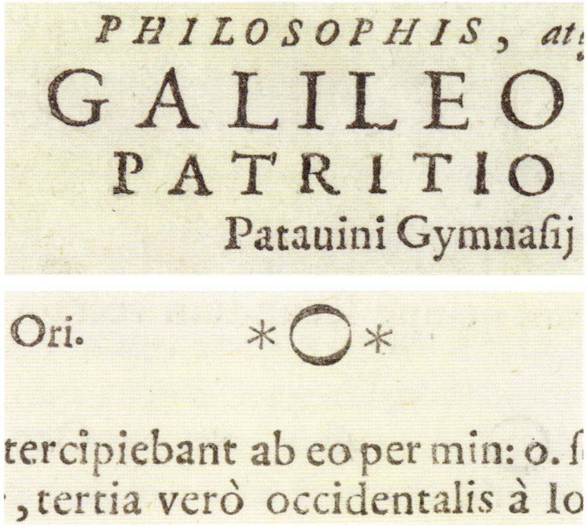

86 A creative typographic illustration: the Capital O from the title page font (in GALILEO), is turned on its side to represent the planet Jupiter. Asterisks denote Jupiter's newly discovered moons.

A COSMIC FORGERY

Something remarkable turned up 395 years later, in the summer of 2005. A proof copy of *Sidereus nuncius* came onto the antiquarian book market in New York. It was the first Venice edition of 1610, but with one crucial and extraordinary difference: this was Galileo's personal copy! Instead of the usual printed etchings of the Moon, in this unique copy they had been substituted with five ink-and-wash drawings, assumed to have been painted by Galileo himself. And, as the cherry on the cake, on the title page in Galileo's own hand was the inscription, '*Io Galileo Galilei f.*', interpreted as 'I, Galileo Galilei, made this.' Richard Lan, the book's owner, thought the book to be worth about $10 million. Space does not permit a fuller account of the ensuing detective story, but thanks to the healthy scepticism and dogged sleuthing of historian Nick Wilding, and later reanalysis by academic librarian Paul Needham and others, who had initially confirmed its authenticity, the book was exposed as an incredibly elaborate, though not particularly sophisticated, forgery. The fake, made in 2005, was the brainchild of unabashed book thief and forger Massimo Marino De Caro who, at the time, was director of the Girolamini Library in Naples.

From the twenty-first-century hubris of forgers to the hubris of the seventeenth-century church. After the publication of *Sidereus nuncius*, dedicated to Cosimo II de' Medici (whom Galileo had very shrewdly courted), in June 1610 Galileo was appointed court mathematician and philosopher and moved from Padua to Florence in September of the same year. It was a highly lucrative and prestigious post, one that set him up for life. But Galileo was not one to rest on his laurels. Being curious but also combative and stubborn by nature, he eventually landed himself in hot water.

In 1632, twenty-two years after *Sidereus nuncius*, Galileo published his *Dialogue Concerning the Two Chief Systems of the*

World, in which he compared the Ptolemaic and Copernican systems, going all in on the latter heterodoxy. By summer, the church had prohibited sales of *Dialogue* and ordered unsold copies to be confiscated. In October, Galileo was 'invited' to appear before the Inquisition in Rome. When he tried to delay by obtaining a doctor's note signed by physicians in Florence, the church was having none of it. The Inquisition rejected Galileo's subterfuge, demanding he come willingly or else be arrested and dragged to Rome in chains. Galileo was left with no choice; he acquiesced and arrived in Rome, in good health, in February 1633. After interrogations throughout April and May, in June Galileo was compelled to recant by reading aloud a pre-prepared statement in which he promised to reject and abandon Copernicanism and to never even speak of it again. The *Dialogue* was banned and Galileo was sentenced to indefinite imprisonment (a week later commuted to house arrest) for 'having wished to publish his new opinions about the motion of the earth against the true consensus of the faith'.[126] He died a decade later, in 1642, aged seventy-seven.

It is impossible to describe adequately the significance of Galileo's remarkable discoveries. One of the world's foremost historians of astronomy, Owen Gingerich, described it as 'perhaps the single most unexpected event in the Scientific Revolution of the sixteenth and seventeenth centuries'.[127] It irrevocably changed how we look at the universe, and even how we contemplate our place in it. Galileo, through the conjunction of his many talents, was able to provide incontrovertible empirical evidence that flew in the face of thousands of years of misconception, speculation and dogma (religious *and* philosophical). Hurriedly printed and published in early 1610, the sixty pages of *Sidereus nuncius* ignited an astronomical revolution. Soon after, almost anyone could buy an inexpensive telescope and see for themselves what even the most storied astronomers of old could only have dreamed of.

Since Galileo, we have walked on the Moon, flown by Jupiter and its eighty *named* moons, and launched space telescopes to peer back across billions of years to the birth of the first stars in our nascent universe – missions pioneered by curious and brilliant minds just like Galileo's.

15

THE BOOK ON THE MOON

KING JAMES BIBLE (1611)

After that, hee moved his Majesty, that there might bee a new Translation of the Bible, because, those which were allowed in the reigne of King *Henry* the Eight, and *Edward* the sixt, were corrupt, and not answerable to the truth of the Originall.

William Barlow, 1604[128]

If your lover is 'the apple of your eye', and your ally is fighting 'the good fight' against enemies who are 'a law unto themselves' and 'a thorn in the flesh', then, whether you know it or not, you are using expressions from the King James Bible, commonly known as the Authorized Version. Since its first publication in 1611, as many as a billion copies have been published. But how did it become the bestselling version of the Bible, and why did it come to have such a profound influence on the English language? Before we answer those questions, it makes sense to briefly revisit the King James Bible's remarkable prehistory.

The Bible is a collection of books written over the course of a thousand years, with some parts sourced from much older oral traditions of the ancient Near East. The Old Testament or Hebrew Bible (with a little Aramaic) began to take shape in the ninth and eighth centuries BCE, and was mostly completed by the time of Alexander the Great's conquests in the fourth century BCE. The book of Daniel, the last of the Old Testament books to be written, although describing events from the sixth century BCE, was composed in the second century BCE. This means completion of the Old Testament canon postdates the works of Aristotle and Plato. A biblical canon was formally settled on or closed in the fourth century, tendentiously approved by various church councils. Or at least that was once the popularly held view. More recent scholarship points to there being an earlier informal consensus concerning a core of generally accepted or canonical texts, with the church councils simply confirming or ratifying that consensus. With some exceptions, most modern Bibles are composed of the

87 Nasa's Lunar Roving Vehicle of Apollo 15 Mission, July 1971. The small red Bible is propped on the central control panel.

same sixty-six core books – thirty-nine from the Old Testament and twenty-seven from the New Testament. The latter was written in Greek, the common language of the eastern Mediterranean world of that time even while under Roman rule.

In 382 CE, Pope Damasus I tasked Jerome with revising Old Latin texts of the four Gospels. Once completed, Jerome went on to revise and translate most of the rest of the Bible. The resulting collection of translations, with other contributors, was later known as the Vulgate and remained the principal Latin translation of the Bible until the Reformation in the sixteenth century.

THE BIBLE IN ENGLISH

It appears that at least parts of the Bible were translated into English by the eighth century, if not sooner. In his *Ecclesiastical History of the English People* (around 731 CE), Bede tells the story of an illiterate Northumbrian cowherd named Cædmon who, inspired by God in dreams, was able to turn biblical stories into English poetry. Among the earliest surviving Old English translations of the Bible is the Macregol Gospels in the Bodleian Library, a Northumbrian tenth-century interlinear gloss (a literal translation) of a Latin Bible penned in Ireland around 900 CE.[129] The Norman Conquest of 1066 CE put an end to English translations of the Bible, when, among the ruling classes, English was largely supplanted by French. That is, until the fourteenth century, when John Wyclif (*c.*1330–84) organized a translation of the Bible into Middle English. At this time there was no explicit ban on translating the Bible into English, but Wyclif's dissident views, especially in regard to challenging the legitimacy of the papacy, made him powerful enemies. In response to Wyclif's preaching about the necessity for vernacular translations of the Bible, a contemporary chronicler protested that making the Bible available to the laity, and 'even to women who can read', was to scatter pearls before swine'.[130] Several decades later, the prohibition of *unauthorized* Bible translations – and reading them – was made explicit in the Oxford Constitution of 1408 by Archbishop Thomas Arundel.

88 Noah's Ark from the Cædmon manuscript: parts of Genesis, Exodus and Daniel in Old English verse, illustrated with Anglo-Saxon drawings, *c.*1000 CE.

REFORMATION

Almost a century and a half later, much of what Wyclif had preached in respect to papal authority and Bible reading was reiterated by Martin Luther in Germany. Luther believed passionately that church reform was possible only through biblical literacy – and that meant translating the Bible, so that everyone might

Noe fremede· swa hine nergend heht· hyrde þam hal
gan heofoncyninge· ongan ofostlice ꝥ hof wyrcan·
micle merecieste· magum sægde· ꝥ wæs þrealic þing·
þeodum toweard· reðe wite· hie ne rohton þæs· ge
seah ymb wintra worn· wærfæst metod· geofon
huses mæst· gearo hlifigean· innan ⁊ utan· eorðan
lime· gefæstnod wið flode· fær noes· þy selestan·
þæt is syndrig cynn· Symle bið þy heardra· þe hit hreoh
wæter· swearte sæstreamas· swiðor beatað·

16 Dicit ei iterum simon iohannis
diligis me ait illi Et iam dne tu scis
17 quia amo te. Dicit ei pasce agnos
meos : Dicit ei tertio simon iohan
nis amas me contristatus est pe
trus quia dixit ei tertio amas me
Et dicit ei dne tu omnia scis quia
amo te. dicit ei pasce oues meas :
18 Amen amen dico tibi cum esses
iunior cingebas te et ambulabas
ubi uolebas. cum autem senueris
extendes manus tuas et alius te
19 cinget et ducet quo non uis. haec
autem dixit significans qua
morte clarificaturus esset dm
Et hoc cum dixisset dicit ei seque
re me.

Þe min bruche gibidde fore owun ðe ðas boc gloesde. Færmen ðæm preoste æt harawuda.

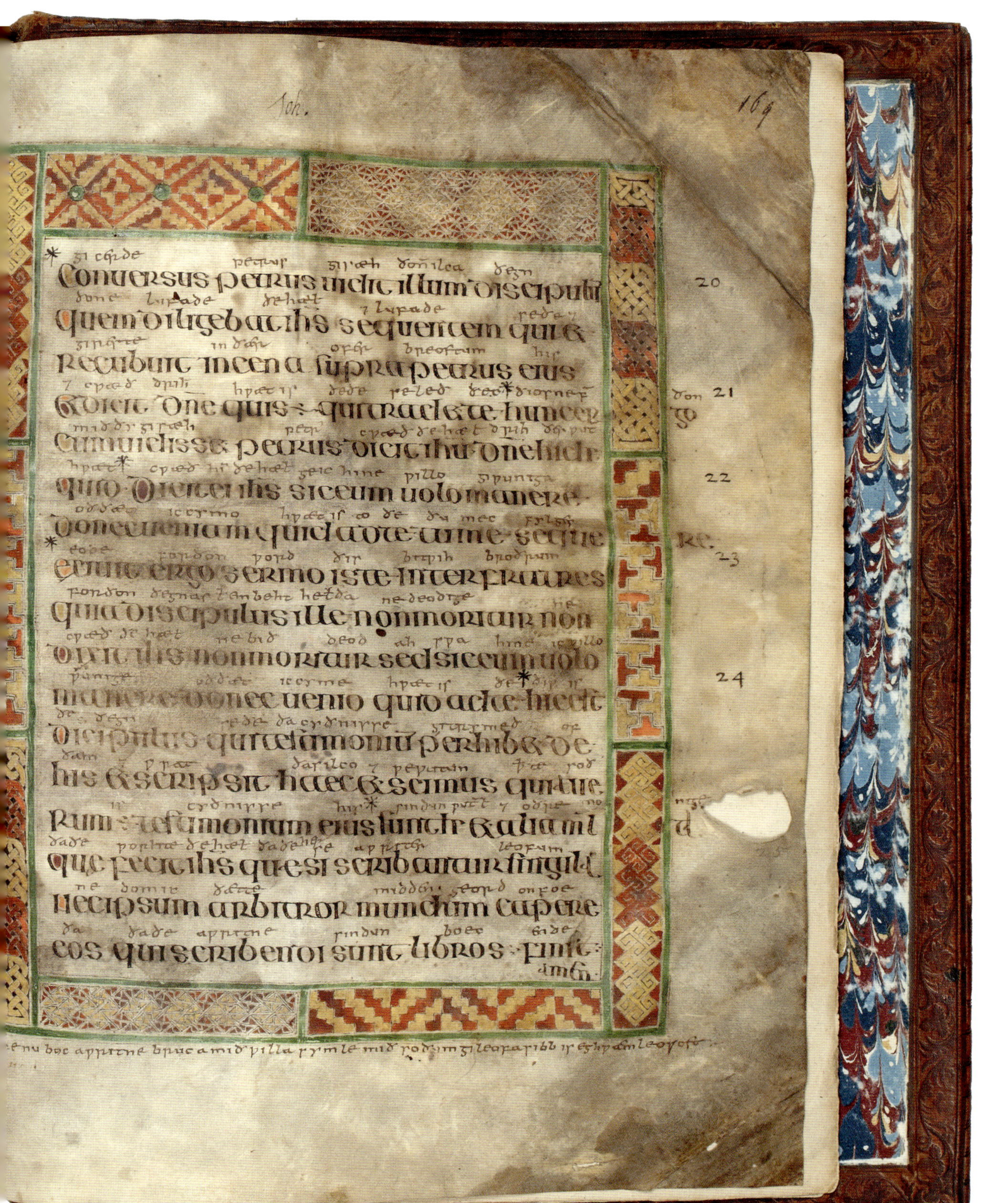

read it in their own language. That way, they would see for themselves how the church had duped them into thraldom and ignorance. England's Reformation was quite different from that experienced elsewhere in Europe when, for personal and political motives, Henry VIII formally abolished papal authority and had himself installed as Supreme Head of the Church of England.

KING JAMES

When Queen Elizabeth I died in the spring of 1603, she was succeeded by King James (James I of England and James VI of Scotland). He was keen to unify his kingdom and resolve simmering religious tensions. On one side there were the Catholics (papists), whose most militant factions would happily have seen James deposed and papal authority over the Church of England restored. But the papists were not the only thorn in James's side. At the other end of the spectrum were the Puritans, who were pressing for another kind of episcopal reform within the Church of England. In January 1604 James convened a three-day conference at Hampton Court. He invited leading bishops and other senior clergy of the Church of England and four moderate members from among leading Puritans. By excluding the nonconformist elements and only inviting influential moderates, James hoped to isolate and undermine radical Puritan dissidence.

It was clear from the outset that James was not going to make any significant concessions to the small Puritan delegation. Over the course of five hours, most of their objections were quickly and sometimes acerbically shot down by James, who believed that many of their grievances were over matters that were little more than quibbles over trifles.

JOHN RAINOLDS

At the close of the second day, the leading Puritan representative, John Rainolds (1549–1607), president of Corpus Christi College, Oxford, proposed a new translation of the Bible. At the time there were two major English versions in use: the Church of England's official Bishops' Bible of 1568, produced during the reign of Elizabeth I, and the considerably more popular Geneva Bible of 1560. The latter owed its popularity to features that made it easier to navigate and to understand; for example, it was the first English Bible to use numbered verses, a feature only recently introduced by the French printer Robert Estienne.[131] The Geneva Bible also included an extensive commentary and references printed in the margins, and was published in a smaller, more handy quarto format. Richard Bancroft, bishop of London,

previous pages

89 Pages from the Gospel of John from the Macregol or Rushworth Gospels, one of the earliest surviving Old English translations of the Bible. Dated before 822, but with Old English gloss added in the tenth century.

opposite 90 Portrait of James I, king of England (1566–1625), unknown artist, seventeenth century.

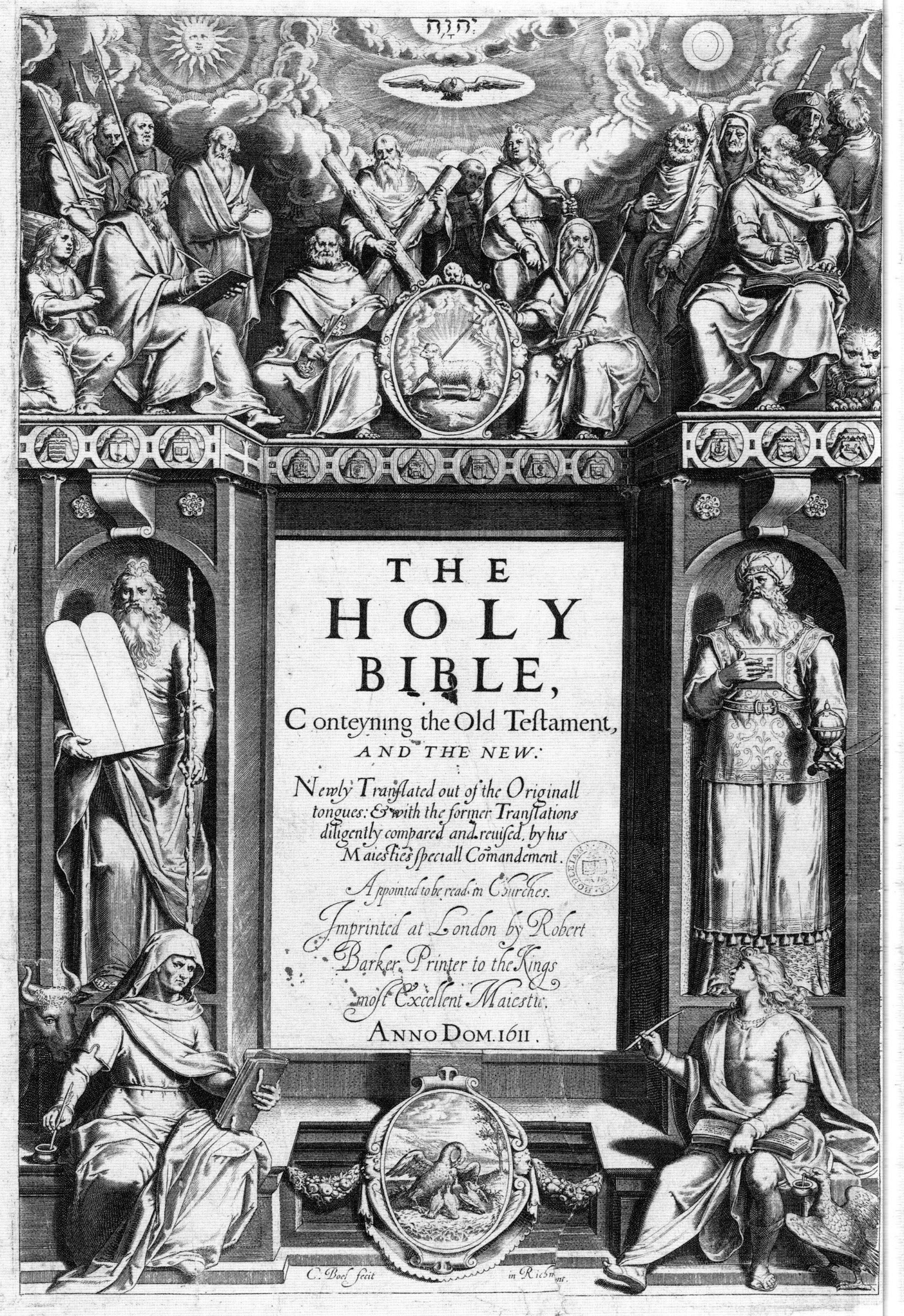

יהוה

THE HOLY BIBLE,
Conteyning the Old Testament,
AND THE NEW:
Newly Translated out of the Originall
tongues: & with the former Translations
diligently compared and reuised, by his
Maiesties speciall Comandement.
Appointed to be read in Churches.
Imprinted at London by Robert
Barker, Printer to the Kings
most Excellent Maiestie.
ANNO DOM. 1611.

C. Boel fecit in Richmont.

who later that year would be enthroned as archbishop of Canterbury, hated the idea of a new translation. Despite Bancroft's objection, and although Bible translation had not been on the agenda, James liked the idea. In this apparent concession to the Puritans, the wily James also saw an ideal opportunity to get rid of the Geneva Bible whose marginal notes he considered 'very partiall, untrue, seditious, and favouring too much of dangerous, and traiterous conceits', [132] including one in the book of Daniel that legitimized resistance to tyrannical kings.[133] This was not exactly the sentiment a king, tyrannical or otherwise, wished his subjects to read in their Bibles!

OXFORD, CAMBRIDGE, WESTMINSTER

A translation committee of about fifty of the nation's best Hebrew and Greek scholars was convened and organized into six companies, with two each at Oxford, Cambridge and Westminster. The Bible was divided up and apportioned to the six translation companies. Bishop Bancroft, supervisor of the project, drafted a set of fifteen rules to be observed during translation. The translators would not be working from the original Hebrew and Greek texts. Forty copies of the Bishops' Bible were distributed among the translators, which was to serve as the base or model text for their translations (rule 1). In addition to the Bishops' Bible, several other English translations were recommended, including Tyndale's, Matthew's, Coverdale's Great Bible and the Geneva Bible, but their renderings should only replace those of the Bishops' Bible if they were deemed closer to the sense of the original (rule 14). James's aversion to the Geneva Bible's expository marginal notes reverberates in rule 6: '*No marginal notes at all to be affixed*, but only for the explanation of the Hebrew or Greek words, which cannot without some circumlocution so briefly and fitly be expressed in the text.'[134] There are 9,000 chapter and verse cross-references printed in the margins of the King James Bible, but ostensibly no expository commentary – only philological notes and cross-references to parallel passages.

The King James Bible was, as its title page states, 'Appointed to be Read in Churches', that is read aloud as part of public or communal worship. Not only did the translation have to be as close to the original as possible, but it had to make sense audibly. When parts of the new translation were completed, one translator read them aloud while the others listened, only interrupting when something did not sound quite right.

RECEPTION

The Bible was completed after seven years, and printed in London in 1611. Hugh Broughton, a

91 Main title page from the King James Bible of 1611.

leading English Hebraist, was scathing and more than a tad melodramatic in his review, arguing that it was better off burned and that he would rather be torn to pieces by wild horses than see the King James Bible used in churches. Broughton's judgement was no doubt coloured by the fact that he had not been invited to participate in the translation, owing to his notoriously eccentric and irascible temperament.

It was some time before the King James Bible was widely adopted outside of churches. Doubtless, many questioned why they should spend their hard-earned money on another Bible when they already had a perfectly good one – probably a Geneva Bible – at home. Measuring approximately 36 cm tall by 23 cm wide, the 1,500-page King James Bible was obviously not for personal use, but rather was designed to be propped on a church lectern. Considerably smaller and eminently more portable quarto (20 × 14 cm) and octavo (16 × 10 cm) editions appeared in the following year, 1612. To boost sluggish sales of the King James Bible, production of the still popular Geneva Bible (many of them cheap imports) was later prohibited. However, shrewd printers on both sides of the English Channel circumvented the prohibition by printing Geneva Bibles with spuriously dated '1599' title pages.

92 Title page introducing the New Testament. From the King James Bible of 1611.

TYNDALE'S LEGACY

Everyone has heard of William Shakespeare, but far fewer are familiar with another William born seventy years before the great bard. William Tyndale (1494–1536), like Martin Luther, believed passionately that everyone had a right to read the Bible in their own tongue – a credo which eventually cost him his life when he was betrayed and executed in 1536 while in exile, in what is today Belgium. But Tyndale's translation would go on to be arguably the most important English translation of the Bible ever produced. Its profound and abiding influence on the English language is second only to Shakespeare's. Many of the King James Bible's most familiar phrases, and indeed entire verses, were lifted straight from Tyndale. 'Eat, drink, and be merry', 'the salt of the earth', 'the powers that be', 'the signs of the times' and even 'filthy lucre' are just some of the phrases coined by Tyndale that found their way into everyday English via the King James Bible.

But if the Bishops' Bible was the translators' main reference text, then how did so much of Tyndale's translation find its way into the King James Bible? By proxy! The Bishops' Bible of 1568 was a revision of Miles Coverdale's Great Bible, produced during the reign of King Henry VIII, which in turn was a revision of Tyndale's New Testament and partial Old Testament

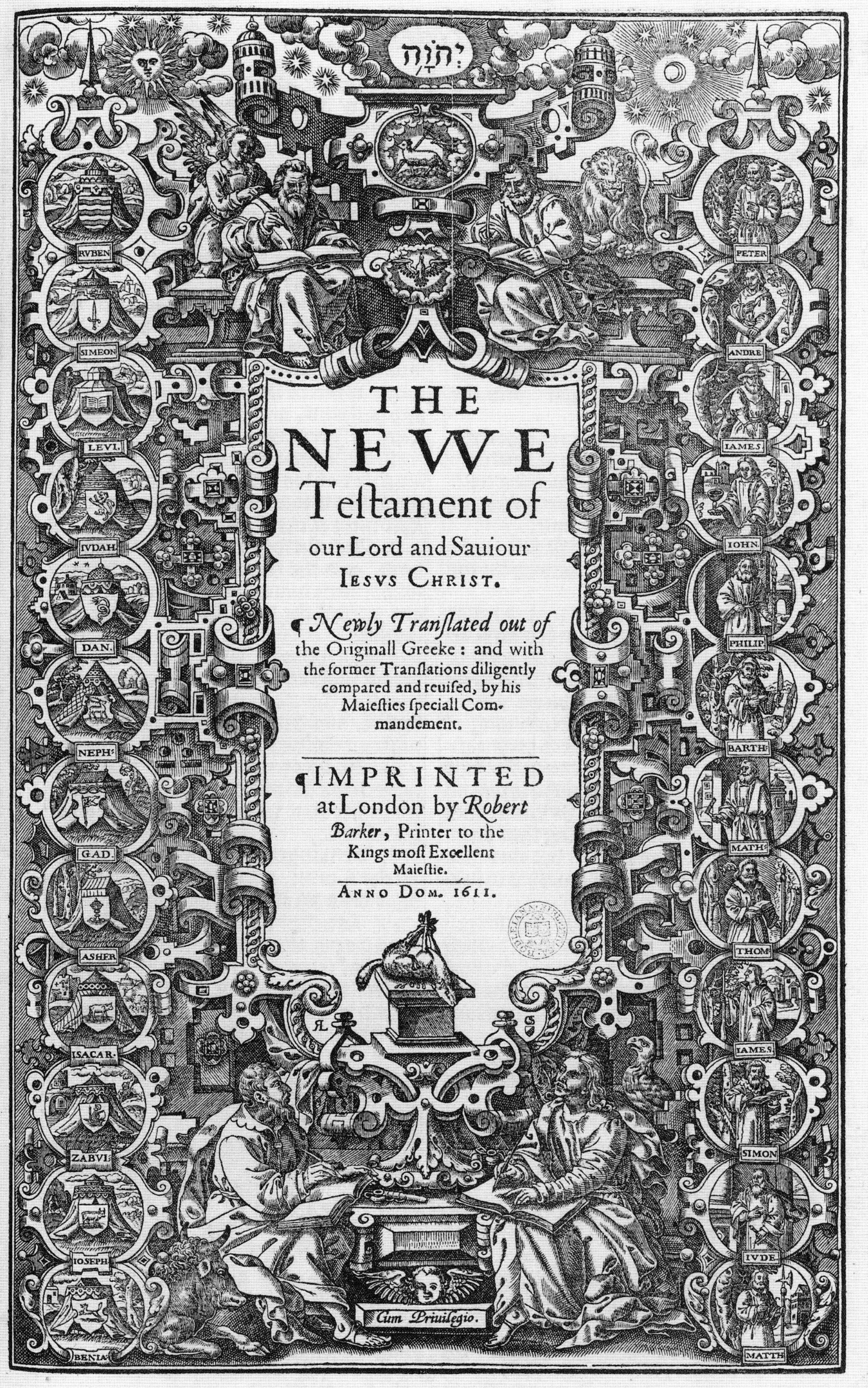

THE
NEWE
Testament of
our Lord and Sauiour
IESVS CHRIST.

¶ *Newly Translated out of* the Originall Greeke: and with the former Translations diligently compared and reuised, by his Maiesties speciall Commandement.

¶ IMPRINTED
at London by *Robert Barker*, Printer to the Kings most Excellent Maiestie.

ANNO DOM. 1611.

translations. In fact, it has been estimated that 84 per cent of the King James Bible New Testament is from Tyndale (word for word), and 76 per cent of the Old Testament.[135]

GENESIS AND THE MOON

Particularly since the nineteenth century, the King James Bible has been celebrated as a masterpiece, as the very pinnacle of English literature. Such sentiments have been repeated up to the present day when, frankly, a good number of those who recycle them have never read more than a handful of verses from any Bible, let alone the King James version. To be truthful, some of the King James Bible's sombre majesty is due to its archaic-sounding early modern English, a sound and register that has over the years become synonymous with 'Bible language'. 'Thou hast ordered fish and chips' lends a certain solemnity or gravitas to an otherwise thoroughly mundane statement. But this in no way diminishes the illustriousness of the King James Bible. It is difficult to imagine better English translations of, say, the twenty-third Psalm, the Lord's Prayer, as recorded in the Gospel of Matthew (6:9–13), or the opening verses of Genesis.

The King James Bible was indeed a remarkable book, but it was not without its flaws. There are roughly 250 typographical and printers' errors in the first edition, plus errors in translation – some owing to the paucity and quality of manuscripts available to the translators. When the King James translators claimed they had consulted the original languages, one might assume they had access to at least some ancient manuscript copies of the Bible. This was not so. For the Greek New Testament, for example, they largely relied on Erasmus's Greek New Testament, first published in 1516. Erasmus was a gifted scholar, but he too had no access to ancient materials, working as he did from a handful of borrowed manuscripts, none older than the twelfth century – copies made a thousand years after the New Testament books were written! Modern scholars now have access to thousands of Bible manuscripts, including quite a few ancient ones.

According to Guinness World Records, the bestselling book of all time is the Christian Bible, with an estimated 5 billion copies sold. Among the scores of Bible translations, the bestselling one, in any language, by a considerable margin, is the King James Bible. It holds another stellar record too. On Christmas Eve 1968, Apollo 8 entered lunar orbit. Its three crew, the first humans to travel to the Moon, took it in turns to read aloud from the first ten verses of the book of Genesis, typed on fireproof paper and inserted into the flight plan ring-binder. The translation? The King James Bible – the first book to orbit the Moon. In August 1971 David R. Scott, commander of the Apollo 15 mission, left a copy of a King James Bible on the Moon, on the control panel of the Lunar Rover, where it remains to this very day.[136]

16

OUT OF EDEN

BESLER, *HORTUS EYSTETTENSIS* (1613)

Les vrais paradis sont les paradis qu'on a perdus.

(The only true paradise is paradise lost.)

MARCEL PROUST, 1927[137]

The word 'paradise' comes from the ancient Greek *paradeisos*. The Greeks in turn had borrowed the word from the Persians. In Old Iranian, *pairidaeza* meant an enclosure or a walled garden. When the Hebrew Old Testament was first translated into Greek, in the third century BCE, its translators used the word *paradeisos* to refer to the Garden of Eden in the book of Genesis. The same word later came to be used in the Greek New Testament to refer to the Christian heaven. By about 1200 CE *paradise* had found its way into Old English via Latin and Old French. It comes as no surprise, then, that when we think of paradise, whether terrestrial or celestial, it is pastoral or garden scenes that most readily come to mind. But what about the first gardens?

The cultivation and domestication of plants for food produced the first agricultural civilizations and the first urban centres, transforming humans from itinerant hunters and foragers to settled city dwellers. It is not difficult to imagine how multipurpose gardens arose in those primordial cities – a few herbs grown within arm's reach of the kitchen, later supplemented by accidental and transplanted flowers for their colour and fragrance, plus some date palms planted both for their sweet fruit and as shade from the scorching Mesopotamian sun.

In Egypt there is evidence for ornamental horticulture dating to the early Dynastic Period of the third millennium BCE. Depictions of formal gardens feature in Egyptian wall and floor paintings, decorative arts and tomb paintings. In the Valley of the Nobles lies the tomb of Sennefer, mayor of Thebes and overseer of the gardens of Amun during the reign of

93 Philipp Hainhofer's notebook drawing of Willibaldsburg, 1611.

Amenhotep II.[138] Sennefer's burial chamber, built in about 1400 BCE, is also known as the Tomb of the Vines after grapevines painted on the ceiling of the tomb's antechamber. The west wall of his tomb is painted with a splendid scene of a large symmetrical garden surrounded by a high mud-brick wall. A sizeable vine-covered trellis or pergola sits at its centre, surrounded by parterres planted with date-palms, sycamore trees and various shrubs surrounding four rectangular ponds (fig. 94).

When the Persian Cyrus the Great (*c.*590–530 BCE) defeated Astyages and the Median Empire at the Battle of Pasargadae in 550 BCE, he chose the site for a new garden-palace – building commenced in 546 BCE. The extensive formal gardens are perhaps the first example of what was later called *chahar bagh* (fourfold garden design). Persian garden design later influenced Greek gardens when the Persian Empire was subsequently conquered by Alexander the Great in 333 BCE. Later Roman gardens incorporated elements of Egyptian and Persian garden designs via the Greeks. While the Roman elite could afford to build vast garden estates on the fringes of the city, the more modest homes of the townsfolk often had small back gardens. As Rome's population grew and houses gave way to *insulae* (apartment buildings), ground-level gardens were supplanted by roof gardens and window-boxes – the latter mentioned by Pliny as the garden of the urban poor.[139]

94 Facsimile of a wall-painting from Sennefer's tomb (Tomb of the Vines), *c.*1450 BCE. From *Monumenti dell'Egitto e della Nubia*, Ippolito Rosellini, 1844.

RENAISSANCE BOTANY

Central to the European Renaissance was the rediscovery and reappraisal of ancient literature, including the botanical works of Theophrastus (371–286 BCE), widely considered the ancient founder of botany. During the sixteenth century, botany began to emerge as a distinct scientific discipline as it began to find its way into university curricula. The universities of Pisa and Padua were the first to establish their own botanical gardens in 1545. In Britain, the first botanical garden was founded at the University of Oxford in 1621. The Physic Garden's first head gardener, Jacob Bobart the elder (who also owned a pub on Oxford High Street), was typically seen about town accompanied by his pet goat. The rise of Renaissance botany was also precipitated by the massive influx of new plant species from the New World and beyond.

THE BISHOP AND THE APOTHECARY

Seventy kilometres south of Nuremberg and perched atop a hill, the fortified Willibaldsburg overlooked the Altmühl valley and the cathedral city of Eichstätt. Built in about 1355 the castle was named after Willibald, the first

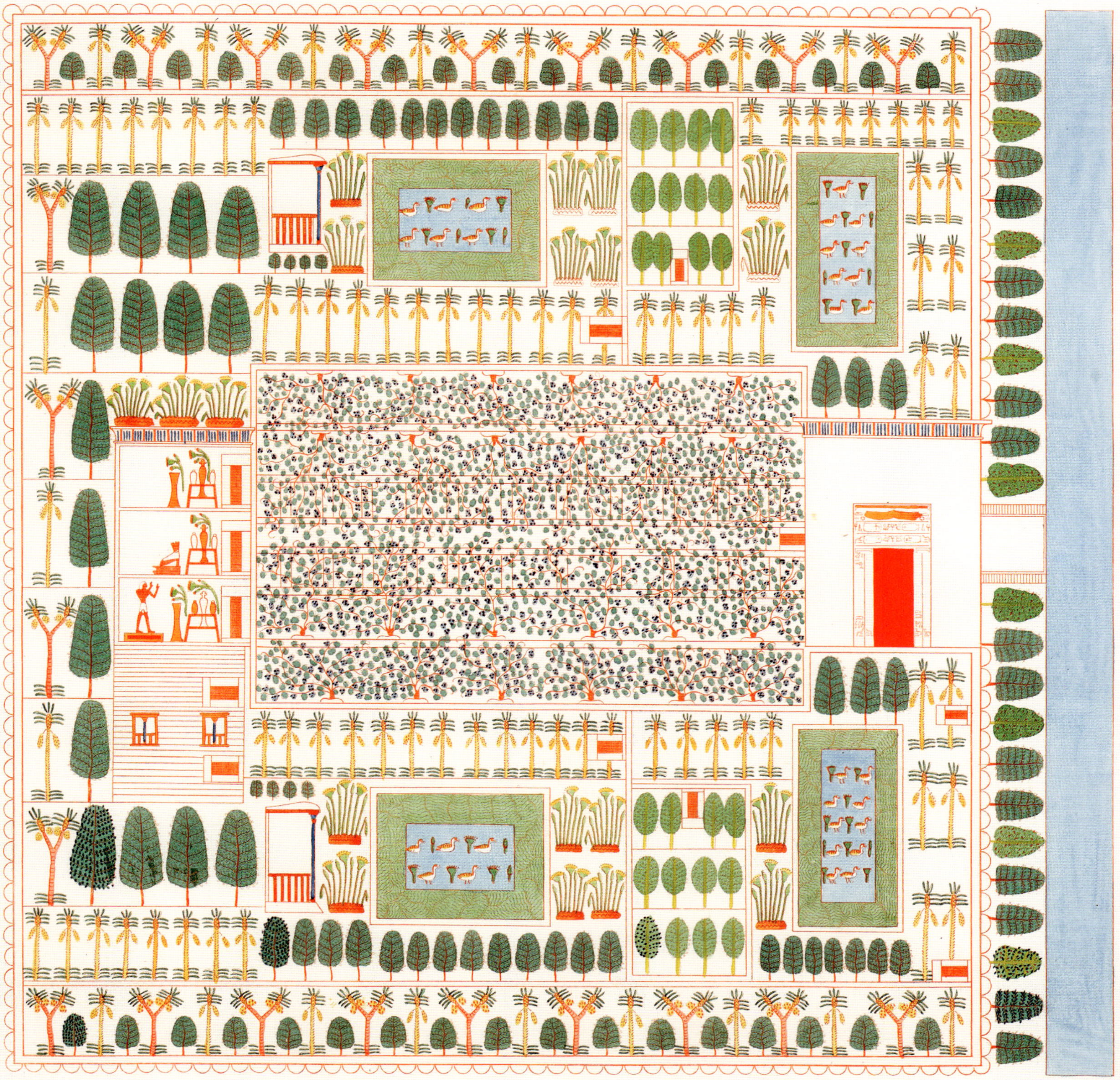

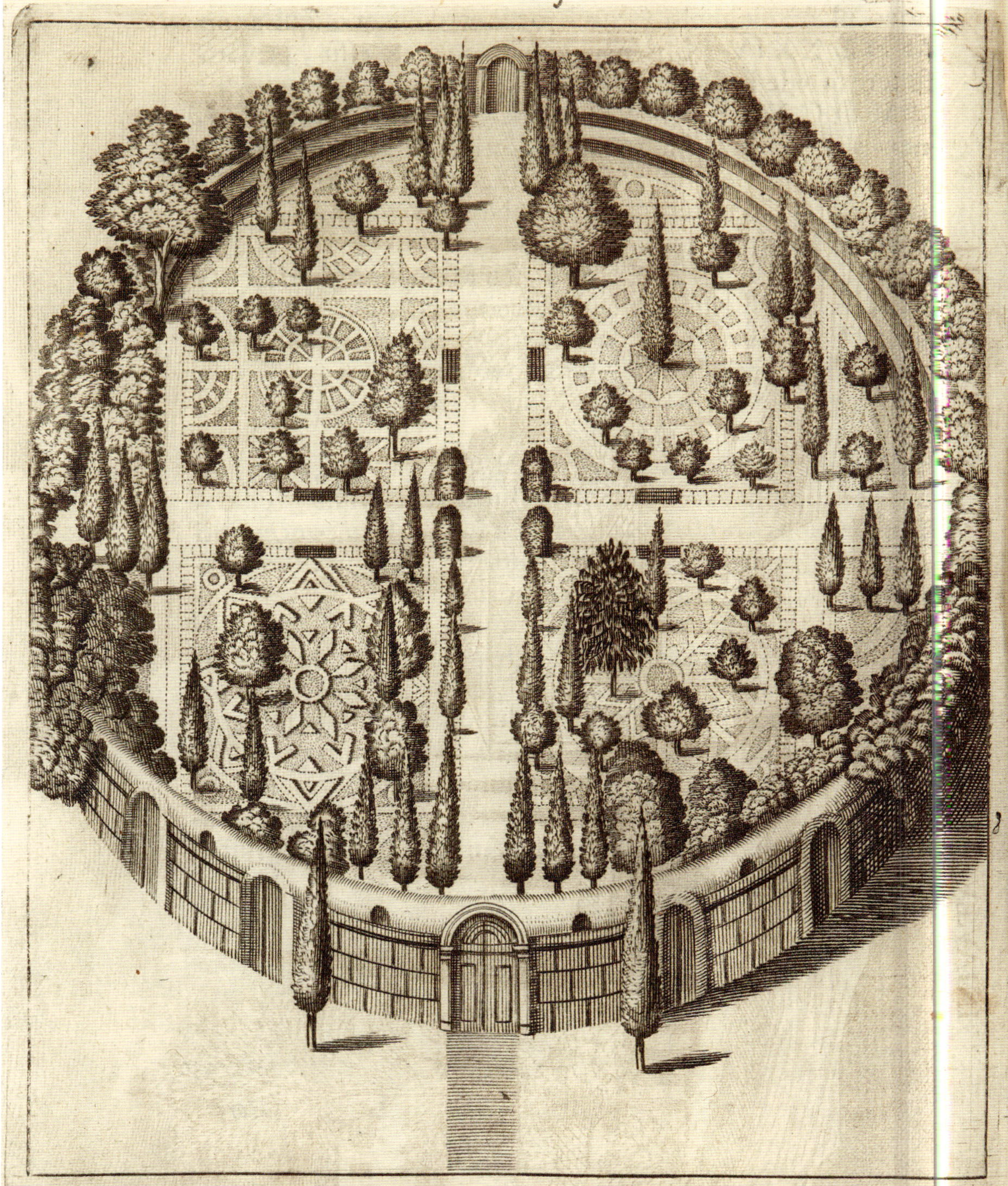

VIRIDARIVM GYMNASII PATAVINI MEDICVM.

Io. Georg. sculps.

bishop of Eichstätt in the eighth century, and served as the seat of successive bishops of the city. When Bishop Kaspar von Seckendorff died in 1595, he was succeeded by Johann Konrad von Gemmingen (1561–1612). Gemmingen was from a noble and wealthy family, well educated and an avid collector of many and varied things, including plants. He was also an exacting man. Unhappy with the east-facing castle he had inherited, he set about building a new west-facing south wing, thus completing its long transformation from medieval castle to Renaissance palace. The palace buildings were only part of the bishop's ambitious plans; he would expand the palace gardens too. For help in designing the gardens and in sourcing plants, he turned to Joachim Camerarius, son of the famed classical scholar and philologist of the same name. Camerarius was a scholar, physician and botanist, and the author of an illustrated herbal cataloguing the plants in his own botanical garden. After Camerarius's death in 1598, the bishop brought on Basilius Besler (1561–1629), a Nuremberg apothecary and thus someone intimately familiar with even the most exotic foreign plants and, perhaps even more crucially, with sourcing them – through major European ports like those in Amsterdam and Antwerp.

In 1611 Philipp Hainhofer (1578–1647), a well-connected diplomat, art collector and art agent, visited Gemmingen. He reported that Willibaldsburg's new wing was still under construction, with 200 workers on the site and stone still being hewn from the quarry below. He also describes eight gardens surrounding the castle, each planted with flowers from different countries, such as roses, lilies and tulips. Among the garden's more exotic plants were some recently introduced to Europe from the Americas. They included the tobacco plant (*Tabacum latifolium*, plate 340), the sunflower (*Flos Solis maior*, plate 204) and the tomato (*Poma amoris fructu luteo*, plate 320) – first domesticated in Peru or Mesoamerica, called *xitomatl* by the Aztec, and brought back to Europe by the Spanish invaders. The physician and botanist Pietro Andrea Mattioli was the first to document tomatoes in Europe, when in 1544 he described the Italians eating tomatoes 'commonly eaten fried in oil, with salt and pepper'.[140] Parts of Europe were slower to acquire a taste for the tomato, but that they were hesitant because they considered them poisonous is often overstated.

BESLER'S FLORILEGIUM

According to Gemmingen, the idea of a book cataloguing the castle gardens had been Besler's, who he said desired to have the plants in the gardens 'engraved in copper, printed,

95 Botanical garden at Padua, from Giacomo Filippo Tomasini's *Gymnasium Patavinum*, 1654.

dedicated to me and to seek his fame and profit with the book'.[141] The bishop accepted Besler's proposal, advancing him 3,000 florins – enough money to buy a sizeable townhouse. The bishop, who was gravely ill, perhaps saw in Besler's proposal an opportunity not only to be a generous patron but to secure his own legacy too. The project was an enormously expensive one with substantial upfront costs. Each week boxes of fresh flowers were sent north to Nuremberg where they were transformed into sketches and final drawings, and then engraved onto 367 copper plates ready for printing.[142] Besler had grand designs for the book. Florilegium were often oversized books, but Besler's would outdo them all. He would print it on the largest size paper then available (57 × 46 cm), thus ensuring that all but one of the plants, the fig tree (*Ficus indica*, plate 359, accompanied by a scale at the bottom left of the page), could be illustrated life-size (fig. 99).

Gemmingen did not live to see the completed book. When he died in November 1612, his successor, Johann Christoph von Westerstetten, secured continued financing, and the book appeared in 1613. *Hortus Eystettensis* (*The Garden of Eichstätt*) was first published in an edition of 300 copies. According to Besler, he had been working on the book for six years. *Hortus Eystettensis* was the largest and most expensive book of its day. The final cost of the project was a staggering 18,000 florins, six times the original outlay and almost a fifth of what Gemmingen had spent on his palace's new wing.[143] Its enormous size prompted one commentator to quip that a wheelbarrow was required to move the book around.[144] One of the Bodleian Library's copies of *Hortus Eystettensis*, bound in a single volume and once owned by none other than Francis Bacon, weighs in at a colossal 16.75 kg. Its 367 plates, illustrating almost 1,100 plants, are organized around the four seasons.

Hortus Eystettensis was available in two main versions. The first was a deluxe copy, expertly and meticulously coloured by hand. The coloured copy now held at the British Library records that its colourist, Georg Mack (the younger), spent a year colouring the 367 colossal plates. The second version was uncoloured, initially costing 35 florins and later rising to 48 florins. The deluxe hand-coloured copy cost the astronomical sum of 500 florins. Even the wealthy bibliophile Herzog August (1579–1666), who wanted a copy for his library at Wolfenbüttel (at the time, the largest library north of the Alps), was taken aback by the price: 'Please be so kind as to tell me whether I have read the sum correctly or whether it should only be 50 [florins]. Should it only cost

96 Title page from *Hortus Eystettensis*, Basilius Besler, 1613.

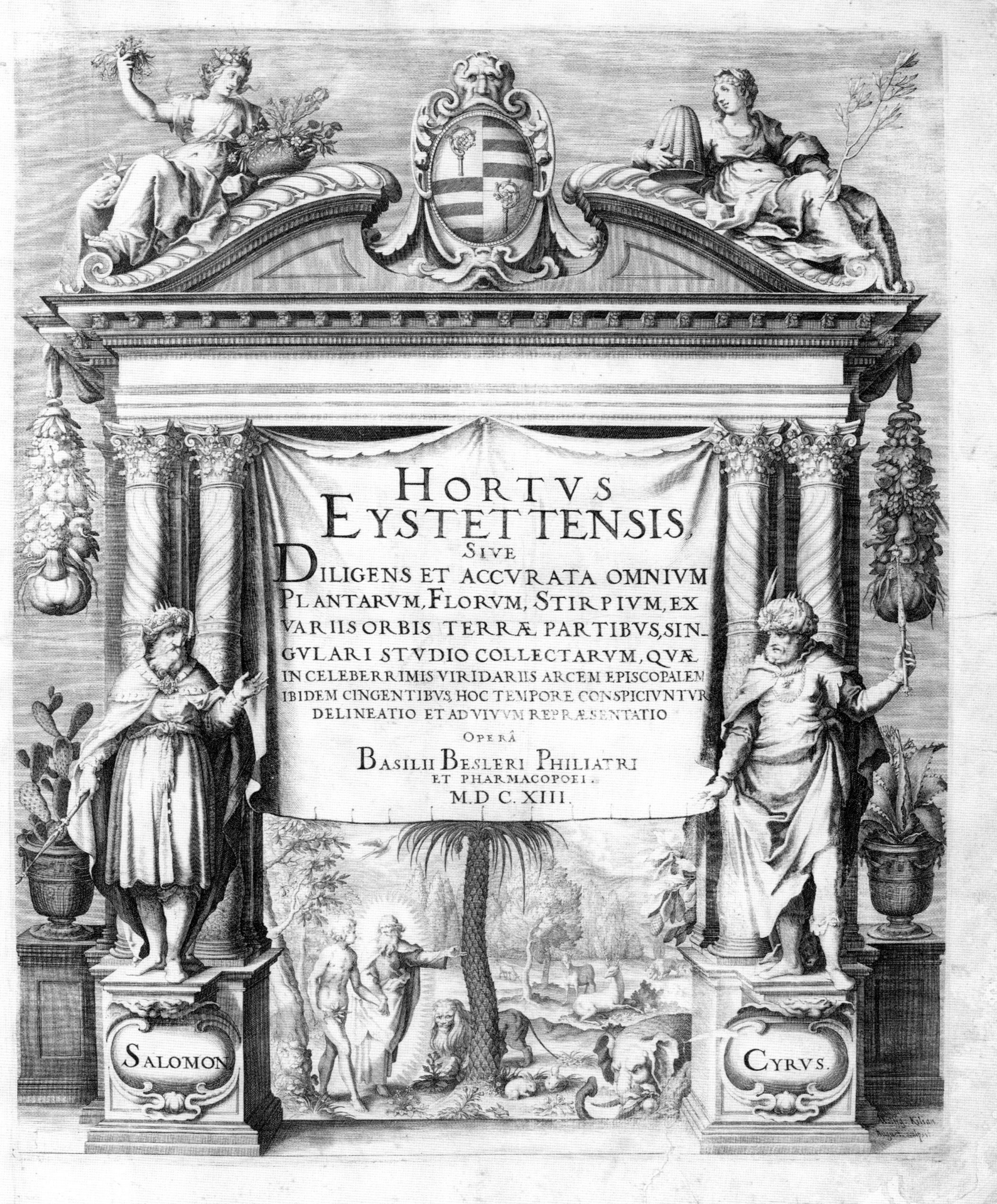
HORTVS
EYSTETTENSIS,
SIVE
DILIGENS ET ACCVRATA OMNIVM
PLANTARVM, FLORVM, STIRPIVM, EX
VARIIS ORBIS TERRÆ PARTIBVS, SIN-
GVLARI STVDIO COLLECTARVM, QVÆ
IN CELEBERRIMIS VIRIDARIIS ARCEM EPISCOPALEM
IBIDEM CINGENTIBVS, HOC TEMPORE CONSPICIVNTVR
DELINEATIO ET AD VIVVM REPRÆSENTATIO
OPERÂ
BASILII BESLERI PHILIATRI
ET PHARMACOPOEI.
M.D C.XIII.
SALOMON
CYRVS.

50 I would prefer the illuminated one; if it costs the greater sum I desire it only the way it is printed [i.e. uncoloured]'.[145] I am not aware of any other printed book of the period costing anywhere near as much – 500 florins is indeed an enormous sum for a book. It should be noted, however, that Herzog ended up buying at least three copies. To put the cost of the book in perspective, consider that the bishop's two head gardeners were paid a salary of 60 florins per year, and in 1601 Besler paid 1,350 florins for a house.

In Besler's day it was not uncommon to break up expensive illustrated books, and to sell the pages piecemeal as art prints or for decoration. Besler warns against this practice in his foreword, cautioning pirates and would-be philistine book butchers: 'might all those who now destroy fine botanical books to make lampshades and table-mats be equally liable!'.[146]

ILLUSTRATING NATURE

Nowadays, it is hard to imagine a book of plants and flowers without illustrations. Although Pliny was not opposed to illustrations as a supplement to text, he was not alone in warning that *pictura est fallax* (a picture is misleading). Throughout the Middle Ages the usefulness of pictures was challenged, with some convinced that they were a distraction from, or even harmful to, learning. Thus, it is not at all unusual to see genres of medieval books that we would now expect to be illustrated produced without any. But the advent of print quickly proved the utility of the printed pictorial image. The seventeenth-century English naturalist John Ray (1627–1705) considered a botanical work without illustrations as ridiculous as a book of geography without maps.

97 Tulips from *Hortus Eystettensis*, Basilius Besler, 1613.

TULIPOMANIA

The tulip was undoubtedly one of Bishop Gemmingen's favourite flowers. He boasted that his garden was home to tulips in 500 different colours. Although he was probably exaggerating a little, their abundance in his gardens is reflected in the book in which fifty-four varieties of tulip appear. The tulip was introduced into Europe from the Ottoman Empire in the 1550s. Conrad Gessner (see pp. 137–47) first saw one in 1559 in a garden in Augsburg, and was the first to publish a description and illustration of the tulip in 1561. The Flemish botanist Carolus Clusius (1526–1609), who supplied plants for the bishop's garden and advised Besler, was foremost among the popularizers of the tulip in Europe. Not only was he enthusiastic in sending bulbs to his vast network of friends, but he wrote an influential six-page monograph on the tulip that was published in 1576. By the early decades of

Qu

CELEBERR
sis horti, Icon

TVlipa serotina effertur
que ad oras utrinque aspersis
Germanicè, Tulipani hochweiß mit

Tulipa præcox Polymita, flor
butis. Interiora enim reflexorum sun
rò rubent.
Germanicè, Tulipa vermischt mit Cir

Hujus Tulipæ flores explicati,
stolonibus & capitulis viridibus: rutilis
apices ferè foliorum conis suis tangenti
Germanicè, Bleichgelbe Tulipani mi

Tulipa conglobatur, florum ex
Germanicè, Tulipa gantz gelbgrün.

Sic ista Tulipa, hiare incipit, flor
Germanicè, Tulipani Purpurfarb mi

1.
Flos Solis maior.

CE

FLo
mu
reâ
elegantiſſima ha
brevi, nec profu
brachialis, fragile
quamvis majora
tuberat in craſſu
rem, amplitudin
luminis (cum qu
reóq; fulgore mi
(at multò major
tur. Diſcus ejus
quinq; denticulis
tis, è medio floris
ſuccreſcit, quaſi i
duo millia trecen
voluit. Sunt aut
terius nigricante

Deſc. à
Lo
Co
Lu
Ni

He
Ep
M
Pl
Pa
Germ.
M
T
D

the seventeenth century the tulip had become prodigiously popular in Europe, leading to one of the most bizarre and extraordinary events in botanical (and economic) history. Between 1634 and 1637 a speculative boom, dubbed 'tulipomania', saw the price of tulip bulbs skyrocket to unprecedented levels, with some going for more than the price of a house.

By the time tulipomania was peaking in the Netherlands, the palace gardens of Eichstätt were in decline. The gardens were damaged during the Thirty Years War when Protestant Swedish troops invaded Eichstätt in 1633, destroying much of the town and massacring 1,000 of its inhabitants. By the eighteenth century the original gardens had all but vanished. But the garden's legacy is immortalized in Besler's magnificent book, produced during the burgeoning golden age of botany.

One of several strands that contributed to the enthusiasm for botany in the sixteenth and seventeenth centuries was the discovery of countless new plant species during the Age of Exploration (and colonization). Almost 1,100 plants are illustrated in *Hortus* – far more than the total number described in ancient sources. The Hippocratic Corpus of the fifth and fourth centuries BCE lists around 300 plants. In the first century CE, Dioscorides' *Materia medica* numbers 600; in the same century, Pliny's *Natural History* contains around 900. The Swiss botanist Caspar Bauhin names 6,000 species in his landmark *Pinax theatri botanici* (*Illustrated Exposition of Plants*), published in 1623. In 1790 Louis-François Jauffret proposes that every plant species in the world, by his estimate 25,000, be reproduced artificially for a universal *cabinet des plantes*, using techniques recently pioneered by Marie Antoinette's florist, Thomas Joseph Wenzel. Today, the World Checklist of Vascular Plants (WCVP) lists 1,434,000 plant names, representing 359,900 species.[147]

Whether it be a utopian Dilmun or Eden, the palace gardens of Cyrus the Great in Pasargadae, the plebeian back gardens of ancient Romans or an inner-city window box in the twenty-first century, the garden is an act of creation, of nature fashioned from our own designs and desires – our very own Eden.

98 The sunflower (*Flos Solis maior*), from *Hortus Eystettensis*, Basilius Besler, 1613.

following pages

99 Barbary fig (*Ficus indica*), from *Hortus Eystettensis*, Basilius Besler, 1613. Note the scale at bottom left.

Ficus Indica Eystetten,
sis ex uno folio enata lu,
xurians.

CELEBERRIMI EYSTETTENsis horti, Icones plantarum Autumnalium.

I

Ficus Indica Eystettensis. Majestatem naturæ, ejúsq; miris modis seipsum superantis Genium, etiam hâc, si ullâ unquam stirpe, palàm fieri, omnium oculis patet, vel illo præcipuo miraculo; ex uno folio, telluri aliquantùm impacto, tantæ altitudinis arborem evadere, quæ etiam octodecim pedum proceritatem evinceret, támq; spaciosam, ut circuitum sexaginta pedum expleret. Inferior caudex trunci humani crassitudinem duplo superabat, lignosus, & fissuris rimarum variis passim dehiscens; rami numerosi inæqualiter & multipliciter divaricabantur, è crassorum, pallidè virentium, latorum, ac spinis albescentibus obsitorum foliorum multijugis cohærentiis, quasi internodiis, sibi invicem impactis, conflati; & quidem tantâ luxuriâ, ut paucis abhincannis tria millia foliorũ simul enumeraverimus. Fructuum annuatim largus proventus est, è lateribus foliorum erumpentium, turbinatâ ficuum effigie, in quorum rudimentis initiò superiùs videndi flores, quos cum Balaustii florum figurâ Lobel. comparat, majores tamen, & in luteo colore, rubedine aliquâ suffusâ, placentes; sub quibus fructus tandem ficuum magnitudinem duplam excedunt, æquè spinulis exasperati, & ad miniatum colorem accedentes, intùs pulpâ sanguineâ involventes semina copiosa sparsim insita, parvis, compressis, albicantibus granis constantia, quæ non minus ac folia, rubicundo germine emisso, temporis successu in arborem evadere queunt, ceu nostra, quam hæc effigies refert, pari proventu in tantam molem & proceritatem excrevit. Mensuram, quâ tàm amplitudo, quàm altitudo stirpis, uti & folia, existimanda sint, nobis hic adjungere visum fuit.

De ficu Indica, Opuntia dicta,

Vid. Dodon. 801.
Cœsalpin. lib. 3. cap. 2. fol. 89.
Lobel. 454. Adv.
Lugdunens. 1795. fol.
Cam. Epit. Matth. 183. fol.
Hort. Med. 110. fol.
C. Bauh. Matth. 234. fol.

Germ. Stachlichter Indianischer Feigenbaum.
Tabern. 664. lib. secundo.
Cam. Matth. Germ. 230. fol.
Durant. 380. fol.

D
A
B
C
A
E
G
H
I
I

17

OF MITES AND MEN

HOOKE, *MICROGRAPHIA* (1665)

All the conduct of our life depends on our senses, and because sight is the noblest and most comprehensive of these, inventions which serve to increase its power are undoubtedly among the most useful there can be.

DESCARTES, 1637[148]

The typical unaided human eye has a maximum resolving power of around 100 microns. In practical terms that means anything smaller than, say, a strand of hair, is pretty much invisible to us. The desire to magnify small things is certainly not a recent idea, and it appears that some ancient cultures were familiar with some form of magnifying lens. The early history of lenses is controversial – when an ancient artefact resembling a lens is unearthed, it is not always possible to know if it is simply a piece of jewellery detached from its setting or some other kind of decorative stone or ornament. Convex, plano-convex or spherical pieces of glass or quartz are able to magnify, but without further corroboration we can only speculate that such things were used as aids to vision.

In the early fifth century BCE, Aristophanes mentions the use of magnifying lenses as fire-starters – designed to concentrate and magnify the sun's rays to ignite kindling. Seneca, in his *Natural Questions* (early 60s CE), writes about another method of magnification: 'Everything is much larger when one is looking through water: writing, however tiny, and difficult, is seen larger and clearer through a glass sphere full of water.'[149] About twenty years later, Pliny, in his monumental encyclopaedia *Natural History*, recalls that Nero watched the gladiatorial games through polished *smaragdus*, a term used to describe emeralds and various other green stones. Apparently this was not for magnification, however, but perhaps to shade his eyes from the sun.

Handheld magnifying glasses were used throughout the Middle Ages. In Basra, in modern-day Iraq, Ibn al-Haytham – better known in the West as Alhazen (965–1040/41)

100 The 'drunken' ant, from Robert Hooke's *Micrographia*, 1665.

– wrote *Kitab al-Manazir* (*Book of Optics*), in which he described the magnifying properties of spheres and lenses. Latin translations of the late twelfth and early thirteenth centuries proved hugely influential right through to the Keplerian revolution in optics almost four centuries later. It is certainly no coincidence that, in the same century in which Alhazen's treatise on optics reached the Latin West, magnifying lenses that could be worn on one's face appeared. Although we do not know who invented spectacles, we do know that they first appeared in the historical record in the 1280s.

But our story begins at the turn of the seventeenth century. Around the time that the telescope was invented, the first compound microscopes appeared. The very earliest microscopes were difficult to use, magnified between about three and nine times, and their rudimentary lenses produced distorted or unevenly focused images. However, by the latter half of the seventeenth century, with improvements in lens-making techniques, microscopes could magnify hundreds of times. Nowadays, the most advanced electron microscope resolves to thirty-five trillionths of a metre – smaller than a hydrogen atom! It is impossible for us, having grown up with photographs and video of the infinitesimally tiny, to fathom just how revolutionary those early microscopical images were. Constantijn Huygens (1596–1687), a precocious young poet at the time, summed up the thrill of pioneering microscopists when he wrote, 'It really is as if you stand before a new theatre of nature, or are on a different planet'.[150] Someone who shared Huygens's sentiment, and who would become one of the foremost popularizers of microscopy, was a peculiar and peculiarly gifted Englishman from a small island off the coast of England.

101 Robert Hooke's microscope and illuminating system. *Micrographia*, 1665.

MICROGRAPHIA

Robert Hooke was born in 1635 in Freshwater on the Isle of Wight. In 1648 his father died and, with an inheritance of £50, the thirteen-year-old Hooke made his way to London where he worked as an apprentice to Peter Lely, former portrait artist to King Charles I. But Hooke soon came to believe that he could teach himself to paint and use the money he had saved for something more profitable. Using his inheritance, he enrolled in the prestigious Westminster School. In 1653 Hooke began his studies, ranging from astronomy to chemistry, at Christ Church, Oxford. Later, after working as an assistant to physician and chemist Thomas Willis, Hooke got his big break when he was taken on as an amanuensis and assistant to the pioneer of modern chemistry Robert Boyle.

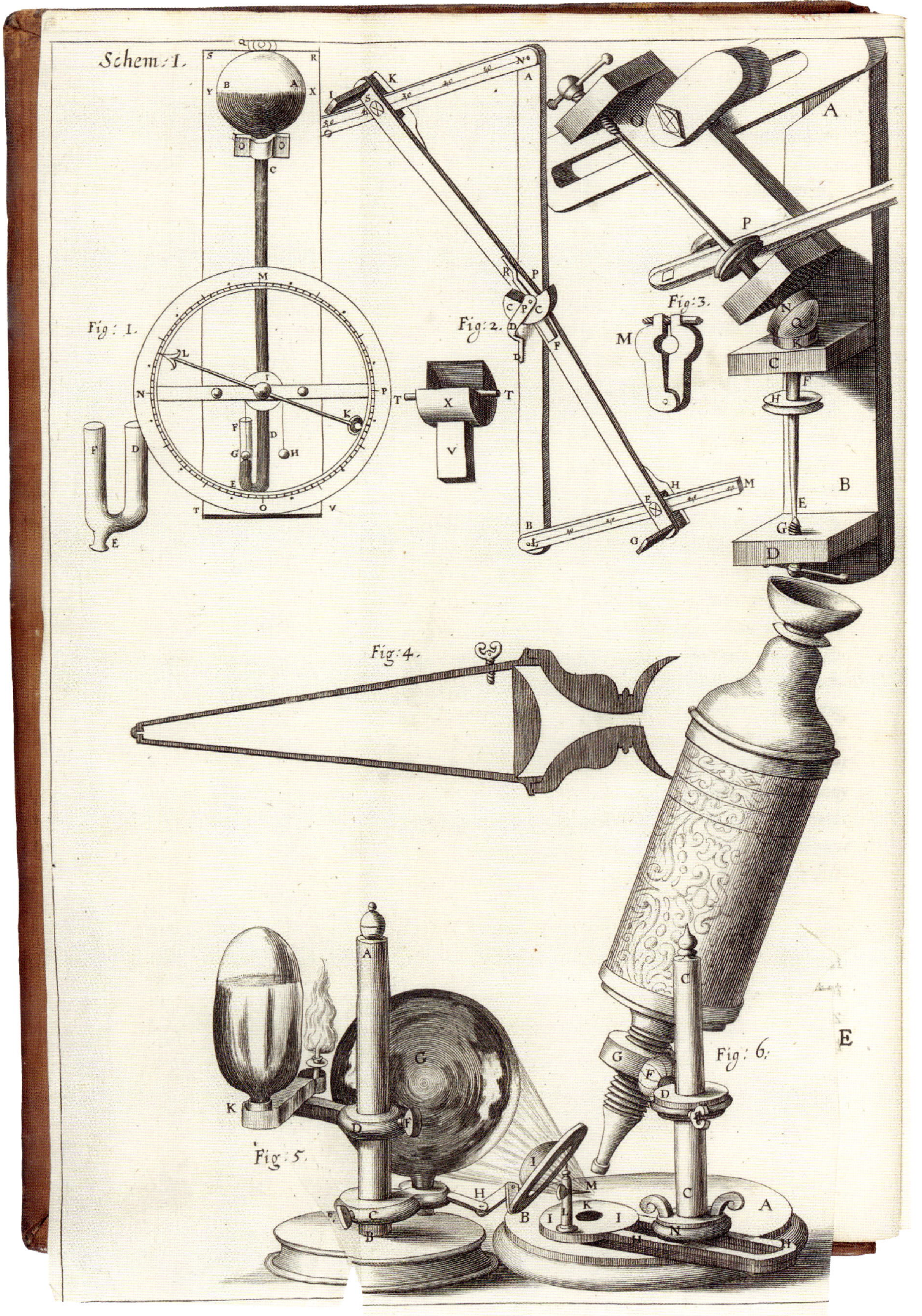
Schem: I.
Fig: 1.
Fig: 2.
Fig: 3.
Fig: 4.
Fig: 5.
Fig: 6.

Their personal and working relationship flourished and led, in November 1662, to Hooke's appointment as the first Curator of Experiments for the newly founded Royal Society of London. The society's motto, *Nullius in verba* (Not words but deeds), epitomises what was expected of Hooke.

In 1661 Christopher Wren, one of the founding members of the Royal Society and an exceptionally skilled draughtsman, presented King Charles II with some drawings of insects as viewed through his microscope. Charles was duly impressed, and the Royal Society suggested Wren draw some more. Wren did not fancy the idea and declined, and the project was handed to Hooke to complete. As Curator of Experiments, Hooke presented his research and experiments at the society's regular meetings held at Gresham College. It was decided that collectively the microscopical parts of his research would make a fine book. In January 1665 it was published as *Micrographia: Some Physiological Descriptions of Minute Bodies Made by Magnifying Glasses with Observations and Inquiries Thereupon*. This large folio format book of 246 pages is organized into sixty chapters (or 'Observations'), accompanied by thirty-eight copperplate illustrations (or 'Schema'), five of which are large fold-outs. The book was printed by John Martyn and James Allestry in London, who had been appointed the official printer-publisher to the Royal Society in 1663.

102 The pointed needle, a printed full stop and a razor blade. Robert Hooke's *Micrographia*, 1665.

following pages

103 Fold-out of flea. Robert Hooke's *Micrographia*, 1665.

A PEDAGOGY OF SIGHT[151]

When Galileo first published his telescopic observations in 1610, many were sceptical. Some even turned to mock him, suggesting he had been fooled by his own eyes and his new-fangled telescopes (see pp. 189–97). Fifty-five years later, Hooke faced a similar challenge. Not only were microscopes quite expensive, but they were not at all easy to use. Lens quality, lighting and the absence of a mechanism for fine-grained focusing made microscopy difficult for professionals, let alone amateurs. Hooke's challenge, then, was to reassure his readers that the microscope was a reliable instrument and that the images it produced were authentic – in short, that they represented reality. Moreover, once their authenticity had been established, he had to convince the naysayers that his drawings were faithful reproductions and not fanciful interpretations.

Hooke was optimistic that with better and more powerful instruments, which could augment our own limited senses, the entirety of nature might be probed – everything from alien civilizations on the Moon to the secrets of 'atoms'. In the preface to his *Micrographia*, he writes: 'there may be yet invented several other

MICROGRAPHIA.

) appears a *broad,blunt*, and very *irregular* end; not resem-
s is imagin'd, but onely a piece of a tapering body, with a
e top remov'd, or deficient. The Points of Pins are yet
d the Points of the most curious Mathematital Instruments
e arrive at so great a sharpness; how much therefore can
demonstrations made onely by the productions of the Ru-
ses, he will be better able to consider that shall but view
d *lines* with a *Microscope*.
this point be commonly accounted the sharpest (whence
d express the sharpness of a point the most *superlatively*, we
a Needle) yet the *Microscope* can afford us hundreds of In-
ts many thousand times sharper: such as those of the *hairs*,
d *claws* of multitudes of *Insects*; the *thorns*, or *crooks*, or
, and other small vegetables; nay, the ends of the *striæ* or
ipeds of *Amianthus*, and *alumen plumosum*; of many of
the Points are so sharp as not to be visible, though view'd
pe (which magnifies the Object, in bulk, above a million of
ubt not, but were we able *practically* to make *Microscopes*
he *theory* of them, we might find hills, and dales, and pores,
bredth, or expansion, to give all those parts elbow-room,
nt top of the very Point of any of these so very sharp bodies.
he *quantity* or extension of any body may be *Divisible in in-*
perhaps not the *matter*.
roceed: The Image we have here exhibited in the
was the top of a small and very sharp Needle, whose
verthelesś appear'd through the *Microscope* above a
inch broad, not round nor flat, but *irregular* and *un-*
it seem'd to have been big enough to have afforded a
d Mites room enough to be rang'd by each other without
he breaking one anothers necks, by being thrust off on ei-
e surface of which, though appearing to the naked eye very
not neverthelesś hide a multitude of holes and scratches and
from being discover'd by the *Microscope* to invest it, several
ualities (as A,B,C, seem'd *holes* made by some small specks of
some *adventitious body*, that stuck very close to it) were *ca-*
est that roughen the surface, were onely so many marks of
nd bungling of *Art*. So unaccurate is it, in all its producti-
hose which seem most neat, that if examin'd with an organ
en that by which they were made, the more we see of their
appearance will there be of their *beauty*: whereas in the
ure, the deepest Discoveries shew us the greatest Excellen-
dent Argument, that he that was the Author of all these
other then *Omnipotent*; being able to include as great a va-
and contrivances in the yet smallest Discernable Point, as in
odies (which comparatively are called also Points) such as
, or *Planets*. Nor need it seem strange that the Earth it self
Analogie call'd a Physical Point: For as its body, though now
so

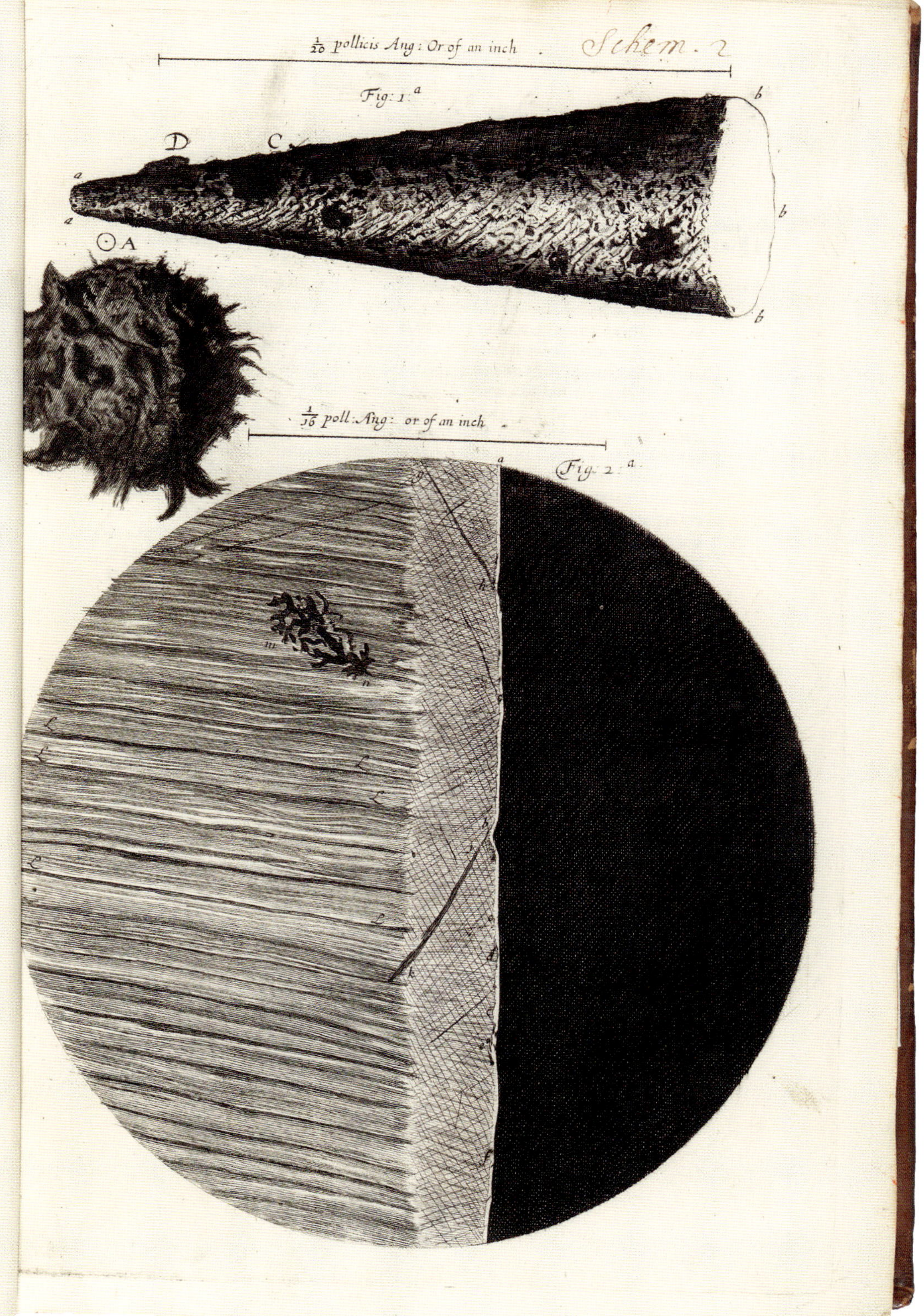

through so many scourings, washings, dressings and dryings, as the parts of old Paper must necessarily have suffer'd; the digestive faculty, it seems, of these little creatures being able yet further to work upon those stubborn parts, and reduce them into another form.

And indeed, when I consider what a heap of Saw-dust or chips this little creature (which is one of the teeth of Time) conveys into its intrals. I cannot chuse but remember and admire the excellent contrivance of Nature, in placing in Animals such a fire, as is continually nourished and supply'd by the materials convey'd into the stomach, and *fomented* by the bellows of the lungs; and in so contriving the most admirable fabrick of Animals, as to make the very spending and wasting of that fire, to be instrumental to the procuring and collecting more materials to augment and cherish it self, which indeed seems to be the principal end of all the contrivances observable in bruit Animals.

Observ. LIII. *Of a Flea.*

The strength and beauty of this small creature, had it no other relation at all to man, would deserve a description.

For its strength, the *Microscope* is able to make no greater discoveries of it then the naked eye, but onely the curious contrivance of its leggs and joints, for the exerting that strength, is very plainly manifested, such as no other creature, I have yet observ'd, has any thing like it; for the joints of it are so adapted, that he can, as 'twere, fold them short one within another, and suddenly stretch, or spring them out to their whole length, that is, of the fore-leggs, the part A, of the 34. *Scheme*, lies within B, and B within C, parallel to, or side by side each other; but the parts of the two next, lie quite contrary, that is, D without E, and E without F, but parallel also; but the parts of the hinder leggs, G, H and I, bend one within another, like the parts of a double jointed Ruler, or like the foot, legg and thigh of a man; these six leggs he clitches up altogether, and when he leaps, springs them all out, and thereby exerts his whole strength at once.

But, as for the beauty of it, the *Microscope* manifests it to be all over adorn'd with a curiously polish'd suit of *sable* Armour, neatly jointed, and beset with multitudes of sharp pinns, shap'd almost like Porcupine's Quills, or bright conical Steel-bodkins; the head is on either side beautify'd with a quick and round black eye K, behind each of which also appears a small cavity, L, in which he seems to move to and fro a certain thin film beset with many small transparent hairs, which probably may be his ears; in the forepart of his head, between the two fore-leggs, he has two small long jointed feelers, or rather smellers, M M, which have four joints, and are hairy, like those of several other creatures; between these, it has a small *proboscis*, or *probe*, NNO, that seems to consist of a tube,

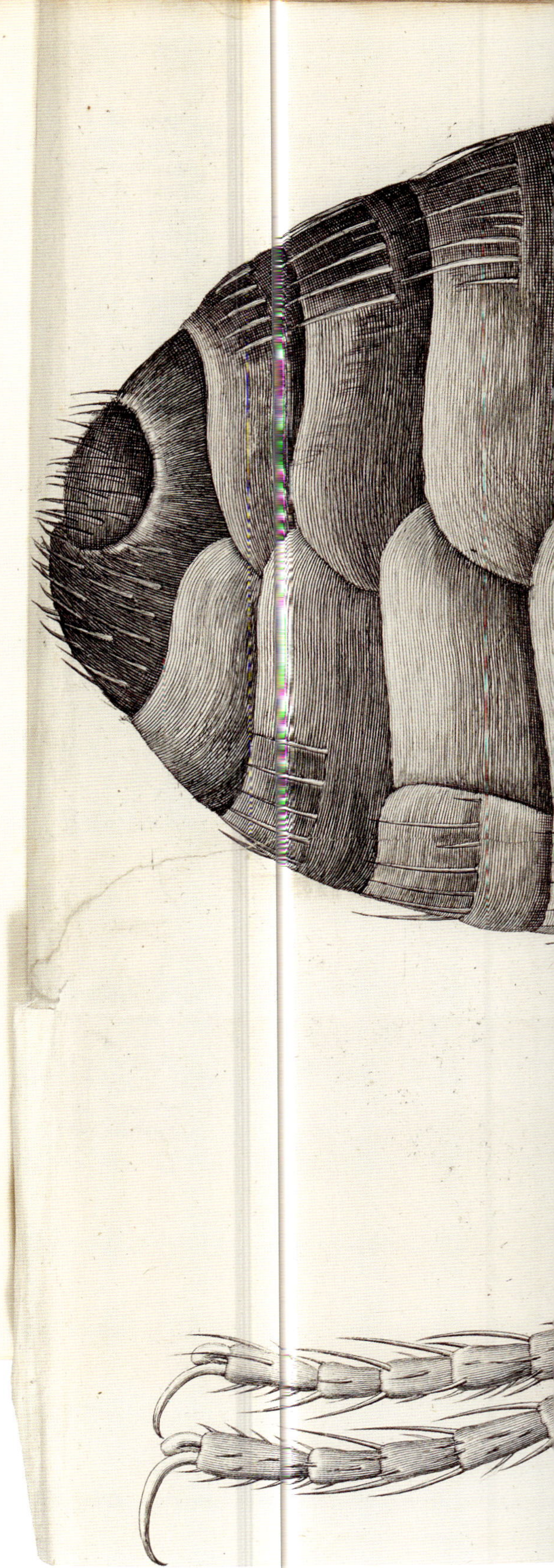

Schem XXXIV
L
K
E
I
F
E
F
D
G
M
H
D
H
A
B
C
B
G
G
A

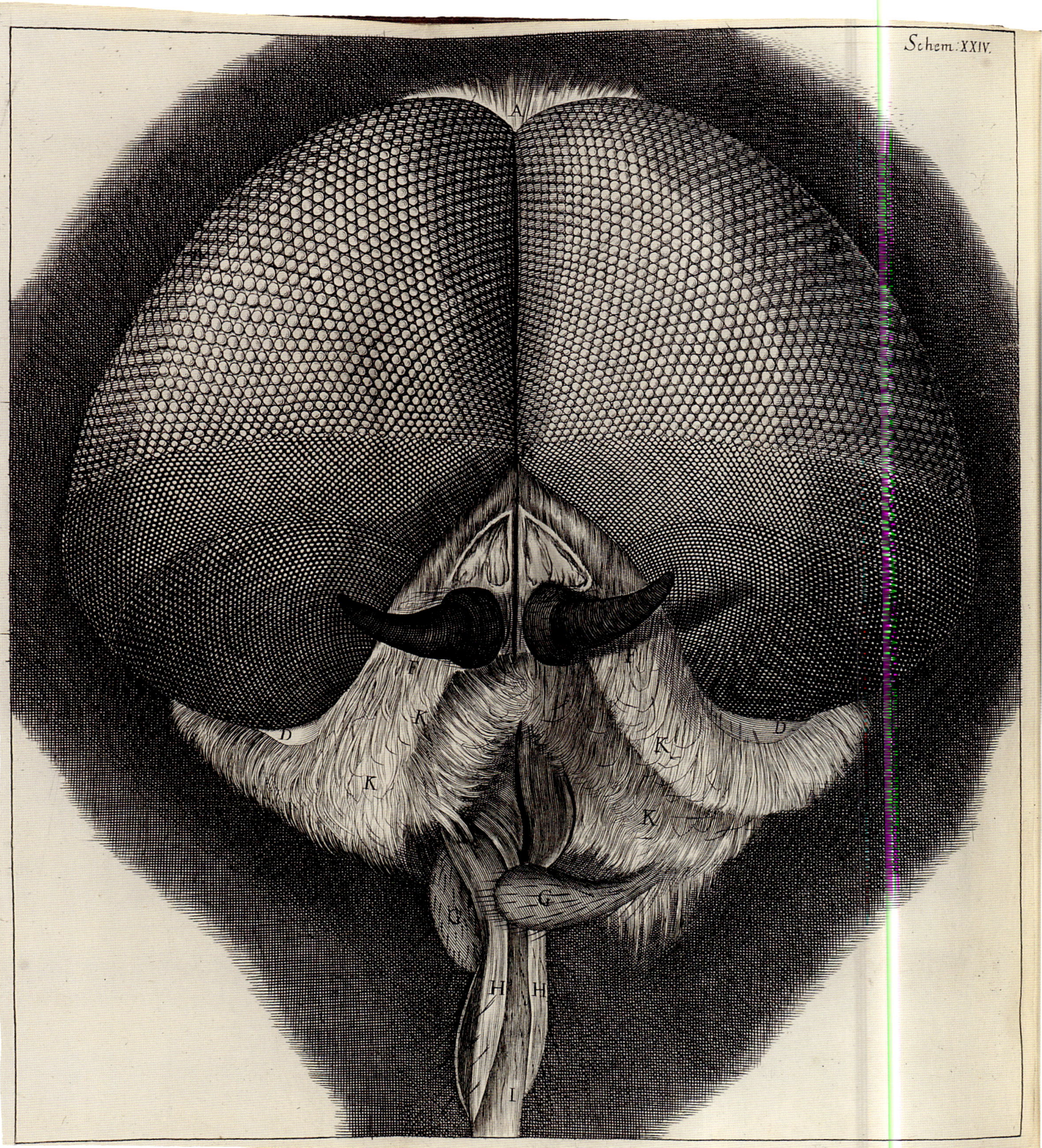
Schem: XXIV.
A
B
B
F
F
D
D
K
K
K
K
G
G
H
H
I

helps for the eye, as much exceeding those already found … which we may perhaps be able to discover living Creatures in the Moon, or other Planets, the figures of the compounding Particles of matter, and the particular Schematisms and Textures of Bodies.'[152]

Throughout the pages of *Micrographia*, Hooke presents his readers with never before seen microscopic marvels, inviting us at every juncture to open our minds to new worlds and our eyes to new perspectives, even on familiar objects. He begins with something as thoroughly ordinary as a needle. To the naked eye, the head of a needle appears perfectly smooth and sharp, but when viewed under a microscope it is anything but. Hooke describes it as 'irregular and uneven', revealing 'a multitude of holes and scratches and ruggednesses'.[153] Next, he examines something that appears right now before our eyes: the full stop. After analysing many kinds, printed and handwritten, he concludes that all of them, under magnification, appear 'like a great splatch of London dirt'. And in typical Hooke fashion, he says he thinks he knows of a method to produce microscopic writing, though he has yet to try it, and that such an invention could be used to convey secret messages – 250 years before the invention of microdots!

However, the star attraction of *Micrographia* is a creature all too familiar to seventeenth-century Londoners, regardless of their social status. Printed on a large fold-out sheet in an already large folio format book, is a flea. The brilliant Dutch polymath Christiaan Huygens (1629–95) remarked that it was as big as a cat – and, as it measured 43 × 33 cm, he was not exaggerating.

For Observation XVIII, Hooke used a razor-sharp penknife to produce a paper-thin slither of cork, which he then placed under his microscope against a black background. What he saw was astonishing: a dense honeycomb structure, leading him to coin the term 'cell'. What he found particularly remarkable was that, according to his calculations, these cells numbered 'above twelve hundred Millions' in a single cubic inch. Albeit without comprehending their true significance or biological function – that would not be understood for another 200 years – Hooke had observed the building blocks of all living organisms.

A large part of the appeal of Hooke's writing is that he is never ponderous or dispassionate. He pauses to comment on how beautiful insect wings are, and how 'prodigiously curious are the works of Nature'. Moreover, he sees in every discovery not so much an answer, an end, but a beginning, a door to yet further discoveries and potential practical applications. For example, in Observation XII – 'Of Gravel

104 Head and compound eyes of grey drone fly. From Robert Hooke's *Micrographia*, 1665.

in Urine' – he suggests that doctors might consider mixing some substance into urine to dissolve bladder stones. This would surely be a treatment preferable to excruciatingly painful pre-anaesthetic lithotomies, or massaging one's genitals with scorpion oil.[154]

When it comes to Hooke's scientific interests, it would probably be quicker to list those things he did not show an interest in. In *Micrographia* he describes the microscopic characteristics of silk and human hair, mouldy leather, charcoal, crystals and snowflakes; discoveres that snails ('a very anomalous creature') have teeth; illustrates the compound eyes of a flies; describes and illustrates the structure of feathers and wings, and the barbed bee's sting; explains how stinging nettles sting; and suggests that fossils are the petrified remains of extinct species. Hooke also strays into non-microscopical territories – from refraction, his 'undulatory' or wave theory of light and the nature of colour, lunar eclipses, gravity and the formation of lunar craters, even experimenting with clay, water and lead bullets to test whether they are the product of bombardment. Ever the optimist, he suggests the possibility of a telescope with a focal length of 10,000 feet (over 3,000 metres)!

Knowing all too well the expansiveness of Hooke's pursuits and passions, and his talent for tangents, the Royal Society insisted that *Micrographia* include a disclaimer for the more theoretical or conjectural aspects of his work. Hooke complied, writing in the dedication: 'And though I desire to have them understood only as Conjectures and Quæries … 'tis fit that I should declare, that it was not done by YOUR Directions.' The modern-day equivalent would be: 'the views expressed are my own and not those of my employer'.

The copy of *Micrographia* reproduced here is from the Bodleian Library. It was owned by Martin Lister (1639–1712), naturalist and Fellow of the Royal Society, and best known for his study of spiders, fossils and shells. Lister bequeathed his books to the Ashmolean Museum in Oxford. When the Ashmolean's books made their way to the Bodleian in 1860, Lister's copy of *Micrographia* was among them.

THE MOST INGENIOUS BOOK

In January 1665, with a copy of *Micrographia* hot off the press, the famed English diarist Samuel Pepys wrote: 'Before I went to bed I sat up till 2 a-clock in my chamber, reading of Mr. Hookes Microscopicall Observations, the most ingenious book that ever I read in my life.'[155] Three weeks later, Pepys joined the Royal Society as a fellow; in 1684, he was elected its president.

Although *Micrographia* was not the first book of microscopy, it was undoubtedly

105 A full-size replica of Robert Hooke's original compound microscope with illuminating system, probably made by John Mayall in the 1880s.

LONDONS fier began September the second, 1666.
To be sold by Tho: Parkhurst Nath: Ranew and Jonath: Robinson

the most influential, capturing not only the attention and respect of his peers in academia but, more crucially, the public imagination too. Until this day, *Micrographia* remains a landmark in the history of microscopy, of science textbooks and scientific illustration – thus paving the way for a new genre of popular science books.

Almost two years after the publication of *Micrographia*, Hooke's career would unexpectedly follow a very different trajectory. On 2 September 1666, following a particularly long, dry summer, a small fire broke out at Thomas Farriner's bakery on Pudding Lane in the City of London. Fanned by high winds, the fire swept through the city at an alarming pace through densely packed thatched-roof timber-framed buildings, crowded around narrow streets. More than 13,000 homes were destroyed, displacing 100,000 Londoners. The Rebuilding of London Act was passed in February 1667, and Hooke, despite no formal training as an architect, was appointed Surveyor of London on 13 March 1667. He worked alongside his close friend Christopher Wren, and together they rebuilt London. (Hooke's diary records 1,000 meetings between them.)

By the end of the seventeenth century, London had been almost entirely rebuilt. And although by that time the microscopy craze had waned, Hooke had already planted a seed that inspired a generation of scientists (or natural philosophers, as they were then known) towards countless new discoveries and entirely new scientific disciplines. Among them were Marcello Malpighi (1628–94), credited as the founder of microscopical anatomy and embryology; Antonie van Leeuwenhoek (1632–1723), a Dutch cloth merchant considered the founder of modern microbiology, who was the first to observe and detail bacteria and sperm cells; and Jan Swammerdam (1637–80), the first to describe red blood corpuscles, and notable for his early study of the anatomy of bees.

Micrographia was – and still is – a paean to nature, an invitation not only to stand before it enthralled, but to seek to probe its secrets, 'To see a World in a Grain of Sand', so to speak.[156] Hooke was one of the greatest experimental scientists of his century, and his restless genius, boundless enthusiasm, unbridled curiosity and sharp wit can be found on every page of *Micrographia*. He recounts that the ant had proven particularly challenging to draw because it would not stay still. His solution was to feed it brandy, which 'knock'd him down dead drunk'. The ant remained inebriated long enough for Hooke to complete his drawings, after which it came to and scuttled off while blowing bubbles.[157]

106 The Great Fire of London, woodcut from *Shlohavot, or, The Burning of London in the Year 1666*, Samuel Rolle, 1667.

18

METAMORPHOSIS

MERIAN, *METAMORPHOSIS INSECTORUM SURINAMENSIUM* (1719)

Therefore I would ask you to write all kinds of books, hesitating at no subject however trivial or however vast. By hook or by crook, I hope that you will possess yourselves of money enough to travel and to idle, to contemplate the future or the past of the world, to dream over books and loiter at street corners and let the line of thought dip deep into the stream.

Virginia Woolf, 1929[158]

The seventeenth-century Belgian chemist Jan Baptist van Helmont is best known as the founder of pneumatic chemistry, for inventing the word 'gas' and for identifying carbon dioxide. Fortunately, for his legacy's sake, he is less well known for proposing that sweaty clothes and wheat left outside in an open-mouthed jar for twenty-one days would spontaneously produce adult mice.[159] This idea of abiogenesis (spontaneous generation) had been popularly held since antiquity. It explained why, for example, maggots and rats suddenly appeared from rotting meat or carcasses. Aristotle, around 350 BCE, in *On the Generation of Animals*, was the first to articulate the theory that living organisms could appear spontaneously from inanimate matter. He claimed that certain animals, among them many insects, 'do not come into being from animals but from putrefying matter … [including] fleas, flies, and cantharides [a kind of beetle]'.[160] More than 2,000 years passed before Francesco Redi (1626–97) revealed how insects hatch from eggs.

A term not coined until the eighteenth century, entomology (the study of insects) was facilitated by the invention of the microscope at the turn of the seventeenth century. The Italian biologist Marcello Malpighi was the first to describe insect respiration in a paper on the anatomy of the silkworm published by the Royal Society in London in 1669. And it was the silkworm, in particular, that captivated the imagination of a rather brilliant German illustrator and entomologist.

107 Banana, moth *Saturniidae*, caterpillar and pupa. *Metamorphosis insectorum Surinamensium*, Maria Sibylla Merian, 1719 (second edition).

A ROOM OF ONE'S OWN

Maria Sibylla Merian was born in Frankfurt am Main in 1647. Her father, Matthäus Merian, was an accomplished painter, engraver and publisher. He died in 1650, when Maria was just three years old. The following year her mother Johanna Heim (also Heyne) married the still-life painter and tulip dealer Jacob Marrel (1613–81). From a young age Merian was fascinated by insects, collecting them, studying them and drawing them. By the age of thirteen she had already begun her study of insect metamorphosis, starting with silkworms. She was also, by this time, a skilled artist – having grown up surrounded by artists, and received instruction in painting, engraving and etching from her stepfather, his apprentices and her half-brothers. In 1665, aged eighteen, Merian married one of those apprentices, Johann Andreas Graff (1636–1701). In 1668 she gave birth to her first daughter Johanna, and the family moved to Graff's hometown of Nuremberg in 1670. Her second daughter, Dorothea, was born in 1678.

After publishing the first two parts of a three-part series of flower pattern books, Merian published the first of a two-volume series on caterpillars, *Der Raupen Wunderbare Verwandelung und Sonderbare Blumennahrung* (*The Wondrous Transformation and Particular Food Plants of Caterpillars*). In these two volumes she demonstrates her particular expertise (besides her evident artistic talents), which is to introduce an ecological aspect to her work, describing insect behaviour and drawing insects in their natural habitats. She describes their life cycles and illustrates their transformation from egg to larva to pupa to adult. Providing further context, she adds flora not simply for decoration, as was then common, but to show the very plants that these insects lived among and fed upon. Later, when in Surinam, she completed the picture in her texts by noting where and when she encountered her living specimens, even recording scents, sounds and taste – the sweet smell of wild jasmine, the watermelon that 'melts in the mouth like sugar', fireflies that sound like lyres, humming wasps dancing about her head while she painted, and the sonorous chorus of myriad other creatures reverberating through the unrelenting heat and humidity of the rainforest. Unlike the wealthy collectors who amass beautiful – dead and articulated – insect specimens for their *Wunderkammer* (cabinet of curiosities), Merian was interested in insects not as static exotica but as living creatures with stories worth telling.

Merian also perfected a novel printing technique called a counterproof. After making a regular print on the roller press, and while the ink was still wet, she would lay another piece of paper on top of it and send it through the press again – thus producing a print of a print. In intaglio printing, lines engraved with a burin are known for their precision and crispness, but a counterproof print yields a silkier, softer line that more closely resembles a hand-drawn line. This method also does not leave a plate impression. Merian by no means invented the counterproof, but she appears to have been the only one at the time to have used it as the basis for hand-coloured copies of her illustrations.[161]

In 1686 Merian – without her husband, but with her two daughters and her mother – moved to live with the Labadists, a pious religious community in the village of Wieuwerd in the Netherlands, named after its French founder and former Jesuit Jean de Labadie (1610–74). Merian's half-brother Caspar had been living there since 1677. When her mother died in 1691 she left the community for Amsterdam, then an incredibly wealthy trade centre owing to the Eastern exploits of the Dutch East India Company (at the time, the world's richest company).

A PERILOUS JOURNEY

In June 1699 Merian, now aged fifty-two, accompanied by her youngest daughter Dorothea, set sail for Surinam on the tropical north-east coast of South America. But why Surinam? The Labadist community, whom Merian had left eight years earlier, lived on the Walta-slot estate, which had been donated by three aristocratic Labadist converts, Anna, Maria and Lucia Aerssen van Sommelsdijk. Their brother Cornelis served as governor of the Dutch colony in Surinam from 1683 until 1688 (when he was shot and killed by mutineers). As governor he had encouraged the Labadists to settle in Surinam, which they did from 1683. Another Surinam connection was that, in 1692, Merian's eldest daughter Johanna had married Jacob Hendrik Herolt, a former Labadist who now traded with the West Indies and Surinam.

Surinam had been inhabited by Indigenous peoples since around 3000 BCE. During the 1650s British colonists established a plantation colony in Surinam, with thousands who had been kidnapped and enslaved from the west coast of Africa. By the early 1660s hundreds of plantations had already been established there. Then, towards the end of 1666, a severe 'raging contagion and wasting sickness' spread through the population.[162] Taking advantage of this, a Dutch fleet of seven ships and a thousand men appeared over the eastern horizon, and a battle ensued. After several

De Surnamse Bank
is Week Moddergront
Brams Punt
Krabbe Bosch
DE LAND
Moerassig
Comowini
Stroom
Cottica Stroom
DE LAND STR
Lant
Moerassig
Cottica Stroom
Batterÿ en Wagthuis
Wilden
t Fort Zeelandia
Gouverneurs Huys
PARIMARIBO of Nieu MIDDELBURG
't Fort Cottica of Sommelsdyk
T EILANT COTTICA
T EILANT SURINO
T EILANT TUINHUISEN
t Fort Para
DE LANDSTREEK VAN PARA
DE LANDSTREEK VAN SURINAME
STREEK VAN COMOWI
Iooden Dorp en Sinagoge
Suriname Stroom
Para Creek
Paramibil of Blauwen berg
Wagthuis
Armadille bergen of Hill
Hangton Hil
Duitsche Mylen 15 in een Graad
Uuren gaans van 20 in een Graad

108 Map of Surinam.
Joachim Ottens, before
1718.

hours of fighting, and once they had all but run out of gunpowder, the British colonists surrendered. Surinam was ceded to the Dutch Republic. In exchange, the British got to keep New Netherlands, including New Amsterdam – present-day New York City.

Maria and Dorothea's journey from Amsterdam to Surinam, with a stopover in the Canary Islands to stock up on supplies, typically took between six and eight weeks. In 1699 it was no pleasure cruise. The quarters were cramped and uncomfortable, and if storms and hurricanes did not sink the ship, then pirates might steal it. It was a perilous journey. Once, a ship carrying Labadist colonists to Surinam had been intercepted by pirates who stole everything, including their ship and cargo, and the clothes they wore. And even when colonists made it to Surinam with their lives and their clothes, most were woefully ill-prepared. The mortality rate was high for European settlers – they succumbed to the stifling heat and humidity, and to tropical diseases, parasitic worms and dietary complaints.[163]

By the time Merian arrived in September 1699, Providence, the Labadist settlement some 80 km inland along the Surinam River, was all but abandoned. She stayed there for some weeks from April to June 1700, but lived in Paramaribo. From this base she ventured out into the rainforest to gather and study tropical insects and plants, aided by Indigenous and African slaves, who in addition to their manual labours taught her about the various dietetic and medicinal properties of local flora and fauna. In her commentary to plate 45, Merian describes how the seeds of the peacock flower (which she calls *flos pavonis*) are used by Arawak and African slaves as an abortifacient:

> The Indians, who are not treated well by their Dutch masters, use the seeds to abort their children, so that their children will not become slaves like they are … In fact, they sometimes take their own lives because they are treated so badly, and because they believe they will be born again, free and living in their own land. They told me this themselves.[164]

BUTTERFLIES AND PINEAPPLES

'I almost had to pay for it with my life', Merian wrote of her time in Surinam.[165] After almost two years, sickness (probably a tropical disease) forced her and her daughter to leave. They set sail from Surinam in June 1701, arriving back home in Amsterdam in late September. Once home, Merian got to work transforming the materials from her field trip into a remarkable book.

following pages

left 109 Pineapple (*Ananas comosus*) in bloom and cockroaches. *Metamorphosis insectorum Surinamensium*, Maria Sibylla Merian, 1719 (second edition).

right 110 Ripe pineapple (*Ananas comosus*). *Metamorphosis insectorum Surinamensium*, Maria Sibylla Merian, 1719 (second edition).

Neither her long and costly journey to Surinam nor her book were sponsored. She had supported herself through commissions and the sale of her paintings, drawings and preserved specimens collected in Surinam and shipped to collectors in Europe. But how would she finance her book, with its substantial upfront costs? Her solution was to kickstart the project by pre-selling copies to subscribers. In 1705 *Metamorphosis insectorum Surinamensium* (*Metamorphosis of Surinamese Insects*) finally rolled off the presses. This deluxe large format book, measuring approximately 53 × 36 cm and weighing more than 6 kg, was available in both uncoloured and hand-coloured versions – for 15 and 45 guilders respectively.

Merian hoped that her book would appeal to a wide audience, 'to art connoisseurs as well as to amateurs of insects and plants' – and she succeeded. *Metamorphosis* is an insect book, an ecological study and a work of art. It's easy to imagine freshly printed and meticulously painted copies of *Metamorphosis* brought to large tables in sun-filled drawing rooms or parlours, their crisp oversized pages turned slowly before wide-eyed visitors.

After a two-page *ad lectorem* (letter to the reader), in which Merian sketches a thumbnail autobiography, she opens with two plates of pineapples – a fruit native to South America. It might appear odd to open a book about insects with pictures of pineapples, but it was the ideal place to begin. This now familiar, though still exotic, emblem of paradise was a rare and expensive delicacy dubbed the 'King of Fruits'.[166] Merian explains in her commentary that the pineapple 'is the most important of all edible fruits, [so] it is only right that it is also the first', and describes its taste 'as though one had mixed grapes, apricots, red currants, apples and pears, and were able to taste all of them at once'.[167]

A second edition of *Metamorphosis* appeared posthumously in 1719, containing an additional twelve plates. Ten were supplied by Merian's daughters, and two appear to have been based on designs found in the collection of Albertus Seba (1665–1736), the apothecary and obsessive collector who owned one of the most impressive cabinets of curiosities in Europe. Among the new plates, perhaps contributed by Dorothea, is the scene of a spectacled caiman battling with a false coral snake that is attempting to steal one of its hatchlings (see fig. 111). The new edition is also supplied with a charming neoclassical frontispiece in which half a dozen putti rifle through specimen boxes, while through the tall archway, in the centre background, Merian chases butterflies in an idealized Surinamese landscape (fig. 113).

LEGACY

In January 1717, several months before her seventieth birthday and after a long illness, Maria Sibylla Merian died in Amsterdam. Her daughters and students continued the trailblazing journey she had begun as a child. Invited by Peter the Great, her daughter Dorothea and her husband Georg Gsell moved to St Petersburg. Her daughter Johanna, along with her husband Jacob Hendrik Herolt, moved to Surinam in 1711. He ran an orphanage in Paramaribo, while she continued to study insects, to paint and to collect specimens for sale in Europe.

Maria Sibylla Merian was acclaimed during her own lifetime. *Metamorphosis* was well received, both in the scientific community and by amateurs well-off enough to afford copies. The pioneering Swedish naturalist Carl Linnaeus (1707–78), famed for his work in taxonomy and who introduced Latin binomial nomenclature (genus + species), frequently cited Merian's work, using it to name about 100 species. Her illustrations (and those of her daughters) too were widely imitated: an almost exact copy of the above-mentioned caiman and snake illustration appears as plate 69 in Linnaeus's *Systema naturae* (*General System of Nature*). Goethe famously praised Merian's ability to move effortlessly 'between art and science, between nature observation and artistic intention'.[168]

111 Spectacled Caiman (*Caiman crocodilus*) and South American False Coral Snake (*Anilius scytale*), from *Metamorphosis Insectorum Surinamensium*, Maria Sibylla Merian, 1719 (second edition).

But during the nineteenth century, Merian's reputation came under attack. After her death in 1717 some uncoloured copies of her books were inexpertly coloured, and in some instances plates from her early floral pattern books (intended purely for decoration and for use by embroiderers and water-colourists) were appended to later editions of her work. These bastardized works and some posthumous mistranslations were wrongly attributed to her, and led to wholly unjustified criticisms of her. Merian lived during a time when women were still barred from universities.[169] Typically, for women, independent travel was difficult and very unusual. While male students often travelled throughout Europe as part of their education (a kind of finishing school), women were encouraged to stay at home and pursue actives that would better prepare them for housewifery.

Thankfully, Merian's reputation has since been restored by less prejudicial and more dispassionate commentators. Determined and independent, she was an autodidact, an entrepreneur and a teacher. The first female entomologist and arguably the first ecologist, she established a new way of looking at insects – an ecological perspective that illuminated

FIG. LXIX.

opposite 112 Pomelo *Pomelmoes* with moth *Uraniidae*, caterpillar and pupa. *Metamorphosis insectorum Surinamensium*, Maria Sibylla Merian, 1719 (second edition).

left 113 Frontispiece to *Metamorphosis insectorum Surinamensium*, Maria Sibylla Merian, 1719 (second edition).

their behaviour and habitats and the symbiotic relationships which sustained them.

There are about 255,000 species of Lepidoptera, the order of butterflies and moths. About 9 per cent are butterflies. These creatures weigh less than a gram and the full stop at the end of this sentence is larger than a butterfly's brain. And yet, each year, thousands of millions of painted ladies (*Vanessa cardui*), the world's most widespread species of butterfly, set off on a 13,000 km round trip between Europe and sub-Saharan Africa. These butterflies live no longer than a month, so their intercontinental migration is completed over six generations.[170] There is still much to be learned about these extraordinary creatures – the systematic study of them was begun by pioneers such as Maria Sibylla Merian.

114 Merian discovered this red flower and caterpillar in January 1701. The butterfly is from the *Nymphalidae* family. *Metamorphosis insectorum Surinamensium*, Maria Sibylla Merian, 1719 (second edition).

EPILOGUE
BACON'S ARK AND WITTGENSTEIN'S GLASSES

Are there not some pursuits that we practise because they are good in themselves … I have sometimes dreamt, at least, that when the Day of Judgment dawns and the great conquerors and lawyers and statesmen come to receive their rewards – their crowns, their laurels, their names carved indelibly upon imperishable marble – the Almighty will turn to Peter and will say, not without a certain envy when he sees us coming with our books under our arms, 'Look, these need no reward. We have nothing to give them here. They have loved reading.'

VIRGINIA WOOLF, 1925[171]

We have come a long way. We have travelled around the world and across centuries. Our eighteen remarkable books were printed over a period of 250 years, from Johannes Gutenberg in the mid-fifteenth century to Maria Sibylla Merian at the beginning of the eighteenth. How much had the world changed during those two and a half centuries? And how much of that change had been wrought by books?

In 1450 the entire world was inhabited by about 400 million people. Europe's population, only just beginning to bounce back from the Black Death pandemic a hundred years before, stood at less than 60 million. During the next 250 years the population of Europe would double, despite massive emigration from Europe to the Americas. The world Gutenberg lived in was at the centre of a small, anthropocentric universe. Much of what was understood about their 6,000-year-old world was inherited from antiquity and the Middle Ages. Gutenberg and his contemporaries were completely unaware that another continent existed across the Atlantic Ocean. No one but the inhabitants of the Americas had any clue that the Americas existed. It was discovered by outsiders accidentally when, in 1492, Columbus, trying to find a westerly route to the East Indies, bumped into what he then christened the West Indies.

115 Painted cover for a manuscript book of Persian poetry, 1582.

By the time this happened, printing in Europe had spread to almost every major European city. But if the growth of printing in Gutenberg's century was impressive, the next century made it pale in comparison. By conservative estimates, 10 million books were printed in the fifteenth century. By the end of the sixteenth, it was more than 150 million. Southern centres, led by the Italian peninsula and Venice, had dominated printing in the fifteenth-century, but the next century marked the rise of northern print centres, notably Paris, Lyon, Basel, Antwerp, London and (the anomalous) Wittenberg.[172] The same century saw printing extend its reach beyond Europe. Printing was introduced to Africa via Fez in Morocco in 1516; the first press in the Western hemisphere was established in Mexico City in 1539 by its first bishop, Juan de Zumárraga, and reached India via Goa in 1556. Printing in North America would not commence for another century, when Stephen Daye printed his first book in the then-British colony of Massachusetts in 1640.

VERNACULARIZATION

Bibles, books of hours, psalters, missals, law books (canon and civil), grammars and the Greek and Roman classics – these were the staples and bestsellers of the fifteenth century. Almost three-quarters of all the books printed in that century were in Latin. If you were a contemporary of Johannes Gutenberg and decided you wanted a book to teach yourself, say, astronomy, then Sacrobosco's hugely popular introductory astronomy textbook, *De sphaera* (*The Sphere*), written around 1230 and available in print from 1472, was the best place to begin. If you did not read Latin, then you would have had to wait until the next century before *De sphaera* was translated into vernacular languages, including English, German, French and Italian. These translations reflected a growing demand for vernacular texts.

Latin had for centuries been the language for writing and learning in Europe, but even before the advent of print, vernacular texts had slowly been on the rise. This steady vernacularization had been propelled by Europe's fragmentation and the consolidation of monarchies and national cultural identities (including the national vernacular), and would be accelerated, albeit unevenly, by events in the early decades of the sixteenth century. The Protestant Reformation, ignited by Luther and propelled by print, not only fomented profound religious and political change but radically 'transformed the dynamics of the printing industry'.[173] Luther had taken theology and biblical exegesis, until then debated by dusty scholastics in turgid and inscrutable medieval Latin, and transformed it into lively, colloquial German prose. The Reformation demonstrated that there was a significant latent demand for cheap printed literature in the vernacular.

PRINTED EVERYTHING

Europe experienced considerable economic growth in the sixteenth century, fuelled directly and indirectly by colonialism and slavery. The same century witnessed an attendant rise in literacy. Some studies indicate that literacy rates rose from around 11 per cent in 1500 to about 60 per cent by 1750.[174] Improved literacy meant more readers, and more readers meant increased demand for books. Publishers soon began to cater for this new and demographically broader readership with new kinds of printed literature: illustrated encyclopaedias, recreational and how-to books, and books for children that for the first time combined learning and entertainment. There was a proliferation of new genres and formats, from religious and political tracts and pamphlets to broadside ballads and chapbooks hawked on busy street corners and in village squares. From this deluge of printed ephemera emerged, in the first decade of the seventeenth century, the newspaper. It was in part made possible by cheaper print, improvements in infrastructure and the expansion of postal systems, which facilitated both the gathering of news and its dissemination in print.

ORGANIZING KNOWLEDGE

In the late sixteenth century, physicians, apothecaries, naturalists and the otherwise curious (and wealthy) began amassing sometimes enormous collections in *Wunderkammer*, known in English as a cabinet of curiosities (fig. 116). At this time, a cabinet also referred to a small room, like a private study or studio. These baroque-style manifestations of *horror vacui* displayed hundreds or even thousands of pieces, mounted on the walls and even across the ceiling. On display were a broad variety of objects and artefacts, including skeletons, stuffed animals, insects, fossils, plant specimens, coins, medals, paintings, drawings and antiquities – and some items with dubious provenance, such as vials of dragon's blood, basilisks and unicorn horns. These cabinets of curiosities were the forerunners of modern museums.

As the world expanded, and the flood of information and books continued to grow, there arose an ever more pressing need for better ways to order and systematize knowledge – a desire later described as *l'esprit géometrique*

(the quantifying spirit).[175] This spirit is exemplified in the Swedish naturalist Carl Linnaeus's taxonomic hierarchy and biological nomenclature, a timely solution for the growing number of newly discovered plant and animal species. The campaign to organize knowledge also found expression in the way books were designed – paratextual elements such as title pages, page numbers, running heads, tables of contents and alphabetical indexes were gradually adopted to facilitate informational wayfinding and retrieval.

AN ARK TO LEARNING

But how about systems for organising and accessing information across hundreds or even thousands of books? The seventeenth century marked the beginning of the golden age of another kind of institution, one concerned with collecting and preserving knowledge – the library. In 1605 the philosopher and statesman Francis Bacon gave the Bodleian Library at the University of Oxford a copy of his new book, *The Advancement of Learning*. He described the library, recently refitted and reopened as 'an Ark to save learning from deluge'.[176] The deluge he spoke of was the Reformation, an event that threatened to drown the whole of Europe. But the Bodleian Library survived that deluge, and others, and thrived owing to the foresight of its visionary founder, Sir Thomas Bodley (1544–1613). In 1587 Bodley married Ann Ball (née Carew), the wealthy widow of a successful pilchard merchant. In 1597, after a successful career as a diplomat and roving ambassador for Queen Elizabeth, Bodley retired from public life, devoting his energies and fortune to the library.

The Bodleian's first librarian, Thomas James, appointed by Bodley in 1602, published the first printed catalogue of the Bodleian Library's collection in 1605. It followed the long medieval tradition of arranging by faculties – arts, theology, law and medicine – but with, for the time, a novel revision. The books within each faculty were arranged in roughly alphabetical order. Broad classification systems had served libraries well for centuries, when even large libraries typically held hundreds rather than thousands of books and catered to only a handful of visitors, but they were beginning to crack under the weight of millions of new printed books. From the early seventeenth century, alphabetical order was beginning to catch on, although Burke suggests that its adoption was more an acknowledgement of 'defeat by the forces of intellectual entropy at a time when new knowledge was coming into the system too fast to be digested or methodized'.[177]

previous pages

116 Woodcut of a cabinet of curiosity in Ferrante Imperato's *Dell'historia naturale*, 1599.

117 The Bodleian Library and Schools Quadrangle from the south. *Oxonia illustrata*, David Loggan, 1675.

All of the remarkable books featured in the preceding chapters live on shelves in that splendid 'ark of learning', the Bodleian Library. Inaugurated on 8 November 1602, with about 2,500 books, it is now home to more than 13 million printed items.

WHAT IS A BOOK?

You might think this question rather overdue. Would it not have made more sense to pose it at the outset? But bear with me, please; it's Ludwig Wittgenstein's fault. I began this book with an epigraph, a quote from that great Austrian philosopher. As a reminder, it reads, 'The aspects of things that are most important for us are hidden because of their simplicity and familiarity. (One is unable to notice something – because it is always before one's eyes.)'[178] Indeed, the most commonplace, ordinary and familiar things are those most readily taken for granted. Books are among those familiar and ubiquitous items. As an object, a printed book is made of ink printed on sheets of paper, folded, collated, sewn or glued, and bound between covers. But all books live lives beyond their pages. The purpose of this book has been to highlight those lives, exposing rich histories and sometimes ancient prehistories, and describing their enduring and profound legacies.

So, then, what is the remedy for our tendency to look past the familiar and ordinary – an antidote to the age-old problem of failing to see the wood for the trees? In an earlier analogy Wittgenstein describes us as philosophizing (or observing the world) through glasses which we never think to take off.[179] The answer is to take off the glasses or, to leave behind the analogy, to look at everything, even the apparently ordinary, afresh – to begin not with preconceptions and assumptions but with an open mind, with boundless curiosity and awe. In highlighting the rich prehistories, lives and legacies of the volumes featured in these pages, it is my hope that the volume now in your hands has sparked more than a little wonder for the ubiquitously familiar, yet remarkable, book.

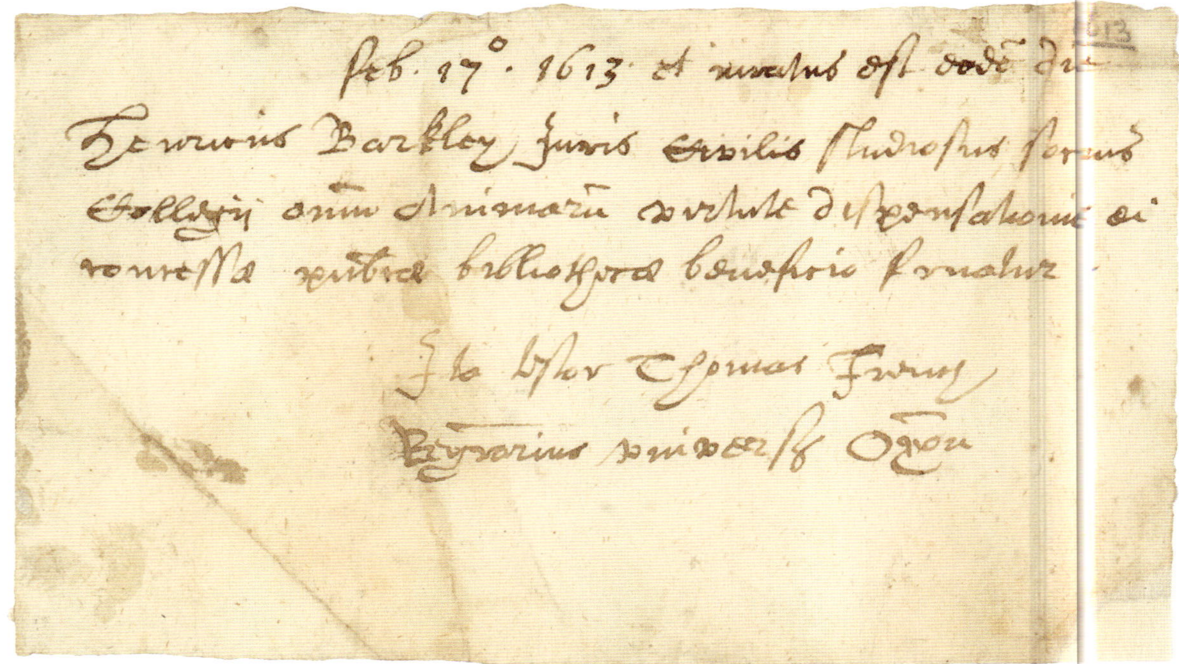

right 118 Earliest known 'reader's card', Oxford. This small slip of paper gave Henry Barkley of All Souls College, Oxford permission to use the Bodleian Library, 1613/14.

opposite 119 Book wheel from Agostino Ramelli's *Le diverse et artificiose machine del capitano*, 1588.

NOTES

Prelims

1. Ludwig Wittgenstein, *Philosophical Investigations,* third edition, tr. G.E.M. Anscombe, Macmillan Publishing, New York, 1958, p. 50.

Introduction

2. Excerpt from 'The Boston Athenaeum', in Louis Untermeyer (ed.), *The Complete Poetical Works of Amy Lowell*, Houghton Mifflin Company, Boston, 1925, p. 22.
3. Plato, *Phaedrus,* 14, 274c–275b. Also Walter Ong, *Orality and Literacy: The Technologizing of the Word*, 30th anniversary (third) edition, Routledge, London and New York, 2012, pp. 78–9.
4. Maryanne Wolf, *Proust and the Squid: The Story and Science of the Reading Brain*, Icon Books, London, 2008, p. 73.
5. 'Reading is not a conversation; it does not discuss, it does not question. It never asks of the book, and still less of the author: "What did you mean exactly? What truth, then, do you bring me?"' Maurice Blanchot, *The Space of Literature*, University of Nebraska Press, Lincoln, NE, and London, 1982, p. 193.
6. Cited in Katja Weirauch and Michele Cammarosano, 'WoW! Writing on Wax in Ancient Mesopotamia and Today: Questions and Results from an Interdisciplinary Project', in Lucia Raggetti (ed.), *Traces of Ink: Experiences of Philology and Replication*, Brill, Leiden and Boston, 2021, p. 13, n. 14.
7. While the traditional date for the invention of modern paper is 105 CE, it might well have been used for wrapping or packaging in the first or second centuries BCE. See James Raven (ed.), *The Oxford Illustrated History of the Book*, Oxford University Press, Oxford, 2020, p. 35. Also Joseph Needham and Tsuen-hsuin Tsien, *Science and Civilization in China, vol. 5: Chemistry and Chemical Technology*, Cambridge University Press, Cambridge, 1985, pp. 38–41.
8. Erik Kwakkel, *Books Before Print,* Arc Humanities Press, Leeds, 2018, p. 8.
9. David Cressy, *Literacy and the Social Order: Reading and Writing in Tudor and Stuart England,* Cambridge University Press, Cambridge, 1980, pp. 159–63, 175–90. Male and female literacy in most of Europe would not begin to reach parity until the twentieth century.
10. From Bacon's *Refutation of Philosophies*, cited in Peter Burke, *A Social History of Knowledge: From Gutenberg to Diderot*, Polity Press, Cambridge, 2000, p. 114. The shortcomings of Aristotle's physics did not go unnoticed during the Middle Ages, but 'the deference that was paid to it during the Middle Ages was a great brake on scientific progress'. Anthony Kenny, *A New History of Western Philosophy*, Oxford University Press, Oxford and New York, 2010, p. 501.
11. Ptolemy in the second century stated the distance to the edge of the cosmos, to the sphere of fixed stars, to be about 20,000 e.r. (Earth radii). Johannes Kepler in the seventeenth century proposed a distance of 60 million e.r. to the stars. Using the present-day measurement of Earth's radius (6,371 km), we arrive at a distance to the stars (or radius of the cosmos) of about 382 billion kilometres.
12. Brian Cowan, *The Social Life of Coffee*, Yale University Press, New Haven, 2005, pp. 25, 30, 90; see also Adrian Johns, 'Coffeehouses and Print Shops', in Katherine Park and Lorraine Daston (eds), *The Cambridge History of Science, vol. 3: Early Modern Science*, Cambridge University Press, New York, 2006, pp. 320–40 (esp. pp. 332–40).
13. Entry dated 21 January 1665. Robert Latham and William Matthews (eds), *The Diary of Samuel Pepys, vol. VI: 1665*, University of California Press, Berkeley, 1974.

1. From Pilgrims to Print

14. Cited in Stephan Füssel, *Gutenberg*, Haus Publishing Ltd, London, 2019, pp. 149–50.
15. 'Tribus digitis scribitur totum corpus laborat. Orate pro me qui istum librum legerit.' Bibliothèque Nationale de France. Département des Manuscrits, Latin 9561, fol. 81v.
16. See Richard Schwab et al., 'Cyclotron Analysis of the Ink in the 42-Line Bible', *The Papers of the Bibliographical Society of America*, 77:3, 1983, pp. 285–315; Richard Schwab et al., 'New Evidence on the Printing of the Gutenberg Bible: The Inks in the Doheny Copy', *The Papers of the Bibliographical Society of America*, 79:3, 1985, pp. 375–410; T.A. Cahill et al., 'Gutenberg's Inks and Papers: Non-destructive Compositional Analyses by Proton Milliprobe', *Archaeometry*, 26, 1984, pp. 3–14.
17. McCarthy suggests that the paper was made elsewhere, in the Duchy of Savoy or in Basel. See Isabel Feder McCarthy, 'Ad Fontes: A New Look at the Watermarks on Paper Copies of the Gutenberg Bible', *The Library,* 17:2, 2016, pp. 115–37.
18. Letter dated 12 March 1455. Cited in Füssel, *Gutenberg*, p. 145.
19. Twelve million is a conservative estimate, based on 30,000 editions and an average print-run of 400 copies per edition. The Incunabula Short Title Catalogue (ISTC, https://data.cerl.org/istc) lists almost 30,000 editions (accessed 2 January 2025). On fifteenth-century print-runs, see Eric Marshall White, 'A Census of Print Runs for Fifteenth-Century Books', *CERL, the Consortium of European Research*

Libraries, 2012: https://www.cerl.org/resources/incunabula/main#e_white_researching_print_runs (accessed 2 January 2025). On manuscript production, see Jacques Verger, 'Schools and Universities', in *The New Cambridge Medieval History, vol. 7: c.1415–c.1500*, Cambridge University Press, Cambridge, 1998, pp. 220–24, 226; E. Buringh and J.L. Van Zanden, 'Charting the "Rise of the West": Manuscripts and Printed Books in Europe, a Long-Term Perspective from the Sixth through Eighteenth Centuries', *Journal of Economic History*, 69:2, 2009, pp. 409–45, Table 1, p. 416, and Table 2 p. 417; Eltjo Buringh, *Medieval Manuscript Production in the Latin West*, Brill, Leiden, 2011, Table 5.6, pp. 262, 315–95.

2. Illuminating Pliny

20. *Natural History,* 2.5. Translation by H. Rackham from Pliny the Elder, *Natural History*, vol. I: Books 1–2, Loeb Classical Library, Harvard University Press, Cambridge, MA, and London, 1949, pp. 180–81.
21. Daisy Dunn, *The Shadow of Vesuvius: A Life of Pliny*, Liveright Publishing Corp., New York, 2019, p. 57, paraphrasing *Natural History*, 7.167.
22. On the *Natural History* as an encyclopaedia, see Aude Doody, *Pliny's Encyclopedia: The Reception of the Natural History*, Cambridge University Press, Cambridge and New York, 2010. Also Aude Doody, 'Pliny's "Natural History: Enkuklios Paideia" and the Ancient Encyclopedia', *Journal of the History of Ideas*, 70:1, 2009, pp. 1–21. Candidates for compiling earlier encyclopaedias include Aulus Cornelius Celsus (*c.*25 BCE–*c.*50 CE). The earliest surviving technical encyclopaedia is the Chinese *Kao Gong Ji* (*The Artificer's Record*), written sometime between the sixth and third centuries BCE. Zengjian Guan and Konrad Herrmann (eds), *Kao Gong Ji: The World's Oldest Encyclopaedia of Technologies*, Brill, Leiden and Boston, 2020.
23. Jacob Burckhardt, *The Civilization of the Renaissance in Italy*, Penguin Books, London, 1990, p. 41.
24. Pliny, *Historia naturale*, 1476, 1v. Translation from Andrea Rizzi, 'Editing and Translating Pliny in Renaissance Italy: Agency, Collaboration and Visibility. Issues in Translation', *Renæssanceforum*, 14, 2018, p. 126.
25. Pliny the Elder, *Natural History*, Preface 6, tr. John F. Healy, Penguin Books, New York, 2004, p. 4.
26. Edler de Roover, 'Per La Storia Dell'arte Della Stampa in Italia: Come Furono Stampati a Venezia Tre Dei Primi Libri in Volgare', *La Bibliofilía*, 55:2, 1953, p. 110.
27. Eve Borsook, 'Filippo Strozzi and the Two Plinys: Civic Pride, Diplomacy, and Private Taste in Quattrocento Naples and Florence', *I Tatti Studies in the Italian Renaissance*, 23:1, 2020, p. 13.
28. From Pliny the Younger's letter to Tacitus (6.16). On the two letters, see Nicholas F. Jones, 'Pliny the Younger's Vesuvius "Letters" (6.16 and 6.20)', *The Classical World*, 95:1, 2001, pp. 31–48.
29. E.J. Kenney and W.V. Clausen (eds), *The Cambridge History of Classical Literature, vol. 2: Latin Literature*, Cambridge University Press, Cambridge, 1992, p. 670.

3. History in Your Hands

30. Cited in Denys Hay, *Annalists and Historians: Western Historiography from the Eighth to the Eighteenth Century*, Routledge, London and New York, 2016, p. 3.
31. Eusebius's Greek manuscript of *Chronicon* has not survived. The earliest surviving manuscripts are of Jerome's translation, of which one of the oldest extant is the Bodleian Library's MS. Auct. T. 26, ascribed to the fifth century. On the dating of the *Chronicon*, see R.W. Burgess, 'The Dates and Editions of Eusebius' "Chronici Canones and Historia Ecclesiastica"', *The Journal of Theological Studies*, 48:2, 1997, pp. 471–504. The *Chronicle* of Eusebius comprised two books: the *Chronography* (a chronographical encyclopaedia) and the *Canon* (chronological tables presented as parallel timelines).
32. On the familiar arguments for why Christians preferred the codex over the roll, see Colin Roberts and T.C. Skeat, *The Birth of the Codex*, Oxford University Press, Oxford, 1983, ch. 9, pp. 45–53; for alternative hypotheses, see ch. 10, pp. 54–61.
33. *The Brill Encyclopedia of the Medieval Chronicle* lists some 2,500 chronicles dating from late antiquity until 1500.
34. The 1493 broadside advertisement, pasted into Schedel's copy of the *Nuremberg Chronicle*, is reproduced and translated in Stephan Füssel, *The Book of Chronicles: The Complete and Annotated Nuremberg Chronicle of 1493*, Taschen, Cologne, 2018, p. 9, fig. 3.
35. From the introduction to the *Nuremberg Chronicle*, fol. 2r.
36. *Liber Chronicarum*, 1493, fol. 201v. For the alleged crucifixion in 1144 of a twelve-year-old English boy by Jews, see also fol. 239v. See E.M. Rose, *The Murder of William of Norwich: The Origins of the Blood Libel in Medieval Europe*, Oxford University Press, Oxford, 2015.

4. Luca and Leonardo

37. Aristotle, *Metaphysics*, XIII, 1078b. Jonathan Barnes (ed.), *The Complete Works of Aristotle: The Revised Oxford Translation*, vol. 2, Princeton University Press, 1984, p. 1705.
38. Caleb Everett, *Numbers and the Making of Us: Counting and the Course of Human Cultures*, Harvard University Press, Cambridge, MA, 2017, p. 125.
39. The two extant copies of the deluxe manuscript edition are now at Biblioteca Ambrosiana (Milan) and the Bibliothèque de Genève.
40. Oxford Bodleian Library shelfmark: Douce VV 42; USTC: 862078. Giorgio Vasari, *The Lives of the Artists*, Oxford University Press, Oxford, 1998, p. 163. Vasari writes that Pacioli came into possession of Piero's manuscripts after Piero's death in 1492 (ibid., p. 163); see also Argante Ciocci, *Luca Pacioli tra Piero della Francesca e Leonardo*, Aboca Museum Edizioni, Sansepolcro, 2009, p. 96.
41. Richard Earl and James Nicholson (eds), *The Concise Oxford Dictionary of Mathematics*, sixth edition, Oxford University Press, Oxford, 2021, p. 431.
42. Euclid, *Elements*, Book II, Proposition 11. Thomas L. Heath (tr.), *The Thirteen Books of the Elements, vol. 1: Books 1–2*, Dover Publications, New York, 1956, pp. 402–3.
43. An expression coined, I believe, by Roger Herz-Fischler. Roger Herz-Fischler, 'The Home

of Golden Numberism', *The Mathematical Intelligencer*, 27, 2005, pp. 69–71.

44. 'Eighty Nautilus shells were measured in the Smithsonian collection. The results show that the Nautilus genus is clearly not the widely quoted 4:3 (1.333), but averaged 1.310 … the Crusty Nautilus [averaged] 1.356.' C. Bartlett, 'Nautilus Spirals and the Meta-Golden Ratio Chi', *Nexus Network Journal*, 21, 2019, p. 641.
45. A. Ciocci, *Luca Pacioli tra Piero della Francesca e Leonardo*, Sansepolcro, AR: Aboca Museum Edizioni, 2009, cited in Alan Sangster, 'Pacioli's Lens: God, Humanism, Euclid, and the Rhetoric of Double Entry', *The Accounting Review*, 93:2, 2018, p. 306.
46. 'Tolle numerum in rebus omnibus, et omnia pereunt.' *Etymologies*, Book III.4. English translation from Stephen A. Barney, W.J. Lewis, J.A. Beach and Oliver Berghof (tr.), *The Etymologies of Isidore of Seville*, Cambridge University Press, Cambridge, 2006, p. 90.

5. Catapults and Cornices

47. Martial, *Epigrams*, Book 5.56. Martial, *Epigrams, vol. I: Spectacles, Books 1–5*, ed. and tr. D.R. Shackleton Bailey, Loeb Classical Library 94, Harvard University Press, Cambridge, MA, 1993, p. 375.
48. Ingrid Rowland and Thomas N. Howe (eds), *Vitruvius: 'Ten Books on Architecture'*, Cambridge University Press, Cambridge, 1999, p. 1.
49. Henry Millon, 'The Architectural Theory of Francesco Di Giorgio', *The Art Bulletin*, 40:3, 1958, pp. 257–61.
50. Jean Paul Richter (ed.), *The Notebooks of Leonardo da Vinci*, Dover Publications Inc., New York, 1970 (Paris Ms. A, 55v).
51. Vitruvius, *De architectura*, 1.6.12. Translation from M.H. Morgan (tr.), *Vitruvius: The Ten Books on Architecture*, Harvard University Press, Cambridge, MA, 1914. In one instance, when Vitruvius attempts to describe the water organ of Ctesibius (a musical instrument), he admits defeat, not even promising pictorial corroboration, but suggesting instead that readers will understand if they just go and look for themselves. 'Quodsi qui parum intellexerit ex scriptis, cum ipsam rem cognoscet profecto inveniet curiose et subtiliter omnia ordinata', *De architectura*, 10.8.6.
52. The Carolingian and earliest extant manuscript of *De architectura* is Harley 2767, now in the British Museum (the drawing is on fol. 16v). Frank Granger, 'The Harleian Manuscript of Vitruvius (H) and the Codex Amiatinus', *Journal of Theological Studies*, 32, 1930, pp. 74–7. Two leaves from Harley 2767 are now in the Oxford Bodleian Library (Rawlinson MS D. 893, fols. 135–136).
53. Leon Battista Alberti, in his own architectural treatise, *De re aedificatoria* (*c.*1450), book 6, ch. 1, famously lampooned Vitruvius for his impenetrable prose: 'What [Vitruvius] had passed on was not refined: for he spoke so that to Latins he would have seemed a Greek, and the Greeks would have guessed him to be a Latin. The book itself will attest that it was neither Latin nor Greek; so he might as well never have written it at all, since he wrote in a way that we don't understand.' Leon Battista Alberti, *L'architettura (De re aedificatoria)*, ed. Giovanni Orlandi, Il Polifilo, Milan, 1966, p. 443.
54. Giorgio Vasari, *Lives of the Most Eminent Painters, Sculptors and Architects*, vol. 4, Philip Lee Warner, London, 1913, p. 138.
55. Cecelia Lahiff, 'Aemulatio and Sprezzatura: Palladio and the Legacy of Vitruvius', *Art Journal*, 1:3, 2018, p. 13.

6. A Wedding and Four Funerals

56. On Francesco de Madiis's *Zornale*, see Cristina Dondi and Neil Harris, 'Best Selling Titles and Books of Hours in a Venetian Bookshop of the 1480s: The Zornale of Francesco de Madiis', *La Bibliofilía*, 115:1, 2013, pp. 63–82; and Cristina Dondi and Neil Harris, 'Oil and Green Ginger. The Zornale of the Venetian Bookseller Francesco de Madiis, 1484–1488', in Malcolm Walsby and Natasha Constantinidou (eds), *Documenting the Early Modern Book World*, Brill, Leiden, 2013, pp. 341–406.
57. Gesamtkatalog der Wiegendrucke (GW08045) ascribes the printing to Johannes Reinhard, *c.*1475.
58. William Ivins Jr, 'Geoffroy Tory', *The Metropolitan Museum of Art Bulletin*, 15:4, 1920, p. 82.
59. 'Alexander the vi pope of Rome hath granted to all them that say this prayer devoutly, in the worship of Saint Anna and our Lady and her son Jesus, v thousand years of pardon for deadly sins, and xx years for venial sins, totiens quotiens.' Edgar Hoskins, *Horæ Beatæ Mariæ Virginis: Or, Sarum and York Primers …*, Longmans, New York, London and Bombay, 1901, p. 123. See also R. Swanson (ed.), *Promissory Notes on the Treasury of Merits: Indulgences in Late Medieval Europe*, Brill, Leiden, 2018, p. 230, n. 57.
60. Martina Bagnoli, *Prayers in Code: Books of Hours from Renaissance France*, Walters Art Museum, Baltimore, 2009, p. 3. By contrast, Jean Gerson (1363–1429) argued that understanding the prayers was not the point – reciting them was: 'In this ritual act, *understanding* mattered less than *fidelity*'. Virginia Reinburg, *French Books of Hours: Making an Archive of Prayer, c.1400–1600*, Cambridge University Press, Cambridge, 2012, pp. 89 and 92; see also Roger S. Wieck, *Time Sanctified: The Book of Hours in Medieval Art and Life*, George Braziller, New York, 1988, p. 40.
61. Cited in Virginia Reinburg, 'Hearing Lay People's Prayer', in Barbara B. Diefendorf and Carla Alison Hesse (eds), *Culture and Identity in Early Modern Europe (1500–1800): Essays in Honor of Natalie Zemon Davis*, University of Michigan Press, Ann Arbor, 1993, p. 19.
62. The concept of books of hours as archives of prayer was introduced by Virginia Reinburg. Virginia Reinburg, *French Books of Hours: Making an Archive of Prayer, c.1400–1600*, Cambridge University Press, Cambridge, 2012, pp. 4–5.
63. Petrarch writing to Giovanni Boccaccio (*Familiaris* XXIII 19), cited in Igor Candido (ed.), *Petrarch and Boccaccio: The Unity of Knowledge in the Pre-modern World*, De Gruyter, Berlin, 2018, p. 17, n. 6. See also B.L. Ullman, *The Origin and Development of Humanistic Script*, Edizioni di Storia e letteratura, Rome, 1960, pp. 12–13.

7. Northern Renaissance

64. Jean Paul Richter (ed.), *The Literary Works of Leonardo da Vinci: Compiled and Edited From the Original Manuscripts*, vol. 1, p. 327 (no. 653), London, 1883. The original Italian reads: 'L'occhio, che si dice finestra dell'anima, è la principale via donde il comune senso può piú copiosamente e magnificamente considerare le infinite opere di natura.'
65. Letter dated October 1506. Albrecht Dürer and Roger Fry, et al., *Dürer's Record of Journeys to Venice and the Low Countries*, The Merrymount Press, Boston, 1913, pp. 26–7. We do not know the identity of the teacher Dürer sought out, but Scipione del Ferro (1465–1526) and Luca Pacioli (see pp. 57–65) have been proposed.
66. Albrecht Dürer and David Price, *De symmetria partium in rectis formis humanorum corporum / Underweysung der Messung*, Octavo, Palo Alto, CA, 2003, p. 84 (A1v).
67. The five Platonic solids are: tetrahedron (or pyramid), cube, octahedron, dodecahedron and icosahedron. Each is an enclosed or convex solid in which each face is an identical regular polygon. Dürer also covers semi-regular polyhedra, also known as Archimedean solids.
68. Albrecht Dürer and David Price, *De symmetria partium*, p. 166 (O6r).
69. In Latin, *velum*. Also known as 'Alberti's window'. Leon Battista Alberti, *De pictura*, 1435–36, Book II.7; Leon Battista Alberti and Cecil Grayson, *On Painting and On Sculpture: The Latin Texts of De Pictura and De Statua*, Phaidon, London, 1972, pp. 68–9.
70. Cited in Giulia Bartrum, *Albrecht Dürer and His Legacy: The Graphic Work of a Renaissance Artist*, The British Museum Press, London, 2002, p. 16. On the so-called 'Dürer renaissance' (*c*.1570–*c*.1630), see pp. 266–7.

8. Paper Cosmos

71. *Georgics*, Book 2. John Dryden, *The Works of Virgil Containing his Pastorals, Georgics and Æneis*, third edition, London, 1709, lines 677–80, p. 144.
72. Recently, parts of Hipparchus's star catalogue were discovered in a medieval palimpsest. Victor Gysembergh, P. Williams and E. Zingg, 'New Evidence for Hipparchus' Star Catalogue Revealed by Multispectral Imaging', *Journal for the History of Astronomy*, 53:4, 2022, pp. 383–93.
73. Ptolemy, *Almagest*, Book 1.7. *Ptolemy's Almagest*, tr. G.J. Toomer, Duckworth, London, 1984, p. 44.
74. Owen Gingerich, 'Apianus's Astronomicum Caesareum', *Journal for the History of Astronomy*, 2, 1971, p. 168.
75. Translation from John North, 'Werner, Apian, Blagrave and the Meteoroscope', *The British Journal for the History of Science*, 3:1, 1966, p. 61, n. 14.
76. USTC: 678038; Oxford Bodleian Library shelfmark: Arch. B d.25.

9. The Walking Dead

77. Francis Bacon, *Novum organum scientiarum*, 1620. Bacon's original Latin reads: 'Melius autem est naturam secare, quam abstrahere.'
78. Peter J. Koehler and Christopher J. Boes, 'A History of Non-Drug Treatment in Headache, particularly Migraine', *Brain*, 133:8, 2010, pp. 2489–500.
79. David C. Lindberg, *The Beginnings of Western Science*, University of Chicago Press, Chicago and London, 1992, p. 120. On Herophilus of Chalcedon and Erasistratus of Ceos, see H. von Staden, 'The Discovery of the Body: Human Dissection and its Cultural Contexts in Ancient Greece', *The Yale Journal of Biology and Medicine*, 65:3, 1992, pp. 223–4; N.S. Bay and B.H. Bay, 'Greek Anatomist Herophilus: The Father of Anatomy', *Anatomy & Cell Biology*, 43:4, 2010, pp. 280–83; and James Longrigg, 'Anatomy in Alexandria in the Third Century B.C.', *The British Journal for the History of Science*, 21:4, 1988, pp. 455–88.
80. 'After the fall of Rome the practice [human dissection] was forbidden by the church'. J.B. Frank, 'Body Snatching: A Grave Medical Problem', *The Yale Journal of Biology and Medicine*, 49:4, 1976, p. 399. The belief that the church prohibited human dissection is refuted in Katherine Park, 'The Criminal and the Saintly Body: Autopsy and Dissection in Renaissance Italy', *Renaissance Quarterly*, 47:1, 1994, pp. 1–33 (esp. p. 7). Later misinterpretation of a bull issued by Pope Boniface VIII in 1299 (reissued in 1300) appears to be the source of misconceptions concerning outright prohibitions on human dissections. However, the bull applied explicitly to the common practice of eviscerating and boiling corpses; the remaining bones were then returned home for burial – no one wanted to lug a rotting corpse halfway across the world! The bull does not prohibit or even reference dissection. See also Nancy Siraisi, *Medieval and Early Renaissance Medicine*, University of Chicago Press, Chicago and London, 1990, pp. 86–90.
81. *Fabrica*, 1543. Translation from Fabio Zampieri, et al., 'Andreas Vesalius: Celebrating 500 years of Dissecting Nature', *Global Cardiology Science & Practice*, 66, 2015, p. 12.
82. Paraphrased from M. Kemp, 'A Drawing for the *Fabrica*; and Some Thoughts upon the Vesalius Muscle-Men', *Medical History*, 14:3, 1979, p. 277.
83. From the charter of ennoblement creating Vesalius a Count Palatine. Charles D. O'Malley, et al., 'Andreas Vesalius, Count Palatine: Further Information on Vesalius and his Ancestors', *Journal of the History of Medicine and Allied Sciences*, 9:2, 1954, pp. 207–8.
84. *Fabrica*, Book 5, 1543. Andreas Vesalius, *On the Fabric of the Human Body: A Translation of De Humani Corporis Fabrica Libri Septem, Book V: The Organs of Nutrition and Generation*, Norman Publishing, Novato, CA, 2007, p. 183.
85. Theodore E. Mommsen, 'Petrarch's Conception of the "Dark Ages"', *Speculum*, 17, no. 2, 1942, pp. 226–42.

10. Unicorns and the Sausage Supper Affair

86. Aristotle, *Parts of Animals*, Book 1, 645a21–23. Jonathan Barnes (ed.), *The Complete Works of Aristotle: The Revised Oxford Translation*, vol. 1, p. 1004.
87. Genesis 1:20–22; 2:19–20.
88. H. Wellisch, 'Conrad Gessner: A Bio-Bibliography', *Archives of Natural History*, 7:2, 1975, p. 194.
89. Christophe Plantin's Antwerp printshop, one of the most acclaimed in Europe, took three months to complete the hand-colouring of a book for Severinus Gobelius (*Plantarum seu stirpium icones*, 1581) with almost 2,200 illustrations, according to a letter dated October 1581, from Plantin to Gobelius.

Correspondance de Christophe Plantin, 1883, pp. 315–16 (letter 954). On the prices of the coloured and plain versions, see Sachiko Kusukawa, 'Gessner's History of Nature', in H. Curry, N. Jardine, J. Secord and E. Spary (eds), *Worlds of Natural History*, Cambridge University Press, Cambridge, 2018, p. 37.

90. Nora Epstein, 'It's all Gucci (and Gessner)', *Preserving the World's Rarest Books* (blog), 29 April 2020 https://pwrb.wp.st-andrews.ac.uk/its-all-gucci-and-gessner (accessed 30 May 2022).
91. Plutarch, *Theseus*, 1.1: 'Just as geographers, O Socius Senecio [a Roman senator], crowd on to the outer edges of their maps the parts of the earth which elude their knowledge, with explanatory notes that "What lies beyond is sandy desert without water and full of wild beasts", or "blind marsh", or "Scythian cold" or "frozen sea", so in the writing of my *Parallel Lives*, … I might well say of the earlier periods "What lies beyond is full of marvels and unreality, a land of poets and fabulists, of doubt and obscurity."'
92. Contrary to popular opinion, the phrase 'here be dragons', or similar, was never used on medieval maps. The phrase in Latin (*hic sunt dracones*) first appeared in about 1510 on the Hunt–Lenox Globe, now at the New York Public Library.
93. Gessner, *History of Animals*, vol. 1, 1551, p. 785, section G. See Laurent Pinon, 'Conrad Gessner and the Historical Depth of Renaissance Natural History' in Gianna Pomata and Nancy G. Siraisi (eds), *Historia: Empiricism and Erudition in Early Modern Europe*, 2005, MIT Press, Cambridge, MA, p. 250.
94. Anna Pavord, *The Naming of Names: The Search for Order in the World of Plants*, Bloomsbury, New York, 2005, p. 287.

11. Renaissance Invention

95. William Ivins Jr, *Prints and Visual Communication*, MIT Press, Cambridge, MA, 1969, p. 3.
96. On the emergence of professional print-publishers, see David Landau and Peter Parshall, *The Renaissance Print, 1470–1550*, Yale University Press, New Haven and London, 1994, pp. 219–20. Also Jan van der Stock, *Printing Images in Antwerp: The Introduction of Printmaking in a City, Fifteenth Century to 1585*, Sound & Vision Interactive, Rotterdam, 1998, pp. 181–2. On peintre-graveurs, see ibid., pp. 106–7.
97. On Luigi Alamanni and his relationship with Stradanus, see Lia Markey (ed.), *Renaissance Invention: Stradanus's Nova Reperta*, Northwestern University Press, Evanston, IL, 2020, pp. 26–37. Also Lia Markey, 'Stradano's Allegorical Invention of the Americas in Late Sixteenth-Century Florence', *Renaissance Quarterly*, 65:2, 2012, pp. 385–442. On their collaboration on an unfinished series of prints on the sport of *calico* (football), see Dorine van Sasse van Ysselt, 'Il Calcio Fiorentino disegnato da Giovanni Stradano', *Mitteilungen des Kunsthistorischen Institutes in Florenz*, 37:2/3, 1993, pp. 481–7.
98. Felipe Fernandez-Armesto, *Amerigo: The Man Who Gave His Name to America*, Random House, New York, 2007, Preface.
99. William M. Denevan (ed.), *Introduction to the Native Population of the Americas in 1492*, second edition, University of Wisconsin Press, Madison, 1992, p. 5. Catherine M. Cameron, Paul Kelton and Alan C. Swedlund (eds), *Beyond Germs: Native Depopulation in North America*, University of Arizona Press, Tucson, 2015, argue compellingly that disease has been overemphasized as a cause of depopulation, while the deliberate erasure of Indigenous identities and systematic genocide has been downplayed.
100. Bacons's *Novum organum*, 1620, book 1, aphorism 129, line 105, cited in Michael Gaudio, *Engraving the Savage: The New World and Techniques of Civilization*, University of Minnesota Press, Minneapolis, 2008, p. xviii. Before Bacon, the Italian polymath Girolamo Cardano (1501–76) had singled out the same three inventions (the *nautica pyxis* or 'mariners' compass', 'printing books with type', and 'military artillery' or gunpowder) in his encyclopaedic *De subtilitate rerum*, 1550 (USTC: 662761). John M. Forrester (ed.), *The 'De Subtilitate' of Girolamo Cardano*, Arizona Center for Medieval and Renaissance Studies, Temple, 2013, p. 823 (this English translation is based on the Basel edition of 1560; USTC 601654; Bodleian Library shelfmarks: Byw. L 2.10,11 and Savile S 11).

12. You Are Here

101. Credited to Gilbert H. Grosvenor, founding editor of *National Geographic* magazine. https://www.nationalgeographic.com/maps/article/about-maps (accessed 2 January 2025).
102. Denis Wood, *Rethinking the Power of Maps*, Guilford Press, New York, 2010, p. 24.
103. Strabo, *Geography, vol. I: Books 1–2*, tr. Horace Leonard Jones, Loeb Classical Library 49, Harvard University Press, Cambridge, MA, 1917, 2.5.10, p. 449.
104. Alexander V. Podossinov (ed.), *The Periphery of the Classical World in Ancient Geography and Cartography*, Peeters, Leuven, 2014.
105. William Dahlman, *William Tyndale: The Translator of the English Bible*, Concordia Pub. House, St Louis, MO, 1904, p. 205.
106. Jeremy W. Crampton, 'Maps as Social Constructions: Power, Communication and Visualization', *Progress in Human Geography*, 25:2, 2001, p. 239.
107. Carl Sagan, *Pale Blue Dot: A Vision of the Human Future in Space*, Ballantine Books, New York, 1994, pp. 6–7.

13. A Star Is Born

108. *Cosmos: A Personal Voyage*, TV series by PBS, 1980–81.
109. Max Caspar, *Kepler*, Dover Publications, New York, 1993, p. 36.
110. Ibid., p. 46.
111. Kepler, *Harmonices mundi* (1619), cited in Aviva Rothman, 'Kepler's Astrological Play', in Patrick J. Boner, *Kepler's New Star (1604): Context and Controversy*, Brill, Leiden, 2021, p. 132 and n. 22.
112. Heading borrowed from Christopher M. Graney, 'Of Mites and Men (and Stars): Kepler on the Question of Star Sizes in *De stella nova*', in Boner, *Kepler's New Star*, pp. 41–62.
113. In his *Almagest* (V.16), Ptolemy calculated the distances to and sizes for the Moon and Sun. In his *Planetary Hypotheses* he addresses the distances to the other celestial bodies.

Ptolemy believed the Earth's radius to be about 28,667 stades, or very approximately 5,230 km (it is actually 6,371 km). Ptolemy's estimated distances were generally accepted until the time of Copernicus. See Albert Van Helden, *Measuring the Universe: Cosmic Dimensions from Aristarchus to Halley*, University of Chicago Press, Chicago, 1985, p. 30, Table 2. Al-Farghani computed a distance to the fixed stars of 20,110 e.r. Al-Battani (*c.*858–929) claimed 19,000 e.r. to the sphere of fixed stars. Bruce Stephenson, 'Distances to the Planets', in *The Music of the Heavens: Kepler's Harmonic Astronomy*, Princeton University Press, Princeton, 1994, Table 4.1, p. 70. On the influence of Ptolemy's planetary distances on medieval Arab astronomers, see W. Hartner, 'Medieval Views on Cosmic Dimensions and Ptolemy's Kitab al-Manshurat', in A. Koyré, *Mélanges Alexandre Koyré, publiés à l'occasion de son soixante-dixième anniversaire*, Hermann, Paris, 1964, vol. 1, pp. 254–82. For Kepler's estimates, see Van Helden, *Measuring the Universe*, pp. 87–8.

114. 'Tycho simply stated that in the Copernican scheme the fixed stars had to be at least 700 times as far away from the Sun as Saturn is, that is, about 7,850,000 e.r.' Ibid., p. 51.

115. 'There is some evidence to suggest that the majority of massive stars above ~20 M may collapse quietly to black holes and that the explosions remain undetected.' Stephen J. Smartt, 'Progenitors of Core-Collapse Supernovae', *Annual Review of Astronomy & Astrophysics*, 47:1, 2009, p. 63.

116. 'An upper limit of 6.4 kpc to the distance [to SN 1604] can be derived based on the lack of H I absorption.' E.M. Reynoso and W.M. Goss, 'A New Determination of the Distance to Kepler's Supernova Remnant', *The Astronomical Journal*, 118:2, pp. 926–9. Nagayoshi et al. adopt a conservative distance of 4 kpc. Tsutomu Nagayoshi, Aya Bamba, Satoru Katsuda and Yukikatsu Terada, 'Detection of the Hard X-ray Non-Thermal Emission from Kepler's Supernova Remnant', *Publications of the Astronomical Society of Japan*, 73:2, 2021, p. 303. Compare the references in D.A. Green, 2022, 'A Catalogue of Galactic Supernova Remnants, (2022 December version), Cavendish Laboratory, Cambridge, United Kingdom, https://www.mrao.cam.ac.uk/surveys/snrs/snrs.G4.5+6.8.html (accessed 27 February 2023).

117. Not all parts of the ejecta or debris from Kepler's Nova are moving at a uniform speed. 'We estimate high radial velocities of up to ~8000 km s^{-1} for some of these ejecta knots.' Matthew J. Millard, et al., 'An Ejecta Kinematics Study of Kepler's Supernova Remnant with High-resolution Chandra HETG Spectroscopy', *The Astrophysical Journal*, 893:2, 2020, p. 1.

14. Forging Heaven

118. *The Song of Hiawatha by Henry Wadsworth Longfellow*, James R. Osgood & Co., Boston, 1874, p. 35.

119. Albert Van Helden, Sven Dupré, Rob van Gent and Huib Zuidervaart (eds), *The Origins of the Telescope*, Knaw Press, Amsterdam, 2010, p. 11.

120. Owen Gingerich and Albert Van Helden, 'From OCCHIALE to Printed Page: The Making of Galileo's Sidereus Nuncius', *Journal for the History of Astronomy*, 34:3, 2003, p. 254.

121. Ibid., p. 251.

122. Galileo Galilei, *Sidereus Nuncius, or The Sidereal Messenger*, tr. with introduction, conclusion and notes by Albert Van Helden, second edition, University of Chicago Press, Chicago and London, 2016, p. 42.

123. Ibid., p. 64. For a concise summary of pre-telescopic views of the Milky Way, see Stanley L. Jaki's illuminating, albeit whiggish, 'The Milky Way Before Galileo', *Journal for the History of Astronomy*, 2:3, 1971, pp. 161–7. For a fuller treatment see, by the same author, *The Milky Way: An Elusive Road for Science*, David and Charles, Newton Abbot, 1973. Also W.J. Wintemberg, 'Myths and Fancies of the Milky Way', *Journal of the Royal Astronomical Society of Canada*, 2, 1902, pp. 235–47. For Aristotle's view, see his *Meteorology*, 345a10–30: *The Complete Works of Aristotle: The Revised Oxford Translation*, vol. 1, pp. 555–66. Also Tofigh Heidarzadeh, 'Aristotle's Theory of Comets', in *A History of Physical Theories of Comets, From Aristotle to Whipple*, Springer, Dordrecht, 2008, pp. 16–17. On North American Indian beliefs, see William B. Gibbon, 'Asiatic Parallels in North American Star Lore: Milky Way, Pleiades, Orion', *The Journal of American Folklore*, 85:337, 1972, pp. 236–47.

124. Galileo, *Sidereus Nuncius*, p. 64.

125. Ibid., p. 61. This might explain the omission of the Orion Nebula (M42). See Michael Hoskin, 'Nebulae, Star Clusters and the Milky Way: From Galileo to William Herschel', *Journal for the History of Astronomy*, 39:3, 2008, p. 364.

126. As recorded in Guido Bentivoglio's *Memorie* (1648; ISTC: 4018660). Bentivoglio was Galileo's former student and one of ten cardinal-inquisitors present at Galileo's trial in 1633. As cited in J.L. Heilbron, *Galileo*, Oxford University Press, Oxford, 2010, p. 31[illegible], n. 251, p. 369. On Galileo's trial, I enthusiastically recommend Thomas F. Mayer (ed.), *The Trial of Galileo, 1612–1633*, University of Toronto Press, Toronto, 2012. Also Richard J. Blackwell, *Behind the Scenes at Galileo's Trial: Including the First English Translation of Melchior Inchofer's 'Tractatus syllepticus'*, University of Notre Dame Press, Notre Dame, IN, 2006.

127. Gingerich and Van Helden, 'From OCCHIALE to Printed Page', p. 251.

15. The Book on the Moon

128. William Barlow, *The Svmme and Svbstance of the Conference ... at Hampton Court Ianu. 14. 1603* [i.e. 1604], John Norton, London, 1638, p. 46.

129. Bodleian Library shelfmark: MS Auct. D.2.19. Kenichi Tamoto (ed.), *The Macregol Gospels or The Rushworth Gospels*, John Benjamins Publishing, Amsterdam and Philadelphia, 2013, pp. xxv–xxxii; the Latin text is the Insular Vulgate version; ibid., pp. xxxii–xxx[illegible].

130. Henry Knighton cited in Alister McGrath, *In the Beginning: The Story of the King James Bible and How It Changed a Nation, a Language, and a Culture*, Anchor Books, New York, 2002, p. 20.

131. In 1551, while Estienne was living in Geneva. Earlier Bibles, such as the Great Bible of 1539, for example, had indicated chapter numbers but not verses. The Geneva Bible of 1560 (substantially revised in 1572) was also the first

English Bible to be printed entirely in roman rather than blackletter type. Subsequent editions, however, returned to using blackletter: 'Evidently some regarded this as too daring an innovation'. Bruce M. Metzger, 'The Geneva Bible of 1560', *Theology Today*, 17:3, 1960, p. 342. Also Bruce M. Metzger, *The Bible in Translation: Ancient and English Versions*, Baker Academic, Grand Rapids, MI, 2001, pp. 65–6.

132. William Barlow, *The Svmme and Svbstance of the Conference ... at Hampton Court, Ianu. 14. 1603* [i.e. 1604], John Norton, London, 1638, p. 47.
133. For example, the marginal note to Daniel 6:22 in the Geneva Bible reads: 'For he did disobey the king's wicked commandment to obey God, and so did no injury to the king, who ought to command nothing whereby God should be dishonored' (spelling modernized). '[T]here were margin notes that appeared to suggest the legitimacy of resistance to overweening rulers, and there was the frequent use of the language of tyrant (a word expressly disallowed in James' Bible) and slave.' Julia Ipgrave, *Adam in Seventeenth Century Political Writing in England and New England*, Taylor and Francis, London, 2017, p. 14; see also Maurice S. Betteridge, 'The Bitter Notes: The Geneva Bible and Its Annotations', *The Sixteenth Century Journal*, 14:1, 1983, pp. 41–62. Specifically on the Geneva Bible's marginal note to Exodus 1:19, see Adam Nicolson, *God's Secretaries: The Making of the King James Bible*, Harper, London, 2003, pp. 58–9.
134. British Library, MS Harley 750, fol. 1v, rule 6 (emphasis added).
135. 'For the New Testament Tyndale's contribution is about 84 per cent of the text, while in the Old Testament about 76 per cent of his words have been retained.' Jon Nielson and Royal Skousen, 'How Much of the King James Bible is William Tyndale's? An Estimation Based on Sampling', *Reformation*, 3:1, 1998, p. 49.
136. For the Bible left on the Moon during the Apollo 15 mission, see https://history.nasa.gov/alsj/a15/a15.clsout3.html (accessed 16 April 2023). St Christopher Episcopal Church in League City, Texas, which donated the Bible to Commander Colonel David R. Scott, confirmed that the Bible was indeed a King James translation (correspondence, 1 July 2023).

16. Out of Eden

137. Marcel Proust, *Le temps retrouvé*, Chatto & Windus, London, 1927.
138. Michael Rice, *Who's Who in Ancient Egypt*, Routledge, London, 1999, pp. 183–4.
139. Ellen Churchill Semple, 'Ancient Mediterranean Pleasure Gardens', *Geographical Review*, 19:3, 1929, p. 441. On Pliny and Roman window-boxes, see J. Linderski, '"Imago Hortorum": Pliny the Elder and the Gardens of the Urban Poor', *Classical Philology*, 96:3, 2001, pp. 305–8. Martial also spoke of 'window gardens' (*Epigrams*, 11.18.1–2).
140. In his Italian translation and commentary of Dioscorides, *Commentarii in sex libros Pedacii Dioscoridis Anazarbei de medica materia*, 1544, p. 327: 'Le Mele adunque insane sono frutti d'una pianta volgare, che nasce per tutto, come fanno i melloni, & le zucche, lequali ai coltivano co'l medesimo modo, & mangiansi volgarmente fritte nell'oglio, con sale, & pepe, come i funghi.' Transcribed from the McGill University Library copy (Osler Room Collection: folio WZ 240 D594dm 1544).
141. Philipp Hainhofer, cited in Nicolas Barker, *Hortus Eystettensis: The Bishop's Garden and Besler's Magnificent Book*, Harry N. Abrams, New York, 1994, p. 3.
142. The first fifty plates were produced in the Augsburg workshop of Wolfgang Kilians. Signatures on other plates suggest that perhaps most of the remainder were produced in Nuremberg. Mara Hofmann and Caroline Zöhl, *Hortus Eystettensis: Studien zur Entstehung des Kupferstichwerks und zum Exemplar des Andrea Vendramin*, Universität Heidelberg, Heidelberg, 2003, pp. 6, 38–9. In 1998, 328 of the 367 original copperplates, including the title page, were discovered in the Albertina Museum in Vienna. R. Doppelbauer, V. Birke and M. Kiehn, 'Die Kupferplatten zum "Hortus Eystettensis"', *Wiener Geschichtsblätter*, 54:1, 1999, pp. 22–32.
143. It was 100,000 florins, according to Philipp Hainhofer's account, cited in Barker, *Hortus Eystettensis*, p. 2.
144. Arthur Harry Church, the British botanist and botanical illustrator, cited in Wilfrid Blunt and William T. Stearn, *The Art of Botanical Illustration: An Illustrated History*, Dover Publications, New York, 1994, p. 95.
145. January 1614. Quoted in Barker, *Hortus Eystettensis*, p. 65.
146. Cited in Blunt and Stearn, *The Art of Botanical Illustration*, p. 96.
147. The World Checklist of Vascular Plants (WCVP), https://doi.org/10.15468/6h8ucr (accessed 4 January 2025).

17. Of Mites and Men

148. 'La dioptrique' in René Descartes's *Discourse on Method, Optics, Geometry and Meteorology*, 1637. Translation from Neil M. Ribe, 'Cartesian Optics and the Mastery of Nature', *Isis*, 88:1, 1997, p. 47.
149. Seneca, *Natural Questions*, 1.6.5–6, tr. Harry M. Hine, University of Chicago Press, Chicago and London, 2020.
150. Constantijn Huygens, father of Christiaan Huygens, quoted in E. Jorink, *Reading the Book of Nature in the Dutch Golden Age, 1575–1715*, tr. Peter Mason, Brill, Leiden, 2011, p. 181.
151. Jordynn Jack, 'A Pedagogy of Sight: Microscopic Vision in Robert Hooke's *Micrographia*', *Quarterly Journal of Speech*, 95:2, 2009, pp. 192–209.
152. Robert Hooke, *Micrographia*, Royal Society, London, 1665, preface.
153. Robert Hooke, *Micrographia*, 1665, p. 2.
154. Jonathan Charles Goddard, 'Goddard's Dropps: A Paradox of the C17th', *Urology News*, 19:6, 2015, p. 2.
155. Entry dated 21 January 1665. Robert Latham and William Matthews (eds), *The Diary of Samuel Pepys, vol. VI: 1665*, University of California Press, Berkeley, 1974.
156. William Blake, 'Auguries of Innocence'.
157. Robert Hooke, *Micrographia*, 1665, p. 204.

18. Metamorphosis

158. Virginia Woolf, *A Room of One's Own*, Hogarth Press, London, 1929, p. 164.
159. 'If a soiled shirt is placed in the opening of a

vessel containing grains of wheat, the reaction of the leaven in the shirt with fumes from the wheat will, after approximately twenty-one days, transform the wheat into mice.' Cited in Louis Pasteur, *Revue des cours scientifics*, 1, 23 April 1864, pp. 257–64.

160. Aristotle, *Animal Generation*, Book 1.16 (720b 6–8). Barnes (ed.), *The Complete Works of Aristotle: The Revised Oxford Translation*, vol. 1, p. 1119.

161. Counterproofs were a well-established technique by the beginning of the sixteenth century. Marie-Christine Seigneur, 'On Counterproofs', *Print Quarterly*, 21:2, 2004, p. 115.

162. Justin Roberts, 'Surrendering Surinam: The Barbadian Diaspora and the Expansion of the English Sugar Frontier, 1650–75', *The William and Mary Quarterly*, 73:2, 2016, p. 235, n. 31, p. 236.

163. Saxby, 'Disaster in the Jungle: Labadist Colonial Enterprise in Surinam, 1683–1719', in *Quest for the New Jerusalem: Jean de Labadie and the Labadists, 1610–1744*, Martinus Nijoff, Dordrecht, 1987, pp. 278–9.

164. Quoted in Londa Schiebinger, 'Feminist History of Colonial Science', *Hypatia*, 19:1, 2004, p. 237.

165. Letter, dated 8 October 1702, to the Nuremberg physician and botanist Johann Georg Volkamer (1662–1744), quoted in Natalie Zemon Davis, *Women on the Margins: Three Seventeenth-Century Lives*, Harvard University Press, Cambridge, MA, 1995, pp. 177, 321, n. 157. Elisabeth Rücker and William T. Stearn, *Maria Sibylla Merian in Surinam*, Prion, London, 1982, p. 65. In her preface to *Metamorphosis* Maria does not specifically mention an illness, but that she was forced to return home because 'the heat did not agree with me' ('… atque hic aestus naturae; meae adversetur: qua de re coacta domum citius reverti, ac mihi antea propositum erat').

166. Dubbed the 'King of Fruits' after King Ferdinand of Spain's reported preference for the fruit. Fran Beauman, *The Pineapple: King of Fruits*, Chatto and Windus, London, 2005, pp. 22–3.

167. 'Gustu fructus hic uvas, mala punica, ribesia, poma atque pyra inter se mista refert, omnium enim horum fructuum saporem quasi in uno illo simul reperies.' *Dissertatio de generatione et metamorphosibus insectorum Surinamensium*, 1719, plate 2, verso.

168. Quoted in Bert van de Roemer et al., *Maria Sibylla Merian: Changing the Nature of Art and Science*, Lannoo, Tielt, 2022, p. 16.

169. With rare exceptions (concentrated in Italy). An example is Laura Bassi (1711–88), professor of physics at the University of Bologna. Londa Schiebinger, *The Mind Has No Sex? Women in the Origins of Modern Science*, Harvard University Press, Cambridge, MA, 1991, pp. 14–17.

170. 'The migratory cycle in this species involves six generations.' Constantí Stefanescu et al., 'Multi-generational Long-Distance Migration of Insects: Studying the Painted Lady Butterfly in the Western Palaearctic', *Ecography*, 36, 2013, pp. 474, 483. For a non-technical summary, see Justin Jackson, 'Tracing the Migration Path of Painted Lady Butterflies across Africa', 13 April 2023, https://phys.org/news/2023-04-migration-path-lady-butterfliesafrica.html (accessed 1 July 2023).

Epilogue

171. Virginia Woolf, *Second Common Reader: Annotated Edition*, Houghton Mifflin Harcourt, Boston, MA, 2003, p. 155.

172. Andrew Pettegree, *Brand Luther: 1517, Printing, and the Making of the Reformation*, Penguin Books, New York, 2015, p. 336.

173. Ibid., p. xii.

174. Data from https://ourworldindata.org/literacy (accessed 2 January 2025).

175. Tore Frängsmyr, J.L. Heilbron and Robin E. Rider (eds), *The Quantifying Spirit in the 18th Century*, University of California Press, Berkeley and Los Angeles, 1990, pp. 1–2; cf. Foster Stockwell, 'Organizing Knowledge', in *A History of Information Storage and Retrieval*, McFarland & Company, Jefferson, NC, and London, 2001, pp. 93–101.

176. Basil Montagu, *The Works of Francis Bacon, Lord Chancellor of England*, vol. 3, Carey and Hart, Philadelphia, 1841, p. 28.

177. Peter Burke, *A Social History of Knowledge: from Gutenberg to Diderot*, Polity Press, Cambridge, 2000, p. 110.

178. See note 1.

179. Wittgenstein, *Philosophical Investigations*, p. 45; see also 'True philosophy consists in relearning to look at the world.' Maurice Merleau-Ponty, *Phenomenology of Perception*, Routledge & Kegan Paul, New York, 1962, p. xx.

FURTHER READING

Ammirati, Serena, 'The Use of Wooden Tablets in the Ancient Graeco-Roman World and the Birth of the Book in Codex Form: Some Remarks', *Scripta*, 6, 2013, pp. 9–15

Baigrie, Brian S., *Scientific Revolutions: Primary Texts in the History of Science*, Pearson Prentice Hall, Upper Saddle River, NJ, 2004

Bakker, Frederik A., et al. (eds), *Space, Imagination and the Cosmos from Antiquity to the Early Modern Period*, Springer Cham, 2018

Barker, Nicolas, *Hortus Eystettensis: The Bishop's Garden and Besler's Magnificent Book*, Harry N. Abrams, New York, 1994

Barton, John, *A History of the Bible: The Story of the World's Most Influential Book*, Viking, New York, 2019

Bartrum, Giulia, *Albrecht Dürer and His Legacy: The Graphic Work of a Renaissance Artist*, The British Museum Press, London, 2002

Beagon, Mary, *Roman Nature: The Thought of Pliny the Elder*, Clarendon Press, Oxford, 1992

Bennett, Jim, Michael Cooper, Michael Hunter and Lisa Jardine, *London's Leonardo: The Life and Work of Robert Hooke,* Oxford University Press, Oxford, 2003

Biagioli, Mario, *Galileo, Courtier: The Practice of Science in the Culture of Absolutism*, University of Chicago Press, Chicago and London, 1993

Biagioli, Mario, *Galileo's Instruments of Credit: Telescopes, Images, Secrecy*, University of Chicago Press, Chicago and London, 2006

Blair, Ann, *Too Much to Know: Managing Scholarly Information before the Modern Age*, Yale University Press, New Haven and London, 2010

Boner, Patrick J., *Kepler's New Star (1604). Context and Controversy*, Brill, Leiden, 2021

Bora, Fozia, *Writing History in the Medieval Islamic World: The Value of Chronicles as Archives*, Bloomsbury Academic, 2019

Boudalis, Georgios, *The Codex and Crafts in Late Antiquity*, exhibition catalogue, Bard Graduate Center, New York, 2018

Bredekamp, Horst, Irene Brückle and Paul Needham (eds), *A Galileo Forgery: Unmasking the New York Sidereus Nuncius*, vol. 3 of *Galileo's O*, De Gruyter, Berlin, 2014

Brown, Michelle P., 'The Role of the Wax Tablet in Medieval Literacy: A Reconsideration in Light of a Recent Find from York', *The British Library Journal*, 20:1, 1994, pp. 1–16

Burgess, R.W., and M. Kulikowski, *Mosaics of Time: The Latin Chronicle Traditions from the First Century* BC *to the Sixth Century* AD, Brepols, Turnhout, 2013

Buringh, Eltjo, *Medieval Manuscript Production in the Latin West: Explorations with a Global Database*, Brill, Leiden, 2010

Burke, Peter, *A Social History of Knowledge: From Gutenberg to Diderot*, Polity Press, Cambridge, 2000

Cammarosano, Michele, 'They Wrote on Wax. Wax Boards in the Ancient Near East', *Mesopotamia*, LIV, 2019, pp. 121–80

Campbell, Gordon, *Bible: The Story of the King James Version, 1611–2011*, Oxford University Press, Oxford, 2010

Campbell, Gordon L., *The Handbook of Animals in Classical Thought and Life,* Oxford University Press, Oxford, 2014

Campopiano, Michele, and Henry Bainton (eds), *Universal Chronicles in the High Middle Ages,* York Medieval Press, York, 2017

Carey, Sorcha, *Pliny's Catalogue of Culture: Art and Empire in the Natural History*, Oxford University Press, Oxford, 2003

Caspar, Max, *Kepler*, Dover Publications, New York, 1993

Chapman, Allan, *England's Leonardo: Robert Hooke and the Seventeenth-Century Scientific Revolution,* Institute of Physics Publishing, Bristol and Philadelphia, 2005

Christy, T. Craig, 'From Badges to Moveable Type: How Gutenberg Came to Bring Mass

Production Technology to the Production of Books', *The International Journal of the Book*, 8:4, 2011, pp. 1–25

Clayton, Ewan, *The Golden Thread: The Story of Writing*, Atlantic Books, London, 2013

Cooper, Michael, and Michael Hunter (eds), *Robert Hooke: Tercentennial Studies*, Routledge, London and New York, 2017

Cowan, Brian, *The Social Life of Coffee*, Yale University Press, New Haven, 2005

Crane, Nicholas, *Mercator: The Man who Mapped the Planet*, Phoenix, London, 2003

Crosby, Alfred W., *Ecological Imperialism: The Biological Expansion of Europe, 900–1900*, Cambridge University Press, Cambridge, 2004

Damisch, Hubert, *The Origin of Perspective*, MIT Press, Cambridge, MA, 1994

Daniell, David, *William Tyndale: A Biography*, Yale University Press, New Haven and London, 1994

Dash, Mike, *Tulipomania: The Story of the World's Most Coveted Flower and the Extraordinary Passions It Aroused*, Three Rivers Press, New York, 1999

Davis, Natalie Zemon, *Women on the Margins: Three Seventeenth-Century Lives*, Harvard University Press, Cambridge, MA, 1995

De Ceglia, F. (ed.), *The Body of Evidence: Corpses and Proofs in Early Modern European Medicine*, Brill, Leiden, 2020

De Hamel, Christopher, *The Book: A History of the Bible*, Phaidon, London, 2002

Delatte, N., 'Lessons from Roman Cement and Concrete', *Journal of Professional Issues in Engineering Education and Practice*, 127:3, 2001, pp. 109–15

Doody, Aude, *Pliny's Encyclopedia: The Reception of the Natural History*, Cambridge University Press, Cambridge and New York, 2010

Dooley, Brendan (ed.), *A Companion to Astrology in the Renaissance*, Brill, Leiden, 2014

Drake, Stillman, *Telescopes, Tides, and Tactics: A Galilean Dialogue about the Starry Messenger and Systems of the World*, University of Chicago Press, Chicago, 1983

Dückers, Rob, and Pieter Roelofs, *The Limbourg Brothers: Nijmegen Masters at the French Court 1400–1416*, Ludion, Ghent, 2005

Duffy, Eamon, *Marking the Hours: English People and their Prayers 1240–1570*, Yale University Press, New Haven, 2006

Dunn, Daisy, *The Shadow of Vesuvius: A Life of Pliny*, Liveright Publishing, New York, 2019

Dunphy, Graeme, *The Encyclopedia of the Medieval Chronicle*, Brill, Leiden, 2010

Edney, Matthew H., and Mary Sponberg Pedley (eds), *History of Cartography, vol. 4: Cartography in the European Enlightenment*, University of Chicago Press, Chicago, 2020

Ellis, Harold, and Sala Abdalla, *A History of Surgery*, third edition, CRC Press, Boca Raton, 2019

Etheridge, Kay, *The Flowering of Ecology: Maria Sibylla Merian's Caterpillar Book*, Brill, Leiden and Boston, 2020

Everett, Caleb, *Numbers and the Making of Us: Counting and the Course of Human Cultures*, Harvard University Press, Cambridge, MA, 2017

Fernandez-Armesto, Felipe, *Amerigo: The Man Who Gave His Name to America*, Random House, New York, 2007

Fudge, Erica (ed.), *Renaissance Beasts: Of Animals, Humans, and Other Wonderful Creatures*, University of Illinois Press, Urbana, 2004

Füssel, Stephan, *The Book of Chronicles: The Complete and Annotated Nuremberg Chronicle of 1493*, Taschen, Cologne, 2018

Füssel, Stephan, *Gutenberg*, Haus Publishing, London, 2019

Galilei, Galileo, *Sidereus Nuncius, or The Sidereal Messenger*, tr. with introduction, conclusion and notes by Albert Van Helden, second edition, University of Chicago Press, Chicago and London, 2016

Gharipour, Mohammad (ed.), *Gardens of Renaissance Europe and the Islamic Empires: Encounters and Confluences*, Penn State University Press, University Park, PA, 2017

Ghyka, Matila, *The Geometry of Art and Life*, Dover Publications, New York, 1977

Gibson, Roy, and Ruth Morello (eds), *Pliny the Elder: Themes and Context*, Brill, Leiden, 2011

Gingerich, Owen, *The Eye of Heaven: Ptolemy, Copernicus, Kepler*, American Institute of Physics, New York, 1993

Grafton, Anthony, *Leon Battista Alberti: Master Builder of the Italian Renaissance*, Harvard University Press, Cambridge, MA, 2002

Grafton, Anthony and Megan Williams, *Christianity and the Transformation of the Book*, Belknap Press, Cambridge, MA, and London, 2008

Grant, Edward, *Planets, Stars, and Orbs: The Medieval Cosmos, 1200–1687*, Cambridge University Press, Cambridge, 1994
Grice, G., *Cabinet of Curiosities: Collecting and Understanding the Wonders of the Natural World*, Workman Publishing, New York, 2015
Griffiths, Anthony, *Prints and Printmaking: An Introduction to the History and Techniques*, University of California Press, Berkeley, 1996

Harnett, Benjamin, 'The Diffusion of the Codex', *Classical Antiquity*, 36:2, 2017, pp. 183–235
Heilbron, J. L., *Galileo*, Oxford University Press, Oxford, 2010
Herz-Fischler, Roger, *A Mathematical History of the Golden Number*, Dover Books, New York, 1998
Herz-Fischler, Roger, 'The Home of Golden Numberism', *The Mathematical Intelligencer*, 27, 2005, pp. 69–71
Hindman, Sandra, and James Marrow (eds), *Books of Hours Reconsidered*, Harvey Miller, London, 2013
Hoskin, Michael (ed.), *The Cambridge Illustrated History of Astronomy*, Cambridge University Press, Cambridge, 1997
Houston, Robert A., *Literacy in Early Modern Europe: Culture and Education, 1500–1800*, second edition, Routledge, London, 2002

Ilardi, Vincent, *Renaissance Vision from Spectacles to Telescopes*, American Philosophical Society, Philadelphia, 2007
Impey, O.R., and Arthur MacGregor, *The Origins of Museums: The Cabinet of Curiosities in Sixteenth- and Seventeenth-Century Europe*, Clarendon Press, Oxford, 1985
Inwood, Stephen, *The Man Who Knew Too Much: The Strange & Inventive Life of Robert Hooke 1635–1703*, Macmillan, London and Oxford, 2002
Isaacson, Walter, *Leonardo da Vinci*, Simon & Schuster, New York, 2017

Jardine, Lisa, *The Curious Life of Robert Hooke: The Man Who Measured London*, Perennial, New York, 2005
Jardine, Nick, J.A. Secord and E.C. Spary (eds), *Cultures of Natural History*, Cambridge University Press, Cambridge, 1996
Jarzombek, Mark M., *Architecture of First Societies: A Global Perspective*, John Wiley & Sons, New York, 2013
Jenkins, Catherine, Nadine M. Orenstein and Freyda Spira, *The Renaissance of Etching*, Metropolitan Museum of Art, New York, 2019

Kanas, Nick, *Star Maps: History, Artistry, and Cartography*, Springer, New York, 2012
Kang, Lydia, and Nate Pedersen, *Quackery: A Brief History of the Worst Ways to Cure Everything*, Workman Publishing, New York, 2017
Karr Schmidt, S., *Interactive and Sculptural Printmaking in the Renaissance*, Brill, Leiden, 2017
Kent, Alexander J., and Peter Vujakovic, *The Routledge Handbook of Mapping and Cartography*, Routledge, Abingdon, 2018
Kessler, Fritz, and Sarah Battersby, *Working with Map Projections: A Guide to their Selection*, CRC Press, London, 2019
King, David A., *Islamic Astronomical Instruments*, Variorum Reprints, London, 1987
Knight, Leah, Micheline White and Elizabeth Sauer (eds), *Women's Bookscapes in Early Modern Britain: Reading, Ownership, Circulation*, University of Michigan Press, Ann Arbor, 2018
König, Jason, and Greg Woolf (eds), *Encyclopaedism from Antiquity to the Renaissance,* Cambridge University Press, Cambridge, 2013
Kurlansky, Mark, *Paper: Paging Through History*, W.W. Norton, New York and London, 2016
Kusukawa, Sachiko, *Picturing the Book of Nature: Image, Text, and Argument in Sixteenth-Century Human Anatomy and Medical Botany*, University of Chicago Press, Chicago, 2011
Kwakkel, Erik, *Books Before Print,* Arc Humanities Press, Leeds, 2018

Landau, David, and Peter Parshall, *The Renaissance Print, 1470–1550*, Yale University Press, New Haven and London, 1994
Leu, Urs B., *Conrad Gessner (1516–1565): Universal Scholar and Natural Scientist of the Renaissance*, Brill, Leiden, 2023
Lindberg, David C., *The Beginnings of Western Science*, second edition, University of Chicago Press, Chicago and London, 2007
Luber, Katherine Crawford, *Albrecht Dürer and the Venetian Renaissance*, Cambridge University Press, Cambridge, 2005

McGrath, Alister, *In the Beginning: The Story of the King James Bible and How It Changed a Nation, a Language, and a Culture*, Anchor Books, New York, 2002

McKitterick, David, *Print, Manuscript and the Search for Order, 1450–1830*, Cambridge University Press, Cambridge, 2003

Margócsy, D., M. Somos and S.N. Joffe, *The Fabrica of Andreas Vesalius: A Worldwide Descriptive Census, Ownership, and Annotations of the 1543 and 1555 Editions*, Brill, Leiden, 2018

Markey, Lia (ed.), *Renaissance Invention: Stradanus's Nova Reperta*, Northwestern University Press, Evanston, IL, 2020

Markowsky, George, 'Misconceptions about the Golden Ratio', *The College Mathematics Journal*, 23:1, 1992, pp. 2–19

Mattern, Susan P., *The Prince of Medicine: Galen in the Roman Empire*, Oxford University Press, Oxford, 2013

Meyer, E.A., 'Roman Tabulae, Egyptian Christians, and the Adoption of the Codex', *Chiron*, 37, 2007, pp. 295–331

Monmonier, Mark, *Rhumb Lines and Map Wars: A Social History of the Mercator Projection*, University of Chicago Press, Chicago, 2004

Moore, Helen, and Julian Reid (eds), *Manifold Greatness: The Making of the King James Bible*, Bodleian Library, Oxford, 2012

Morgan, Joyce, and Conrad Walters, *Journeys on the Silk Road: A Desert Explorer, Buddha's Secret Library, and the Unearthing of the World's Oldest Printed Book*, Lyons Press, Guilford, CT, 2012

Muhanna, Elias, *The World in a Book: Al-Nuwayri and the Islamic Encyclopedic Tradition*, Princeton University Press, Princeton, 2018

Mun, Seung-Hwan, 'Printing Press Without Copyright: A Historical Analysis of Printing and Publishing in Song, China', *Chinese Journal of Communication*, 6:1, 2013, pp. 1–23

Murphy, Trevor M., *Pliny the Elder's Natural History: The Empire in the Encyclopedia*, Oxford University Press, Oxford, 2009

Neugebauer, O., *A History of Ancient Mathematical Astronomy*, Springer, New York, 1975

Nicolson, Adam, *God's Secretaries: The Making of the King James Bible*, Harper, London, 2003

North, John, *The Norton History of Astronomy and Cosmology*, Norton and Co., New York, 1994

Nuovo, Angela, *The Book Trade in the Italian Renaissance*, Brill, Leiden, 2013

O'Malley, Charles D., *Andreas Vesalius of Brussels, 1514–1564*, University of California Press, Berkeley, 1964

Ong, Walter J., *Orality and Literacy: The Technologizing of the Word*, 30th anniversary (third) edition, Routledge, London and New York, 2012

Ovenden, Richard, *Burning the Books: A History of Knowledge Under Attack*, The Belknap Press of Harvard University Press, Cambridge, MA, 2000

Panofsky, Erwin, *The Life and Art of Albrecht Dürer*, Princeton University Press, Princeton, 1955

Park, Katherine, 'The Criminal and the Saintly Body: Autopsy and Dissection in Renaissance Italy', *Renaissance Quarterly*, 47:1, 1994, pp. 1–33

Park, Katherine, 'The Life of the Corpse: Division and Dissection in Late Medieval Europe', *Journal of the History of Medicine and Allied Sciences*, 50:1, 1995, pp. 111–32

Park, Katherine, and Daston, Lorraine (eds), *The Cambridge History of Science, vol. 3: Early Modern Science*, Cambridge University Press, New York, 2006

Pavord, Anna, *The Naming of Names: The Search for Order in the World of Plants*, Bloomsbury, New York, 2005

Pettegree, Andrew, *The Book in the Renaissance*, Yale University Press, New Haven and London, 2010

Pettegree, Andrew, *The Invention of News: How the World Came to Know about Itself*, Yale University Press, New Haven, 2014

Pettegree, Andrew, *Brand Luther: 1517, Printing, and the Making of the Reformation*, Penguin Books, New York, 2015

Pettegree, Andrew, and Arthur der Weduwen, *The Library: A Fragile History*, Basic Books, New York, 2021

Pliny the Elder, *Natural History: A Selection*, translated with an introduction and notes by John F. Healy, Penguin Books, New York, 2004

Purrington, Robert D., *The First Professional Scientist: Robert Hooke and the Royal Society of London*, Springer, London 2009

Raven, James, *What is the History of the Book?*, Polity Press, Cambridge, 2018

Reinburg, Virginia, *French Books of Hours: Making an Archive of Prayer, c.1400–1600*, Cambridge University Press, Cambridge, 2012

Reitsma, Ella, *Maria Sibylla Merian & Daughters: Women of Art and Science*, Waanders, Zwolle, 2008

Riggs, Timothy A., *Hieronymus Cock, Printmaker and Publisher*, Garland, New York and London, 1977

Roberts, Colin, and T.C. Skeat, *The Birth of the Codex*, Oxford University Press, Oxford, 1983

Rowland, Ingrid D., and Thomas N. Howe (eds), *Vitruvius: Ten Books on Architecture*, Cambridge University Press, Cambridge, 1999

Sangster, Alan, 'The Life and Works of Luca Pacioli (1446/7–1517), Humanist Educator', *Abacus*, 57, 2021, pp. 126–52

Schiebinger, Londa, *The Mind Has No Sex? Women in the Origins of Modern Science*, Harvard University Press, Cambridge, MA, 1991

Schmidt, Suzanne Karr, and Edward H. Wouk (eds), *Prints in Translation 1450–1750: Image, Materiality, Space*, Routledge, New York and London, 2016

Sinisgalli, Rocco, *Perspective in the Visual Culture of Classical Antiquity*, Cambridge University Press, Cambridge, 2012

Siraisi, Nancy, *Medieval and Early Renaissance Medicine*, University of Chicago Press, Chicago and London, 1990

Siraisi, Nancy, *Medicine and the Italian Universities, 1250–1600*, Brill, Leiden, 2001

Sohn, Pow-Key, 'Printing Since the 8th Century in Korea', *Koreana*, 7:2, 1993, pp. 4–9

Stijnman, Ad, *Engraving and Etching, 1400–2000: A History of the Development of Manual Intaglio Printmaking Processes*, Archetype, London, 2012

Taylor, Andrew, *Gerard Mercator: The Mapmaker who Revolutionized Geography*, Harper Perennial, London, 2004

Thomas, Hugh, *The Slave Trade: The Story of the Atlantic Slave Trade 1440–1870*, Simon & Schuster, New York, 1997

Todd, Kim, *Chrysalis: Maria Sibylla Merian and the Secrets of Metamorphosis*, Harcourt, Orlando, FL, 2007

Tsien, Tsuen-Hsuin, *Written on Bamboo and Silk: The Beginnings of Chinese Books and Inscriptions*, second edition, University of Chicago Press, Chicago, 2004

Van Helden, Albert, *Measuring the Universe: Cosmic Dimensions from Aristarchus to Halley*, University of Chicago Press, Chicago, 1985

Wagner, Bettina (ed.), *Worlds of Learning: The Library and World Chronicle of the Nuremberg Physician Hartmann Schedel (1440–1514)*, Allitera Verlag, Munich, 2015

Wieck, Roger S., *Time Sanctified: The Book of Hours in Medieval Art and Life*, George Braziller, New York, 1988

Wilkinson, Alix, *The Garden in Ancient Egypt*, Rubicon, London, 1998

Wolf, Maryanne, *Proust and the Squid: The Story and Science of the Reading Brain*, Icon Books, London, 2008

Woodward, David (ed.), *The History of Cartography, vol. 3: Book 1, Cartography in the European Renaissance*, University of Chicago Press, Chicago, 2007

Zhou, He, 'Diffusion of Movable Type in China and Europe: Why were there two fates?', *International Communication Gazette*, 53:3, 1994, pp. 153–73

PICTURE CREDITS

1 © The Trustees of the British Museum. All rights reserved

2 The Metropolitan Museum of Art, New York. Purchase, Raymond and Beverly Sackler Gift, 1988, 1988.433.3

3 The Metropolitan Museum of Art, New York. Rogers Fund, 1914, 14.2.4a–d

4 British Library / Bridgeman Images, MS. Or.8210/P.2

5 Oxford, Bodleian Library, B 1.9 Art.Seld., frontispiece

6 Oxford, Bodleian Library, MS. Douce 219, fol. 16v

7 Oxford, Bodleian Library, Arch. B b.10, fol. 5r (and p. 6)

8 Germanisches Nationalmuseum, Nürnberg, Inv.-Nr. Gm143, Leihgabe Bayerische Staatsgemäldesammlung. Foto: G. Janssen

9 Ashmolean Museum, University of Oxford, AN 1997.20

10 Oxford, Bodleian Library, MS. Douce 51, fols 58v–59r

11 © State Russian Museum / Bridgeman Images

12 Oxford, Bodleian Library, Arch. G b.6, fol. 5r

13 Bayerische Staatsbibliothek, Munich, Inc. c.a 529

14 Oxford, Bodleian Library, Arch. G b.6, fol. 21r

15 Oxford, Bodleian Library, Arch. G b.6, – fols 402v, 5r, 108r, 21r

16 Library of Congress / Bayerische Staatsbibliothek, Munich, Rar. 287 fol. 262v

17 Oxford, Bodleian Library, MS. Auct. T. 2. 26, fols 82v–83r

18 Oxford, Bodleian Library, MS. Laud misc. 636, fol. 1r

19 Oxford, Bodleian Library, Auct. Q sub. fen. 1.7b, fol. XIr

20 Oxford, Bodleian Library, Douce 221, fols iiii verso–v recto

21 Capodimonte Museum, Naples, inv. Q 58

22 Veneranda Biblioteca Ambrosiana/Metis e Mida Informatica/Mondadori Portfolio/Bridgeman Images

23 Bibliothèque de Genève, Ms. l.e. 210, fol. 1r

24 Oxford, Bodleian Library, Arch. B d.24 (2)

25 Oxford, Bodleian Library, Arch. B d.24 (2), plate XXII

26 Gallerie dell'Accademia, Venice / Bridgeman Images

27 Oxford, Bodleian Library, Arch. Antiq. B 2.15, fol. XLIXr

28 Oxford, Bodleian Library, Arch. Antiq. B 2.15, fols XVv–XVIr

29 Prints and Photographs Division, Library of Congress, ADE - UNIT 2463

30 Oxford, Bodleian Library, Arch. Antiq. B 2.15, fol. LXIIIr

31 © Photo Josse / Bridgeman Images, Musée Condé, Ms.65, fol. 1v (and pp. 8–9)

32 University Library Vrije Universiteit Amsterdam, LL.06979gk

33 Oxford, Bodleian Library, MS. Douce 219, fol. 133r (and p. 2)

34 Bibliothèque nationale de France, Paris RESERVE8-T-2547, title page

35 Oxford, Bodleian Library, Douce BB 142, fols D3v–D4r

36 Oxford, Bodleian Library, Douce BB 142, fols O3v–O4r

37 Oxford, Bodleian Library, Douce BB 142, fol. M7r

38 Oxford, Bodleian Library, Douce 25, fol. 41

39 © The Trustees of the British Museum. All rights reserved

40 Oxford, Bodleian Library, Douce D subt. 41, fol. 5r

41 Oxford, Bodleian Library, Vet. D1 c.24, fol. M6v

42 Oxford, Bodleian Library, Vet. D1 c.24, fol. Q2r

43 Oxford, Bodleian Library, Vet. D1 c.24, fols Q2v–Q3r

44 Oxford, Bodleian Library, Vet. D1 c.24, fol. L6v

45 Oxford, Bodleian Library, Vet. D1 c.24, fol. K2v

46 Oxford, Bodleian Library, MS. Ashmole 370, fol. 27v

47 Oxford, Bodleian Library, MS. Ashmole 370, fol. 25r

48 Oxford, Bodleian Library, Arch. B b.7, fols B3r

49 Oxford, Bodleian Library, Arch. B b.7, fols N4v–O1r

50 Oxford, Bodleian Library, Arch. B b.7, fols M2v–M3r

51 © Bridgeman Images / Photo Josse

52 Oxford, Bodleian Library, Arch. B b.7, fols G3v–G4r

53 Oxford, Bodleian Library, B 1.16 Med., title page

54 The Metropolitan Museum of Art, New York. Harris Brisbane Dick Fund, 1938, 38.52

55 Oxford, Bodleian Library, B 1.16 Med., p. 169 and p. 65[illegible]

56 Oxford, Bodleian Library, B 1.16 Med., p. 164

57 Oxford, Bodleian Library, B 1.16 Med., p. 170

58 Oxford, Bodleian Library, B 1.16 Med., p. 178 and p. 190

59 Wikimedia

60 Oxford, Bodleian Library, MS. Ashmole 1511, fol. 15v

61 Oxford, Bodleian Library, G 1.7 Med., p. 345

62 Oxford, Bodleian Library, G 1.7 Med., p. 953

63 Oxford, Bodleian Library, G 1.7 Med., p. 781

64 Oxford, Bodleian Library, G 1.9 Med., p. 139

65 Bridgeman Images

66 Oxford, Bodleian Library, Don. b.8, pl. 19

67 Oxford, Bodleian Library, Don.b.8, title page

68 Oxford, Bodleian Library, Don. b.8, pl. 1

69 Oxford, Bodleian Library, Don. b.8, pl. 8

70 Oxford, Bodleian Library, Don. b.8. pl. 18

71 Oxford, Bodleian Library, Arch. B b.19, fols 131v–132r

72 © The Trustees of the British Museum. All rights reserved

73 Oxford, Bodleian Library, MS. Tanner 170, fol. 15v

74 Oxford, Bodleian Library, Arch. B b.12, title page

75 Oxford, Bodleian Library, Arch. B b.12

76 Oxford, Bodleian Library, Arch. B b.1277 Oxford, Bodleian Library, MS. Douce 390, fols 7v–8r

78 NASA / Chandra X-ray Center, Operated for NASA by the Smithsonian Astrophysical Observatory

79 Prints and Photographs Division, Library of Congress, G1000.2 .C4 1708, pl. 6

80 Oxford, Bodleian Library, Savile Y 3, p. 86

81 Oxford, Bodleian Library, Savile Y 3, p. 76, foldout

82 Bridgeman Images

83 Pictorial Press / Alamy

84 Oxford, Bodleian Library, Savile Cc 8 (15), pp. 18–19

85 Oxford, Bodleian Library, Antiq.e.I.1610.1, fols D5v–D6r

86 Oxford, Bodleian Library, Antiq.e.I.1610.1, title page and fol. E3r

87 NASA https://www.nasa.gov/wp-content/uploads/static/history/alsj/a15/AS15-88-11901HR.jpg

88 Oxford, Bodleian Library, MS. Junius 11, p. 66

89 Oxford, Bodleian Library, MS. Auct. D. 2. 19, fol. 168v

90 Oxford, Bodleian Library, LP 82

91 Oxford, Bodleian Library, Bib. Eng. 1611 b.1, title page

92 Oxford, Bodleian Library, Bib. Eng. 1611 b.1, NT title page

93 Herzog August Bibliothek, Wolfenbüttel Cod. Guelf. 23.3. Aug. 2°, fols 13v & 14r (and p. 4)

94 Oxford, Bodleian Library, W.H.F. Talbot 203, plate LXIX

95 Oxford, Bodleian Library, Douce T 265, p. 82

96 Oxford, Bodleian Library, MS. Arch. Selden. B. 1, title page

97 Oxford, Bodleian Library, MS. Arch. Selden. B. 1, quartus ordo, fol. 7

98 Oxford, Bodleian Library, MS. Arch. Selden. B. 1, quintus ordo, fol. 1

99 Oxford, Bodleian Library, MS. Arch. Selden. B. 1, quartus ordo, fol. 6

100 Oxford, Bodleian Library, Lister E 7, pl. XXXII

101 Oxford, Bodleian Library, Lister E 7, pl. I

102 Oxford, Bodleian Library, Lister E 7, pl. II

103 Oxford, Bodleian Library, Lister E 7, pl. XXXIV

104 Oxford, Bodleian Library, Lister E 7, pl. XXIV

105 © Board of Trustees of the Science Museum, London

106 London Museum, 42.39/56

107 Oxford, Bodleian Library, Arch. Nat. hist. E 10, pl. XII

108 Rijksmuseum Amsterdam, NG-501-94

109 Oxford, Bodleian Library, Arch.Nat. hist. E 10, pl. I

110 Oxford, Bodleian Library, Arch.Nat. hist. E 10, pl. II

111 Oxford, Bodleian Library, Arch.Nat. hist. E 10, pl. LXIX

112 Oxford, Bodleian Library, Arch.Nat. hist. E 10, pl. XXIX

113 Oxford, Bodleian Library, Arch.Nat. hist. E 10, frontispiece

114 Oxford, Bodleian Library, Arch.Nat. hist. E 10, pl. VII

115 Oxford, Bodleian Library, MS. Elliott 239, lower board

116 Oxford, Bodleian Library, Lister E 1, frontispiece

117 Oxford, Bodleian Library, John Johnson Collection: Oxford folder IV, 1

118 Oxford, Bodleian Library, Library Records c. 1693

119 Oxford, Bodleian Library, M 3.10 Art., Fig. CLXXXVIII

INDEX

Pages with illustrations are denoted by numbers in *italic* type.

This publication has been generously supported by the Martin J. Gross Family Foundation.

For Quỳnh

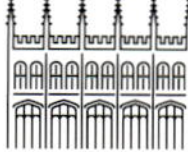

First published in 2025 by Bodleian Library Publishing
Broad Street, Oxford OX1 3BG
www.bodleianshop.co.uk

ISBN: 978 1 85124 548 2

Publisher: Samuel Fanous
Managing Editor: Susie Foster
Editor: Janet Phillips
Picture Editor: Leanda Shrimpton
Designed and typeset by Dot Little at the Bodleian Library in 11/17pt Minion
Printed and bound by Printer Trento S.r.l. on 150gsm Gardamatt Art paper

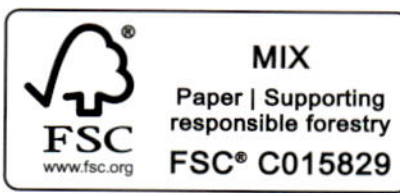

British Library Catalogue in Publishing Data
A CIP record of this publication is available from the British Library